Nonbinary
Gender Identities

Nonbinary Gender Identities

History, Culture, Resources

CHARLIE McNABB

ROWMAN & LITTLEFIELD
Lanham • Boulder • New York • London

3053

Published by Rowman & Littlefield
A wholly owned subsidiary of The Rowman & Littlefield Publishing Group, Inc.
4501 Forbes Boulevard, Suite 200, Lanham, Maryland 20706
www.rowman.com

Unit A, Whitacre Mews, 26-34 Stannary Street, London SE11 4AB

British Library Cataloguing in Publication Information Available

Library of Congress Cataloging-in-Publication Data

Names: McNabb, Charlie, 1983- author.
Title: Nonbinary gender identities : history, culture, resources / Charlie McNabb.
Description: Lanham : Rowman & Littlefield, [2018] | Includes bibliographical references and index.
Identifiers: LCCN 2017028732 (print) | LCCN 2017040955 (ebook) | ISBN 9781442275522 (electronic) | ISBN 9781442275515 (cloth : alk. paper)
Subjects: LCSH: Gender identity—United States. | Gender nonconformity—United States. | Sexual minorities—Identity. | Sexual minorities—United States—History.
Classification: LCC HQ73 (ebook) | LCC HQ73 .M36 2018 (print) | DDC 305.30973—dc23
LC record available at https://lccn.loc.gov/2017028732

∞™ The paper used in this publication meets the minimum requirements of American National Standard for Information Sciences—Permanence of Paper for Printed Library Materials, ANSI/NISO Z39.48-1992.

Printed in the United States of America

For Seren, and for nonbinary people everywhere.

Contents

List of Figures

Foreword

A guide that illuminates pathways to the incredible wisdom, wit, storytelling, scholarship, and history of nonbinary folks has been needed for some time. Finding and contextualizing this knowledge has been a challenge for researchers, regardless of their personal connections to the topic or research experience with other LGBTQ identities. I am glad that this guide has finally been published, and particularly so that Charlie McNabb is the one who created it. Charlie brings scholarship, knowledge, compassion, and pride to this showcase of people and works that have historically been excluded from the research process.

Several factors make it hard to find nonbinary works. Search engine algorithms have historically placed more value on delivering cissexism, binarism, and pornography than true nonbinary and trans experiences. School districts use software that blocks positive representations of nonbinary and transgender people. In libraries, people who use public computers to find this information are surveilled both by computer software and people sitting next to them. Library catalogs—the tools that are supposed to act as guides to library collections—have been built with the assumption that all authors are either male or female, and that terms like "nonbinary" and "genderqueer" have no place in research. For example, the Library of Congress received a proposal to add "genderqueer" as a subject heading more than ten years ago, and has still not created a way to describe books that discuss nonbinary gender identities.[1] As a result, trans and gender nonconforming people have often taken it upon ourselves to connect our peers to the resources they need. Fortunately, it turns out that when we take on this role, the results are fabulous.

The present volume fits into a long genealogy of gender nonconforming, nonbinary, and transgender people guiding their peers toward useful information. Since the 1970s—and perhaps earlier—transgender magazines and newsletters have regularly featured book recommendations and abstracts of scholarly articles. By 1994—only two years after the release of the first widely used web browser—trans woman Julia Case had created an online directory of useful links called GenderWeb "so that we could all share some knowledge and educate those around us."[2] In 2016, activists and scholars collaborated to create a massive crowdsourced bibliography highlighting Latinx identity, LGBTQ communities, and gendered violence as part of the #PulseOrlandoSyllabus project. When at their best, bibliographies can bring healing to harmed communities, knowledge to uninformed ones, and a humble sense of inquiry to all their readers.

Bibliographies have the power to bring people together. In fact, Charlie McNabb and I first met through constructing bibliographies on the Resources Committee of the American Library Association's GLBT Round Table. As we worked together, I was struck by Charlie's dogged commitment, scholarly approach, and intersectional awareness. They bring these qualities to the present volume as well—what a treat for you readers!

I encourage my fellow library workers to use the bibliographic components of this volume to work toward a collection that is accountable to a wide variety of nonbinary perspectives. But please don't stop once the books are ordered. Make sure that you read those books as soon as they arrive at your library. Display these books prominently and talk them up with your colleagues and patrons. Get to know the other chapters of Charlie's work, and challenge yourself with the questions they pose.

To every reader: take time to savor the beautiful, passionately pluralistic landscape that this volume paints. Get to know the incredible people, genders, and histories profiled in this book. It is my hope that this book will help you to find community, learn compassion, and build up a deeper acquaintance with the wisdom of nonbinary people.

—Jane Sandberg
Electronic Resources Librarian
Linn-Benton Community College

NOTES

1. Sanford Berman, "Personal LCSH Scorecard," last modified April 5, 2008, http://jenna.openflows.com/files/lcshscorecard080415.pdf.

2. Julia Case, "Julia's Page," GenderWeb, last modified May 2, 1998, http://web.archive.org/web/20000819003830/http://genderweb.org/julie.

Preface

Nonbinary gender identities are those that are not exclusively male or female. Nonbinary people can identify as being a combination of male and female, shifting between male and female, or off the male-female continuum altogether. Nonbinary is an umbrella term and can also be used as a discrete identity term; other terms include genderqueer, genderfluid, and bigender.

Nonbinary people are becoming more visible in popular culture, library media, and politics. Gender nonconformity is celebrated in popular culture, with rock musicians, actors, and models combining traditionally masculine and feminine styles. Popular and scholarly media are gaining greater representation of nonbinary identities, particularly in young adult fiction, queercore music and zines, and journal literature. Nonbinary people are making strides in the political and legal realms, with a small but growing number of individuals being granted legal nonbinary status. They are also fighting for new gender markers on identity documents, gender-neutral restroom access, trans-competent health care, and hate crimes and discrimination legislation.

Despite the relatively recent growth of representation, these people have existed for centuries. Indigenous cultures around the world have recognized alternate gender roles and identities that do not fit neatly within the Western binary. Some First Nations and Native Americans use the term "nonbinary," while others prefer to identify as Two-Spirit, an umbrella term encompassing sexual and gender diversity in the indigenous Americas. In some countries, third genders are recognized socially and legally; the hijras of India, for example, have a specialized role in their society to bless infants, and they have a third gender marker on identity documents.

The Anglo-European gender system, on the other hand, is a rigid binary of male and female. However, there have always been people who did not fit within this binary. There has been considerably less traditional recognition, but visibility has increased since the Stonewall riot cast light on the wider transgender community. The advent of the Internet, with the possibility of forming relationships across space and time, has allowed people to meet one another, organize politically, share ideas and resources, and create and disseminate their own media. Since the introduction of participatory social media, nonbinary culture has exploded, with the creation and evolution of identity terms and ways of communicating about these identities.

Although there is a great deal of formally and informally published material relevant to nonbinary identities, library cataloging systems do not yet have a distinct classification. Therefore, people seeking these materials must search using keywords, finding related works in bibliographies, and locating materials through peer recommendations and reviews. It is my hope that this book will aid people in locating library and popular culture materials about and for nonbinary people. It is crucial for marginalized people to see themselves represented in media; representation validates minoritized identities and allows readers to imagine, understand, and celebrate human difference.

THIS GUIDE AND ITS ORGANIZATION

Nonbinary Gender Identities: History, Culture, Resources is a pathfinder for nonbinary people and those who wish to educate themselves about nonbinary identities. Nonbinary people have unique identities and rich cultures, but they are not yet easily discoverable in library cataloging systems. Nevertheless, there are thousands of resources pertaining to nonbinary identities. This book is an attempt both to articulate nonbinary histories and cultures, and to provide annotated bibliographies of nonbinary-relevant resources. As a nonbinary person myself, I have struggled to find myself within the library, and each new find has been cause for rejoicing. With this book, nonbinary people can learn their histories and locate pertinent resources by media type and genre.

Part 1, "(Hir)stories," focuses on the histories and cultures of nonbinary people and communities. Chapter 1 provides an introduction to nonbinary gender. Chapter 2 discusses the cultural and political history of nonbinary gender identities in the United States. Chapter 3 articulates a history of culturally specific genders around the world, as well as the impacts of colonialism and conquest. Chapter 4 explores visibility of nonbinary gender identities in popular culture, looking at both self-identified nonbinary people and celebrities "read" as nonbinary by fans. Chapter 5 introduces six notable nonbinary people: Vaginal Davis, Kate Bornstein, Leslie Feinberg, Justin Vivian Bond, Riki Wilchins, and Qwo-Li Driskill.

Part 2, "Resources," provides annotated bibliographies of nonbinary-relevant media. Chapter 6 focuses on archives and special collections and is organized by geographic location. Chapter 7 focuses on nonfiction books and is organized by genre. Chapter 8 focuses on journal literature and is organized by academic discipline. Chapter 9 focuses on theses and dissertations and is also organized by academic discipline. Chapter 10 focuses on fiction books and is organized by genre. Chapter 11 focuses on organizations and associations and is organized by geographic location. Chapter 12 focuses on online resources and is organized by type of resource. Chapter 13 focuses on multimedia and is organized by genre.

I located resources using highly relevant keywords including "genderqueer," "transgender," and "androgynous." For scholarly materials, I searched for keywords in titles and abstracts. I selected resources based on currency, citations, and relevance to nonbinary identities. For books, I searched queer-relevant awards and review blogs. I selected fiction based on the presence of a nonbinary character with dialogue, and nonfiction based on a strong focus on nonbinary identities. For all other resources, I searched the internet using the keyword "nonbinary gender" and the resource type. I searched many nonbinary-specific resource sites and blogs to find other resources. I also asked for recommendations in nonbinary and transgender social and scholarly groups.

Nonbinary Gender Identities: History, Culture, Resources is a treasure trove of library and popular resources pertaining to nonbinary gender identities. I sincerely hope that nonbinary people and our allies use part 1 to learn more about our fascinating histories and cultures, and use part 2 to find us in media. In addition, I hope that librarians and others who build collections and create resource guides use part 2 for collection development and media recommendations. Most of all, I hope that this guide increases visibility for the nonbinary population.

Acknowledgments

This book was not written alone. I wish to thank my editor, Charles Harmon, for his excellent advice and coaching; the Gay, Lesbian, Bisexual, and Transgender Round Table of the American Library Association for the volunteer experience that led to the idea for this book; interlibrary loan staff at Haverford College and Wheaton College for assisting me in locating so many resources; my grandfather, for being willing to listen, learn, and engage; and my beef, Seren Birch, for their love and support through the entire process. Thanks also to Seren for creating figures 1.1, 1.2, and 1.3.

I

(HIR)STORIES

Introduction to Nonbinary Gender

Prior to the so-called transgender tipping point codified in *Time* magazine[1] and eagerly capitalized upon by news outlets and social media, the majority of the American public considered gender to be a simple duality, implicitly connected to the physical body and recognizable from birth. Consider the typical demographic collection instrument found on a medical or school form: two ticky boxes indicating M or F.

FIGURE 1.1

After becoming acquainted with a very specific transgender narrative via media portrayals, national awareness of gender has thankfully widened to include people assigned as one gender at birth who transition to the opposite gender. Let's put a line connecting the two ticky boxes to indicate this potential for movement.

FIGURE 1.2

But what if there were more options than male and female? What if someone identified somewhere in the middle of that line, or even off the line completely? I like to think of gender as a complex constellation of infinite possibilities.

This is getting pretty complicated. Let's start with one concept at a time.

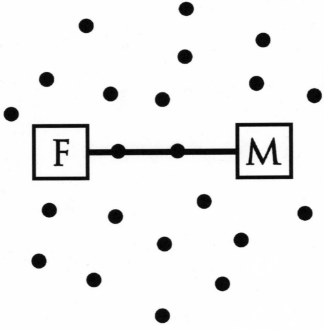

FIGURE 1.3

WHAT IS GENDER?

There are probably as many gender theorists as there are genders,[2] so this discussion will be simplified out of consideration for the aim of this book and the audience's time.

Untangling Gender from Sex

Sex and gender are not necessarily connected, although most people do identify with the gender they were assigned at birth. What typically happens is that the midwife or doctor performs a brief visual inspection of the external genitals during the birth examination. The genital appearance dictates the biological sex of the infant, and this in turn dictates the gender assignment. There is a lot wrong with this. For one thing, biological sex is a lot more complex than genitals; it involves chromosomes, hormones, reproductive organs, and secondary sex characteristics in addition to the external genitalia. And biological sex is not binary, despite the prevalence of the dual ticky-box classification.[3]

So we have a system where infants with vulvas are determined to be girls and infants with penises are determined to be boys. But what does it mean to be a girl or a boy? Until well into the twentieth century, American scientific literature distinguished "anatomical" sex (genitals and reproductive organs) from "mental or psychological" sex (behavior and personality), connecting the two with the model of biological determinism.[4] In 1949, anthropologist Margaret Mead was the first to use the term "sex roles" to discuss the ways in which men and women are expected to behave.[5] This concept was further developed in the 1950s and 1960s, when psychiatrists began using the word "gender." "Gender identity" referred to an individual's internal sense of their gender, and was separated from behaviors deemed masculine or feminine.[6]

Gender Is a Performance

These supposed masculine and feminine behaviors include such things as conversational style, clothing choice, emotional and mental intelligence, skills, desires, and orientation to the world. It seems silly to consider that the size of a child's phallus could dictate whether they prefer to play with trucks or dolls, but until relatively recently this was a widely accepted truism. It is sometimes difficult to separate gendered behaviors from the expectations that shape them. For example: If a girl is at the toy store, and all of the available choices in the "girl aisle" are pink dolls, she will probably choose a pink doll. If a boy exhibits nurturing behavior toward a stuffed animal and is sneered at for being a sissy, he will probably curtail that behavior.

In 1990, feminist theorist Judith Butler argued that neither sex nor gender is politically neutral, that both are produced within a set of power relations that favors a binary heterosexuality. She asserts that gender is an action rather than a state: "Gender proves to be performative—that is, constituting the identity it is purported to be."[7] This is perhaps most evident in drag performance, but everyday gender signifiers are just as powerfully performative, maybe more so because they are unquestioned.

TRANSGENDER IDENTITIES

Sometimes, the baby that is assigned a particular gender grows up to identify as a different gender. This realization may occur in early childhood or anytime in adulthood, and the individual may or may not transition to live as the gender they identify with.

Transvestite to Trans(s)exual to Transgender

Identity terms have a tendency to shift fairly rapidly, and scientific terminology does not always match community terminology. The word "transvestite," which today refers only to cross-dressing, was once used as a gender identity term. Rather quickly, though, the term "transsexual" came into use, to describe the identification from one sex to another. As pioneering sexologist Harry Benjamin wrote in 1966, "The transsexual (TS) male or female is deeply unhappy as a member of the sex (or gender) to which he or she was assigned by the anatomical structure of the body, particularly the genitals."[8] In this time period, the term was defined by distress and a desire to physically change the body.

Individuals used the term with or without the double "s" to self-refer, though in medical texts, it was always spelled "transsexual." For some, the term specifically referred to the postsurgical state; for others, it was a more general term, encompassing identity with or without transition. In the early 1990s, the term "transgender" began to be used, both to reject psychological and medical classification and to serve as a broader umbrella term.[9] This term emphasizes gender rather than physical sex, widening the community to those who did not experience any particular distress with their physical bod-ies. Today, some people use the term "trans(s)exual," some use "transgender," and some use "trans."[10] It is considered best practice to ask a trans person which term they prefer.

Many Ways to Transition

Transitioning can include any combination of social, medical, surgical, and legal processes. It's important to note that a person can be trans even if they decide not to transition, or if their transition does not look normative. Not every trans person desires to "pass" for cisgender[11] or nontrans. Many trans folks cannot afford expensive medical and surgical procedures or have determined that such procedures would not be suitable for their needs. And not every trans person feels uncomfortable with their body or appearance.

Social transition is all of the social actions people take to express their identity via sartorial choices and other interactive signals. This may include coming out, requesting the use of different pronouns and honorifics, a name change, and different gender expression. For example, a trans woman may start using "she/her" pronouns and "Ms." or "Mrs." honorifics; drop her masculine name and start using a feminine one; and grow her hair longer and wear skirts and dresses. Of course, just like how cisgender people don't always follow rigid gender expectations, trans people don't have to conform to them, either.

Medical transition involves treatments that feminize or masculinize a person's sex characteristics. Hormone replacement therapy (a regimen of estrogen and anti-androgens or testosterone) requires a medical professional, which often entails a diagnosis of "gender identity disorder." For children and adolescents, puberty blockers can delay the onset of puberty until they are at the age of consent for permanent transition measures. Other treatments include speech therapy, to train the voice to a different register; and hair re-moval, including epilation and laser treatments.

Surgical transition, also called gender confirmation surgery and sexual reassignment surgery, includes what are colloquially called "top surgery" and "bottom surgery," as well as various facial surgeries. Top surgery for men is mastectomy (breast tissue removal), with or without chest reconstruction or shaping. Top surgery for women is breast augmentation to enlarge the breasts. Bottom surgery for men may include hysterectomy (removal of the uterus), oophorectomy (removal of the ovaries), vaginectomy (removal of the vagina), metoidioplasty (release of the clitoris from the labia minora), and phalloplasty (construction of a penis). Bottom surgery for women may include penectomy (removal of the penis), orchiectomy (removal of the testicles), and vaginoplasty (construction of a vagina and vulva). Facial surgeries reshape the forehead, trachea, jaw, chin, nose, or ears.

Legal transition is the process by which a trans person becomes legally recognized as their gender. This may include name or sex changes on documents such as the birth certificate, Social Security card, driver's license, or passport. Some document changes require a court order; some require evidence of transition; others have no requirements. Rules vary by country, state, and sometimes county. Because of this, many trans people have different name and sex markers on different identity documents.

NONBINARY GENDER

"Binary gender" refers to the idea that there are only two genders, male and female. And while many people (both cisgender and trans) do identify as binary male or female, some people identify as a different gender. Because nonbinary people identify as a different gender than the one they were assigned at birth, they are included under the trans umbrella.

Indigenous Gender Systems

Nonbinary gender is not new. Nor is it a Western invention. Many cultures traditionally recognize three or more genders. In the late nineteenth century, European and American anthropologists were fascinated by gender variance in First Nations and Native American communities, and produced a great deal of literature on what they called the "berdache." This term and the literature that accompanied it are ethnocentric and offensive. Not only is the term itself insulting and inaccurate, as it was derived from an Arabic word relating to prostitution, but the colonial lens of these scholars distorted indigenous systems and meanings, using Western gender and sexuality understandings to frame the Other.[12]

Because of this fraught colonial history, which has included forcible removal of children to boarding schools, nonconsensual sterilization, punishment for engaging in traditional cultural activities, and genocide, it is inappropriate to use Western labels to define indigenous genders. Two-Spirit or two-spirit is the preferred umbrella term for First Nations and Native Americans, as it emerged from those communities;[13] however, many tribes, as well as non-Western cultures outside the United States and Canada, have more specific community terms. I include indigenous gender systems in my discussion because they are valuable and relevant. My use of the term "nonbinary" is intended to be a neutral label simply indicating gender variance outside the binary model. See chapter 3 for a more comprehensive discussion of culturally specific genders.

Flourishing Terminology

Among nonbinary people in the West and the United States in particular, the terminology has shifted over time. Prior to medical advances that allowed for surgical transition and spurred the proliferation of transgender narratives, there were individuals who identified outside the binary but had no community terminology with which to label themselves. It wasn't until 1995 that the term "genderqueer" was coined by Riki Wilchins; it came to be the umbrella term for nonbinary gender variance through the first decade of the 2000s.[14] Sometime in the early 2010s, the term nonbinary gained popularity and quickly became a new umbrella term. Since this time, there has been an explosion of terminology relating to gender variance: identity terms such as neutrois, gender expansive, genderfluid, and bigender; gender-neutral pronouns including ou, ey, ze, and they; and honorifics like Mx and Per have all been added to the nonbinary lexicon.[15]

But How Do You Transition If There's No Opposite Gender to Transition To?

So if a person does not identify as either a man or a woman, how do they transition? While it is true that there is no publicly recognized alternate gender in the West, nonbinary people can and do transition in a variety of ways. Almost all of the transition options available to binary trans people are possibilities for nonbinary people. Some nonbinary people change their names and request different gender pronouns; gender-neutral pronouns are preferred by some, traditional pronouns by others. Mannerisms and clothing and hairstyles vary according to the expression or presentation the individual identifies with. Medical treatments and surgical options may be pursued, depending on an individual's personal sense of their sexed body in relation to their internal gender identity. Legal transition can be trickier for nonbinary people; no U.S. states currently offer a third option for sex markers on driver's licenses. However, this may soon change: Oregon recently became the first state to legally recognize nonbinary gender.[16]

WHY DOES IT MATTER?

Many cisgender people consider gender identity to be a private affair and wonder why it should matter so much. If you think about it, though, cisgender people are just as concerned about gender as trans people are. The clothing industry has created gender-specific clothing designed to enhance secondary sex characteristics. Many cisgender men and women spend quite a lot of time on gendered grooming, to ensure that their gender expression is not just appropriate but aesthetically pleasing to whomever they seek to attract. For those who feel that their body does not fit the gender ideal, there is cosmetic surgery to augment or reduce gendered tissues. There are entire magazines devoted to helping readers attain a more appealing gender presentation. There are separate aisles for gendered toys, and children sometimes even get scolded for playing with a toy inappropriate to their perceived gender.

Gender is clearly important, and even when it's not being reinforced by rigid expectations, most cisgender people still have a strong internal knowledge of their gendered selves and would not very much like to be mistaken for the "opposite" gender. Gender is important to nonbinary people, too, but there are some factors that make it more challenging.

Dysphoria

Being misgendered (perceived as a gender you are not) can be a painful experience. Being deadnamed (called by one's birth name), referred to with incorrect pronouns, or told you are in the wrong bathroom can trigger dysphoria. Dysphoria is an intense feeling of distress associated with misgendering or with one's sexed body not feeling aligned with one's gender. Dysphoria is often the catalyst that motivates transition. That said, not every trans person experiences dysphoria, and dysphoria is not a necessary "symptom" to determine whether somebody is authentically trans.

Human Rights

Gender identity is still not a protected characteristic for many states' hate crimes legislation. Nor is it protected against employment or housing discrimination or bullying in school. This means that many nonbinary people can be legally discriminated against: they can be denied housing, fired for being trans, or not have bullies held accountable.[17] And yet, trans status is one of the top factors in school bullying,[18] and trans and gender nonconforming people (particularly transfeminine people of color) are being attacked and murdered for no other reason than their gender identities.[19]

Being Seen

Finally, I can think of very few people who do not yearn to be truly seen by their loved ones and communities. It is a part of relationship building to disclose important personal experiences and characteristics. Loving somebody and being loved involves appreciating each other at our most authentic and real. Nonbinary people want to be seen and known just as much as anybody else, and this is why coming out is important.

NOTES

1. Katy Steinmetz, "The Transgender Tipping Point," *Time*, May 29, 2014.

2. This is hyperbole, of course; there are probably as many genders as there are people.

3. In Melanie Blackless et al., "How Sexually Dimorphic Are We? Review and Synthesis," *American Journal of Human Biology* 12 (2000): 151–66; the authors determined that as many as 1 percent of people's bodies differ from the standard male or female.

4. Joanne Meyerowitz, *How Sex Changed: A History of Transsexuality in the United States* (Cambridge, MA: Harvard University Press, 2002), 98–129.

5. Margaret Mead, *Male and Female: A Study of the Sexes in a Changing World* (New York: William Morrow, 1949).

6. Meyerowitz, *How Sex Changed*, 115.

7. Judith Butler, *Gender Trouble: Feminism and the Subversion of Identity* (New York: Routledge, 1990), 33.

8. Harry Benjamin, *The Transsexual Phenomenon: A Scientific Report on Transsexualism and Sex Conversion in the Human Male and Female* (New York: Julian, 1966), 13.

9. Leslie Feinberg, *Transgender Liberation: A Movement Whose Time Has Come* (New York: World View Forum, 1992).

10. I will be using "trans" as an umbrella term for this book.

11. Non-transgender.

12. Serena Nanda, *Gender Diversity: Crosscultural Variations* (Long Grove, IL: Waveland, 2000), 11–13.

13. For a rich discussion of Two-Spirit traditions, see http://www.dancingtoeagle spiritsociety.org.

14. As described by Marilyn Roxie, "Genderqueer History," http://genderqueerid .com/gqhistory.

15. See appendix A for a glossary of terminology and appendix B for more information about gender pronouns.

16. Christopher Mele, "Oregon Court Allows a Person to Choose Neither Sex," *New York Times*, June 13, 2016, http://www.nytimes.com/2016/06/14/us/oregon -nonbinary-transgender-sex-gender.html.

17. For up-to-date equality maps, see http://www.lgbtmap.org.

18. Joseph G. Kosciw, Emily A. Greytak, Neal A. Palmer, and Madelyn J. Boesen, "The 2013 National School Climate Survey: The Experiences of Lesbian, Gay, Bisexual and Transgender Youth in Our Nation's Schools," Gay, Lesbian & Straight Education Network, 2014, http://www.glsen.org/article/2013-national-school -climate-survey.

19. Too many citations to count. See the Trans Day of Remembrance for a list of names from 2007 to the present at https://tdor.info.

2

Nonbinary Visibility in the United States

Conceptualizing nonbinary history is inherently problematic. Not only do identity terms change rapidly, but gender as a concept is fairly new. Behaviors and styles that might be labeled nonbinary today had no such labels even in the fairly recent past. And it is impossible to truly classify a historical person's gender without a good amount of evidence. That said, gender nonconformity is not new, and it is possible to trace a shaky lineage of nonbinary ancestors through history. This chapter attempts to bring together some of this history, including the transgender liberation movement, nonbinary-specific activism, culture, health, and the activities of the current generation. The geographic location of this chapter is the United States; although this history might be more properly labeled Western, there is currently very little historical record outside the United States to analyze. See the following chapter for a discussion of culturally specific nonbinary genders, which have been separated in order to avoid a colonialist mentality of subsuming indigenous categories into Western ones.

THE TRANSGENDER MOVEMENT

In the early years of the transgender movement, the term "nonbinary" had not yet been applied to gender, making it difficult to pick out the nonbinary-specific strands from the rich tapestry of trans struggle and liberation. Nevertheless, nonbinary gender identities have always been part of the transgender community. Therefore, an understanding of the broader trans history is essential to contextualize contemporary nonbinary identities.

Early Visibility

Sexual behavior and gender identity were not neat categories in the late nineteenth century. Genitals dictated gender roles, which were complementary in order to ensure both reproduction and marital harmony. Cross-sex identification was theorized to be due to confused homosexual tendencies; such people were often labeled inverts.[1] It wasn't until 1910, when German physician Magnus Hirschfeld published his pivotal book *Transvestites*, that cross-sex identification was separated from homosexuality.[2] At his Institute for Sexual Science in Berlin, Hirschfeld pioneered surgical sex alteration in the 1920s and early 1930s until the rise of the Nazi regime.[3]

While surgery to remove diseased reproductive organs was not unknown in the United States, it was rare for a physician to perform surgery for cross-sex identification. Only a handful of case studies exist before 1952, when New Yorker Christine Jorgensen made her public debut after surgery in Copenhagen.[4] With her carefully curated public persona, Jorgensen both humanized the idea of sex change for the cisgender American public and allowed other "transvestites" to hope for the same. By the 1960s, American scientific scholarship began to use the term "transsexual" and surgical intervention started becoming acceptable.[5]

Meanwhile, trans woman Louise Lawrence had been living as a woman in San Francisco since the 1940s. She worked with Alfred Kinsey in the 1950s to collect data in order to understand the histories and needs of trans people.[6] Prior to this work, Kinsey believed that transsexual women were actually homosexual men.[7] In addition to assisting with increasing behavioral and medical knowledge, Lawrence also started a trans correspondence network and mentored Virginia Prince, who founded peer support groups and publications for cross-dressing men.[8]

In all of the scientific literature up to this point, the primary concepts involved biological and psychological *sex*. The concept of *gender* arose from anthropological and medical conversations about sex roles and social learning. John Money and his colleagues were the first to use the term "gender" in their scholarship about intersex children; they defined this term as "outlook, demeanor, and orientation."[9] The concept was developed further by Robert

FIGURE 2.1
Photo of Christine Jorgensen, taken by Maurice Seymour in January 1954.

Stoller and Ralph Greenson, who distinguished "gender identity" from "gender role," explicitly differentiating feelings and behaviors.[10]

Riots and Organizing

While trans people's identities were being theorized, their activities were also being criminalized. Many cities had anti-cross-dressing laws that were invoked to harass and arrest trans people, particularly trans women. Trans women and drag queens were vulnerable to assault and rape by male inmates, unless they were housed in the so-called queens' tank.[11] Relentless marginalization by police, which also included arrest for nuisance crimes such as prostitution and loitering, gradually fomented more and more resentment and anger in the trans and drag communities.

The first known instance of group resistance occurred in May of 1959 in a Los Angeles coffeehouse called Cooper's Donuts. Police often made sweeps of popular social establishments, demanding identification and arresting those whose identity didn't match their gender marker. This time, though, there was spontaneous opposition: customers threw donuts at police, which led to fighting and many arrestees escaping.[12] In 1966, a similar incident occurred in San Francisco, at Compton's Cafeteria in the Tenderloin district. The manager, irritated by a group of boisterous queens, called the police to evict them. But when an officer roughly grabbed one of them, she threw her coffee in his face, starting a riot that destroyed the interior of the café as well as a police car and newspaper stand outside. Witnesses and participants recall queens using their purses to hit police officers and kicking them with their heels.[13]

Three years later, the most widely known queer and trans riot erupted in New York. The Stonewall Inn in Greenwich Village was a hot spot for dancing and cruising for mostly Black and Latinx[14] trans women, drag queens, gay men, and some lesbians. The bar was Mafia run and police raids occurred whenever payoffs were late. But on June 28, 1969, the raid was anything but routine: people began throwing coins at officers to shame them for their corruption. When Sylvia Rivera was sharply prodded with a baton, she retaliated by throwing a beer bottle, starting a dramatic riot that lasted for hours and involved more than two thousand people.[15]

After these instances of spontaneous direct action, trans people began to organize. Sylvia Rivera, with fellow Stonewall activist Marsha P. Johnson, founded Street Transvestite Action Revolutionaries (STAR) in 1969. Drag

FIGURE 2.2

Marsha P. Johnson (L, holding cooler) and Sylvia Rivera (R, holding banner) march-
ing with the Street Transvestite Action Revolutionaries (STAR) in the 1973 Gay Pride
Parade in New York City. Photographer Leonard Fink; reprinted with permission of the
Lesbian, Gay, Bisexual & Transgender Community Center Archives.

queen Lee Brewster founded Queens Liberation Front (QLF) in 1970. The same year, trans woman Judy Bowen started Transsexuals and Transvestites (TAT) and trans woman Angela Douglas started the Transvestite/Trans-sexual Action Organization (TAO). In 1971, an androgynous organization called AND/OR was founded by trans woman Lee Ann Charlotte. These and other organizations existed primarily to assist trans people with legal aid and medical care, as well as to protest medical gatekeeping and exploitation.[16]

Fissures within the LGBT Community

The term "LGBT community" is a bit of a misnomer. Although an umbrella is supposed to cover everybody, many individuals feel most strongly about their own particular issues, and some even seek to expel those whose identities are unfamiliar. In 1973, trans lesbian Beth Elliot was ousted from the West Coast Lesbian Feminist Conference because the community did not want to include trans women. In 1979, cisgender feminist hatred of trans women was codified in Janice G. Raymond's *Transsexual Empire: The Making of the She-Male*, which characterized trans women as male rapists attempting to infiltrate women's spaces.[17] Lesbian transphobia was again sanctioned in 1991, at the Michigan Womyn's Music Festival: producers Barbara Price and Lisa Vogel stated that only "womyn-born womyn" were permitted.[18]

Of course, cisgender lesbians were not the only bullies. Some cisgender gay men sought to distance themselves from trans politics, arguing that effeminacy damaged the reputation of the gay community. Even within the trans community, political and identity differences resulted in fallings out. Several organizations that had started as alliances between transvestites and transsexuals changed their focus to transsexual rights when cisgender drag queen members rejected medical aid measures. The differences between transsexual and transgender politics created another schism. More recently, nonbinary and gender-nonconforming trans people have been criticized by binary trans people for not passing.[19]

The Emergence of Genderqueer

There have always been people who have rejected binary gender. In fact, transsexual poster child Christine Jorgensen apparently saw herself (and everybody else, for that matter) as being both male and female. In answer to an interviewer in 1957 asking her if she was a woman, Jorgensen responded,

"You seem to assume that every person is either a man or a woman. . . . Each person is actually both in varying degrees. . . . I am more of a woman than I am a man."[20] But the term "genderqueer" wasn't innovated until 1995, when Transexual Menace cofounder Riki Anne Wilchins used the term in a newsletter:

> The fight against gender oppression has been joined for centuries, perhaps millennia. What's new today is that it's moving into the arena at open political activism. And nope, this is not just one more civil rights struggle for one more narrowly-defined minority. It's about all of us who are genderqueer: diesel dykes and stone butches, leatherqueens and radical fairies, nelly fags, crossdressers, intersexed, transsexuals, transvestites, transgendered, transgressively gendered, and those of us whose gender expressions are so complex they haven't even been named yet.[21]

The new term gained popularity quickly. The word "queer" is associated with political activism; people who use it are reclaiming it from earlier derogatory usage. Queering gender is the practice of challenging gender binary norms. This practice may include presenting an androgynous style,[22] or deliberately mixing gender markers in order to confuse or confound.[23] The term is not perfect; some people do not identify their gender as being inherently political, and many people of color consider genderqueer to be a White academic term.[24] For these and other reasons, a great many other terms have proliferated.

NONBINARY ACTIVISM

In using the term "nonbinary," I refer to all identities that fall under the umbrella of "not solely male or female." Activism in this community has included refusing to conform to binary gender norms, insisting on being seen and validated, fighting against data systems that falsely dichotomize, and liberating restrooms.

Hate Crimes and Microaggressions

People that transgress gender norms are often policed, harassed, and sometimes even assaulted. Policing can include subtle digs from peers ("You should really shave your legs so you don't look so weird in that dress") to actual police attention. Trans activist Dean Spade, for example, was arrested in

2002 for failing to pass as a man when using a men's restroom.[25] People who are visibly ambiguous or who do not pass are often subjected to humiliating comments from strangers ("What is that? Is that a boy or a girl?") and called "it" and "he-she."

Occasionally, hatred crosses the line from harassment to assault. So-called corrective rape, wherein a person is raped in order to pressure them to conform to gender norms, happens to cisgender lesbians who are too butch, trans people who do not pass, and nonbinary people who are visually gender nonconforming. Sometimes, a person or group of people will attack somebody simply for existing in a shared space. In 2013, high school student Sasha Fleischman was asleep on a bus when their skirt was set on fire by another student. Sasha survived with second- and third-degree burns to the legs.[26]

While it could be said that media coverage of harassment against nonbinary people lends visibility and community support, the effects of discrimination and violence are devastating to individuals and the community as a whole. Microaggressions, those subtle and often unconscious forms of bias against marginalized people, have a heavy impact on mental health, including lower self-esteem, higher rates of depression, and a higher prevalence of alcohol abuse.[27] Implicit or explicit bias on the parts of police officers or medical personnel has the potential to severely alter a nonbinary person's well-being, from an officer choosing which cell to house an arrestee to a doctor not taking a medical complaint seriously.

Fighting Data Systems

Data systems pertaining to health care, government, and schools generally presume a binary gender identity. In health care, most intake forms have two ticky boxes for male and female. Insurance policies often omit trans-specific services. Providers often range from ill informed to actively discriminatory. Government data systems, including driver's licenses, passports, and other identity documents, only have two gender markers in the United States.[28] While most people can successfully change their gender marker from one binary sex to another, there does not yet exist a nonbinary marker. And in K–12 schools and colleges, the gender binary persists in application paperwork, digital content management environments, and class registration forms.

Changes are being made, slowly but surely, thanks to long-term activist efforts and individual resistance. In Oregon, Jamie Shupe was legally classified as nonbinary on June 10, 2016, after a legal sex/gender change petition was granted by a judge.[29] This historic first has already been followed by many other petitioners seeking the same.[30] And many colleges and universities are expanding their policies to allow students to self-identify their names and pronouns. Harvard University, Ohio University, the University of California system, University of Vermont, and others are now allowing students to choose their gender identities and pronouns on application and registration forms. Many colleges and universities allow students to enter their "preferred name" into content management systems. Some are even offering pronoun primers on their websites to help students learn how to use epicene pronouns.[31]

Restroom Liberation

Restrooms have long been a point of contention for nonbinary people. Most public facilities are gendered according to the binary, so nonbinary people have to make a choice to be uncomfortable and avoid using the restroom at all or be uncomfortable and use a restroom that denies their identity and may also result in harassment or violence. A person who is androgynous and very visually ambiguous may be subjected to stares; a person who was assigned female at birth may be sexually assaulted if they use the men's restroom; a person who was assigned male at birth may be yelled at or physically assaulted if they use the women's restroom. These things happen to binary trans people, too, of course. But binary people generally want to use the appropriate binary restroom, while for many nonbinary people, there *is* no appropriate restroom.

Luckily, this is changing, too. Some public facilities have gender-neutral or gender-inclusive restrooms. The trend has increased in colleges and universities and in public libraries and other government buildings. Most of these restrooms are single-user restrooms, because of the idea that cisgender users may not want to share a multiple-user restroom with a transgender person. And many of these restrooms are located in the basement, or other difficult-to-access locations. But these problems, too, are slowly getting better, as activists continue to educate policy makers, educators, and business owners.[32]

FIGURE 2.3
Comic reprinted with permission of Jason Gross; appeared on http://artdweeb.tumblr.com in 2012.

NONBINARY CULTURE

Although nonbinary people often integrate easily into the wider queer culture, there are several cultural markers that are uniquely nonbinary. Perhaps most obvious is the proliferation of identity terms and other linguistic phenomena. Many nonbinary people also follow a distinctive nonbinary style. And there are many nonbinary culture creators innovating, remixing, and disseminating nonbinary representations.

Evolving Language

In a 2008 study by the National Center for Transgender Equality, the question "What is your primary gender identity today?" resulted in a plethora of write-in responses. Respondents identified as in-between, nongendered, fluid, bigender, third gender, genderfuck, rebel, birl, neutrois, gender blur, radical, and more.[33] The creative language surrounding identity is both serious and playful: people are invested in being authentic and understood while they are clearly enjoying wordplay. Indeed, the researchers in the study concluded that

> while much of the data in the study catalogs serious and widespread violations of human rights, this data testifies to resilience, humor, and a spirit of resistance to gender indoctrination and policing among respondents.[34]

Language play is especially evident on the Internet, where communities innovate, disseminate, and evolve pronoun sets, identity terms, and etiquette practices. Any individual can participate in creating new terms; whether that new term takes off depends on the community as a whole. Posts that get shared and remixed have a wider audience, and the language within is thus more likely to be incorporated. Essentially, language is alive, and the incredible reach and speed of the Internet accelerates its evolution.

Nonbinary pronouns have been particularly important to the community. When the term "genderqueer" began to be used in the late 1990s, many genderqueer people started using the pronouns ze and hir.[35] Although some people are still using these pronouns, many others found them to be clunky in practice, and began playing with other nongendered pronouns. Some pronouns were taken from science fiction novels; some from other languages; and some sprang into existence seemingly from nowhere. Currently, singular "they" seems to have gained the most popularity.

Sartorial Choices

Many nonbinary people present in an androgynous way, with short hair, trousers, and a suppression of secondary sex characteristics (binding chests, tucking genitals, and removing facial hair). Overtly queer signifiers such as gingham, bowties, handkerchiefs, and asymmetrical hairstyles are popular. However, some nonbinary people question the unspoken assumptions about androgyny: that it leans more masculine; that it is typically embodied in White people; that it can only be pulled off by people who have a slim body shape.

For this group, dresses and skirts can be androgynous, people of color can be androgynous, and fat people can be androgynous. What's more, androgyny doesn't have to be the target expression. Femme styles can be nonbinary, and so can butch styles. Just because a cisgender person may not be able to "read" a nonbinary expression doesn't invalidate it. For some people, deliberately confusing cisgender society by mixing gendered style markers is both resistance and fashion. This discussion, and many questions and lines of investigation originating from it, are propagating in community spaces and on the Internet, and can be seen most vividly in curated style blogs.

Art and Technology

Since the advent of the Internet, marginalized people have had greater opportunities to socialize, support one another, and participate in media creation. For nonbinary people, the image-oriented microblogging platform Tumblr has been a key means for community building. As a relatively accessible network for self-representation, many nonbinary youth with intersectional identities have achieved visibility. With Tumblr, people can curate portraits, interviews, and quotes, creating ever-changing art installations focusing on the intersections of gender, race, ability, and size.[36]

Before the Internet (and still today, to a lesser extent), nonbinary people expressed themselves through zine[37] creation and other DIY cultural modes of production. Scrapbooking and collage were in vogue during the post–World War II era.[38] When nonbinary people are not visible in mainstream media, they create and circulate their own images—or they "read" genderqueerness in celebrities and media representations. For example, many people saw the musician Prince as a nonbinary icon, for his blending of feminine and masculine styles and behaviors. See chapter 4 for a deeper discussion of nonbinary gender in popular culture.

NONBINARY HEALTH

We've come a long way from desperate letter writing to surgeons to do experimental surgeries. After the first public cases of transsexual surgeries, the medical community created a model for working with trans patients. Early models were deeply pathologizing, constructing the trans patient as mentally ill. In order to gain access to transition-related care, trans people were forced to work within a strict pathological structure, acquiescing to a clinical label and a rigid path of specific medical and surgical treatments.

Developing Best Practices

In 1979, the World Professional Association for Transgender Health (WPATH), created a standards of care document to educate clinicians on transgender health and promote evidence-based care. Over time, this document has been updated as research and practice has evolved. Today, the seventh version of this document, released in 2012, is the most inclusive to date. Gender-nonconforming people are included in the title, and health care specific to the nonbinary population is incorporated throughout the entire document. Furthermore, being trans is explicitly stated to be a matter of natural human diversity rather than pathology.[39]

Ways to Transition

As previously stated, there are many ways to transition, and not everybody can or wishes to. However, the possibilities have been greatly expanded by the recent update to the WPATH standards of care. For trans and gender-nonconforming youth, hormone suppression therapy can prevent irreversible pubertal changes such as breast development or facial hair growth. These adolescents are gifted with more time to explore their gender identities before deciding whether to transition.[40] Many nonbinary people transition, although no two transitions look alike. Some people mix and match medical and surgical interventions, selecting which feel necessary to alleviate dysphoria or align the individual with their self-image. For others, medical and surgical treatment is unnecessary, but social transition is paramount. And for some people, transition is either unimportant or inaccessible due to financial or social burdens.

Despite having such different experiences with transition, nonbinary people do have similar developmental milestones, regardless of assigned sex at birth. Nonbinary people tend to know that they are different at a young age; some but not all express their different gender identity either through behavior, presentation, or by telling the adults in their life. At some point comes the realization that their gender identity is valid. They may meet another nonbinary person or see themselves reflected in literature or other media. Then there is a period of exploration in which the individual decides whether and how to express their gender identity to others. Nonbinary gender presentation leads to societal resistance: a refusal to accommodate gender-neutral pronouns and use new names is especially common. Much of this resistance comes from the wider queer community, so at this point the nonbinary individual often feels alienated from their former community. In the final milestone, the nonbinary individual creates their own support network within or outside of the wider queer or transgender community.[41]

THE NEW GENERATION

As media representations of nonbinary people increase, gender nonconformity is normalized. Young people growing up today are more likely to question strict gender roles, wear the clothes that they like without worrying about societal disapproval, and accept and support transgender peers. Nonbinary children are coming out earlier and have more support at home and in the classroom. Social justice movements are embracing multiple identities. And youth are moving away from gendered language.

Early Self-Awareness

Young children generally know exactly who they are, and they will tell parents and other adults if they have not been disciplined out of doing so. Many children will have gender-nonconforming behaviors but will not necessarily grow up to be transgender—because gender norms are socially constructed. In her work with youth, developmental psychologist Diane Ehrensaft has come up with several terms to help caregivers understand their gender-creative children. Gender hybrids are children who experience themselves as a combination of girl and boy. Genderfluid children move along the gender spectrum or outside of it. Protogay children may play with gender before they realize they are gay. And prototransgender youth first come out as gay before later realizing they are transgender.[42]

Children and adolescents who are gender nonconforming are at risk for bullying and intolerance at school, as well as family rejection. This in turn is associated with higher risk of depression and other mental illness later in life.[43] However, children whose gender identities are affirmed by family have better health outcomes, including increased self-care and lower incidence of risk behavior.[44] Pediatricians and other providers are now better educated about gender variance in youth, and can help caregivers understand and provide much-needed gender affirmation. Furthermore, the recent abundance of supportive children's books has the potential to have a positive impact on family support and individual self-esteem.

New Activisms

The younger generation is moving away from one-issue politics.[45] Intersectionality, a term coined by Kimberlé Crenshaw in 1991,[46] describes the system of overlapping oppressions that Black women face. In response to the lived experience of the doubly (or triply, or . . .) marginalized, new activisms are focusing on intersectional justice. Black Lives Matter, for example, has explicitly embraced trans and gender-nonconforming Black identities. Rallies across the nation have included "Black Trans Lives Matter" signs, and cisgender BLM activists have supported nonbinary politics, and vice versa. The Portland, Oregon, chapter, among others, has publicly stated support for all gender identities and expressions:

> We reject cis-heterosexism—we are queer, trans, and non-binary Black/
> Africans and we struggle beside and for queer, trans, and non-binary Black/
> Africans. We embrace and fight for the full and free expression of the entire
> spectrum of Black/African gender, sexuality, and identity.[47]

Many other social justice organizations focus on the intersections between gender identity, sexuality, race, class, ability, nationality, and so on—with the intent to make these interlocking oppressions visible and to provide support and advocacy.[48] It's clear that for many nonbinary youth, gender is not the only political issue, and centering the voices of the multiply marginalized is of the utmost importance.

Eschewing Labels; Embracing Fluidity

More and more youth are exploring gender expression and questioning gender norms without necessarily identifying as nonbinary. And more and more youth are accepting gender nonconformity in others, and changing their use of gendered language to support their peers. For example, in 2004, middle and high school students in Baltimore spontaneously innovated a new gender-neutral pronoun, "yo."[49] This word is commonly used as a greeting or attention-focusing device, but these populations expanded its use. It's interesting to note that students using "yo" as a pronoun applied it to all genders, a supportive phenomenon that is also occurring with the use of "they" in other populations. It seems that youth seeking to support nonbinary friends often elect to simply use nongendered language throughout their peer groups.

NOTES

1. For a deeper explanation of the various theories and categories of the time, see chapter 1 in Joanne Meyerowitz, *How Sex Changed: A History of Transsexuality in the United States* (Cambridge, MA: Harvard University Press, 2002).

2. Meyerowitz, *How Sex Changed*, 18–19.

3. Meyerowitz, *How Sex Changed*, 19–21.

4. Meyerowitz, *How Sex Changed*, 62.

5. Meyerowitz, *How Sex Changed*, 97.

6. Susan Stryker, "Transgender Activism," in *GLBTQ Encyclopedia Project*, ed. Claude Summers (2004).

7. Meyerowitz, *How Sex Changed*, 171.

8. Stryker, "Transgender Activism."

9. Cited in Meyerowitz, *How Sex Changed*, 114.

10. Meyerowitz, *How Sex Changed*, 115.

11. Meyerowitz, *How Sex Changed*, 137.

12. Susan Stryker, *Transgender History* (Berkeley, CA: Seal, 2008), 59–61.

13. Stryker, *Transgender History*, 63–65.

14. Latinx is a gender-neutral term for people of Latin American descent.

15. Stryker, *Transgender History*, 82–85.

16. Meyerowitz, *How Sex Changed*, 235–39.

17. See Sandy Stone, "The Empire Strikes Back: A Posttranssexual Manifesto," in *Body Guards*, ed. Julia Epstein and Kristina Straub (New York: Routledge, 1991), 280–301 for a brilliant rebuttal.

18. Riki Anne Wilchins, *Read My Lips: Sexual Subversion and the End of Gender* (Ithaca, NY: Firebrand Books, 1997), 109.

19. Dianne Dentice and Michelle Dietert, "Liminal Spaces and the Transgender Experience," *Theory in Action* 8, no. 2 (April 2015): 74.

20. Quoted in Meyerowitz, *How Sex Changed*, 98.

21. Riki Anne Wilchins, *In Your Face*, Transexual Menace newsletter, Spring 1995.

22. For an explanation of the term and styles associated with it, see Tina Gianoulis, "Androgyny," in *GLBTQ Encyclopedia Project*, ed. Claude Summers (2004).

23. Brett Genny Beemyn, "Genderqueer," in *GLBTQ Encyclopedia Project*, ed. Claude Summers (2005).

24. Megan Davidson, "Seeking Refuge under the Umbrella: Inclusion, Exclusion, and Organizing Within the Category *Transgender*," *Sexuality Research & Social Policy: Journal of NSRC* 4, no. 4 (December 2007): 70. See also Rocko Bulldagger's list of people excluded from the genderqueer scene; people of color are number one. Rocko Bulldagger, "The End of Genderqueer," in *Nobody Passes: Rejecting the Rules of Gender and Conformity*, ed. Matt/Mattilda Bernstein Sycamore (Emeryville, CA: Seal, 2006), 146.

25. Dean Spade, "Undermining Gender Regulation," in Sycamore, *Nobody Passes*, 65.

26. Tracey Taylor, "Supporters Rally for Berkeley Student Set on Fire on Bus," *Berkeleyside*, November 6, 2013, http://www.berkeleyside.com/2013/11/06/supporters-rally-for-berkeley-student-set-on-fire-on-bus.

27. Kevin L. Nadal et al., "Microaggressions toward Lesbian, Gay, Bisexual, Transgender, Queer, and Genderqueer People: A Review of the Literature," *Journal of Sex Research* 53, no. 4–5 (May–June 2016): 489.

28. However, as of this writing, the Oregon DMV is considering a third gender marker.

29. Christopher Mele, "Oregon Court Allows a Person to Choose Neither Sex," *New York Times*, June 13, 2016, http://www.nytimes.com/2016/06/14/us/oregon-nonbinary-transgender-sex-gender.html.

30. As of this writing, petitioners in Oregon, California, and Colorado have been granted legal nonbinary status.

31. Collin Binkley, "He? She? Ze? Colleges Add Gender-Free Pronouns, Alter Policy," *Seattle Times*, September 18, 2015, http://www.seattletimes.com/nation-world/nation/he-she-ze-colleges-add-gender-free-pronouns-to-forms.

32. See, for example, Isaac West, "PISSAR's Critically Queer and Disabled Politics," *Communication and Critical/Cultural Studies* 7, no. 2 (2010): 156–75.

33. Jack Harrison, Jaime Grant, and Jody L. Herman, "A Gender Not Listed Here: Genderqueers, Gender Rebels, and OtherWise in the National Transgender Discrimination Survey," *LGBTQ Policy Journal at the Harvard Kennedy School* 2 (2011–2012): 13–24.

34. Harrison et al., "A Gender Not Listed Here," 20.

35. See appendix B for a discussion of epicene pronoun usage.

36. Although, while projects like this can disrupt cultural norms, the sharing mechanism tends to reinforce norms, such as Whiteness, able-bodiedness, and thinness in relation to nonbinary fashion. For further discussion, see Marty Fink and Quinn Miller, "Trans Media Moments: Tumblr, 2011–2013," *Television & New Media* 15, no. 7 (2014): 617–19.

37. Zines are informal, do-it-yourself (DIY) publications, often created by cutting and pasting text and images and then photocopying.

38. Fink and Miller, "Trans Media Moments," 619.

39. Eli Coleman et al., "Standards of Care for the Health of Transsexual, Transgender, and Gender-Nonconforming People, 7th Version," World Professional Association for Transgender Health (2012), www.wpath.org.

40. Jamie Feldman and Katherine Spencer, "Medical and Surgical Management of the Transgender Patient: What the Primary Care Clinician Needs to Know," in *Fenway Guide to Lesbian, Gay, Bisexual, and Transgender Health*, 2nd ed., ed. Harvey J. Makadon et al. (Philadelphia: American College of Physicians, 2015): 508–9. See also Coleman et al., "Standards of Care," 18–20.

41. Genny Beemyn and Susan Rankin, *The Lives of Transgender People* (New York: Columbia University Press, 2011), 146–55.

42. Diane Ehrensaft, *Gender Born, Gender Made: Raising Healthy Gender-Nonconforming Children* (New York: Experiment, 2011), 9.

43. Scott Leibowitz, Stewart Adelson, and Cynthia Telingator, "Gender Nonconformity and Gender Discordance in Childhood and Adolescence: Developmental Considerations and the Clinical Approach," in Makadon et al., *Fenway Guide*, 431.

44. Joanne G. Keatley et al., "Creating a Foundation for Improving Trans Health: Understanding Trans Identities and Health Care Needs," in Makadon et al., *Fenway Guide*, 465.

45. Which is not to say that members of older generations are all old fuddy-duddies who focus solely on their own political issues.

46. Kimberlé Crenshaw, "Mapping the Margins: Intersectionality, Identity Politics, and Violence against Women of Color," *Stanford Law Review* 43, no. 6 (1991): 1241–299.

47. Black Lives Matter PDX. "Unbroken, Black, and Free: A Statement on the Politics and Principles of Black Lives Matter Portland." http://blmpdx.tumblr.com.

48. See, for example, the Audre Lorde Project (http://alp.org), Black and Pink (http://www.blackandpink.org), and the Silvia Rivera Law Project (http://srlp.org).

49. Elaine M. Stotko and Margaret Troyer, "A New Gender-Neutral Pronoun in Baltimore, Maryland: A Preliminary Study," *American Speech* 82, no. 3 (Fall 2007): 262–79.

3

Culturally Specific Genders

Many precolonial societies recognized more than two genders, and many still do, despite colonization and the attendant forcible Eurocentric restructuring of indigenous gender concepts. On every continent but Antarctica, multiple genders have held important social and often religious roles within their particular cultures.[1] For these cultures, the existence of more than two genders was and is normal and accepted, meaning that the concept of transgender does not fit within these worldviews. Because culturally specific genders do not arise out of a binary gender concept, though, they can fit within a conversation about nonbinary gender—provided, of course, that culturally specific terms are used and Eurocentric gender constructs are stringently avoided.

This is not to say that European cultures have not recognized multiple genders. In Italy, for example, the femminiello (literally, "little woman-man") is a traditional alternate gender role for feminine males; these people are considered both useful and lucky.[2] In Albania and other Balkan regions, the burrnesha or "sworn virgins" swear a vow of chastity and wear traditional men's clothing in order to access patriarchal privileges such as land ownership.[3] And in nineteenth-century Anglo-America, masculine female persons proudly identified as tommies, tribades, female husbands, and inverts—all terms that encompass same-sex romantic and sexual attractions but connote a subtle gender shift away from the binary.[4]

While many cultural groups accept more than three genders, few nations grant legal recognition. In Australia, a nonbinary person can use the gender marker "X" on their passport; this change requires a statement from a medical practitioner without specific details.[5] In Bangladesh, there is a unique third gender category on passports.[6] Denmark allows adults to apply for gender marker "X" on passports without any medical gatekeeping.[7] In India, people can use gender marker "O" for other on voter registrations[8] and gender marker "T" for transgender on their passports.[9] Nepal allows gender marker "X" for indeterminate on passports.[10] In New Zealand, passports offer gender marker "X" for unspecified or indeterminate,[11] and government organizations have begun collecting data on gender-diverse residents in order to advance human rights.[12]

As of this writing, these six are the only countries to offer legal recognition on identity documents. Having a passport that reflects one's gender identity, however, does not necessarily mean that a nonbinary person can easily travel to countries that do not recognize their identity. In 2015, for example, the U.S. Consulate held one Indian traveler's visa application for two days because the "T" on her passport was confusing.[13]

This chapter will describe culturally specific gender systems in the Americas, Polynesia, India, and Southeast Asia, providing historical and contemporary details of social and religious roles. These regions were chosen because of the abundance of scholarship on this topic; this focus certainly does not indicate that other regions have fewer or less important genders. Because so much of this scholarship was produced by White cisgender men many decades ago, many sources are woefully ethnocentric, a fact that necessitates the following discussion.

EUROCENTRISM AND THE CONCEPT OF THE BERDACHE

When European colonial forces arrived in the Americas, they were concerned with documenting every aspect of the cultures they encountered in order to subjugate the indigenous people and assimilate them into their own ways of thinking about the world. And when anthropologists and other social researchers enter a foreign research space, they, too, document cultural differences, though generally for loftier reasons. Both of these groups of people, at different times, encountered alternate gender identities and roles in the Americas and took special notice.

Colonial History

During the Spanish Conquests, Spanish soldiers and missionaries settled in the Americas from the early sixteenth century through the early nineteenth century, building missions and military forts in order to establish control over the land and people. Governing officials, soldiers, and missionaries alike were horrified by the unfamiliar social and sexual roles that they encountered in indigenous communities. Sexual behaviors that they perceived as homosexual were labeled sinful; cross-gender dress and work were criticized as inferior and evidence of weakness as well as decadence.

In the colonial literature, a new term arose to describe these troublesome individuals: berdache. The word "berdache" comes from the Arabic *bardag* and Persian *bardaj*, meaning a captive or prisoner; this term became *bardaje* in Spanish and came to mean the passive partner in homosexual anal intercourse. In the highly religious and patriarchal colonial Spanish culture, this role was repellant and immoral; indigenous persons engaged in this activity received the label, and the term was codified to refer to them.[14]

In the colonial imagination, the berdache was a male who dressed as a woman, performed women's labor, and served a prostitutional role to preserve young girls' chastity and marriageability. Sources describe berdaches being offered to colonial officials and soldiers for sexual service, in addition to being used as sexual slaves among their own people. Shocked missionaries claimed that these poor souls were "selected" (in other words, coerced) as children to be raised as girls and then prostituted. Disgusted soldiers asserted that the berdache was "despised" because of his cowardice in avoiding warfare by taking the inferior feminine role.[15]

Because the indigenous people were viewed as primitive *gente sin razon*, simpleminded near animals who did not have the capacity to understand sin, colonial missionaries undertook a project to convert them—both to Christianity and to the rightful heterosexual binary gender system. Conversion was a long, slow process of religious instruction, confession, sermons, and rigid rules governing clothing, language, behavior, and work. Through these rituals and structures, European gender and sexuality structures were imposed on the new colonial subjects.[16] And because colonization is inextricably entwined with economic and political power, converts were not only subordinated with religion but also with labor exploitation.[17]

FIGURE 3.1

Valboa Throws Some Indians, Who Had Committed the Terrible Sin of Sodomy, to the Dogs to Be Torn Apart (1594). Theodor de Bry's *America* Collection, reprinted with permission of Special Collections, University of Houston Libraries.

Early Anthropologists

While anthropologists and other ethnographic researchers do not make a practice of subordinating their subjects, historically, they have had a colonial lens through which to document their data and analysis.[18] Early anthropologists were just as fascinated by the gender diversity they encountered, and while many also recorded the culturally specific terms for these identities, it is very telling that they continued to use the unfortunate term "berdache."

From the early 1900s to the late 1950s, anthropologists published a smattering of case studies and surveys of berdache roles and status in the United States. Many mistakenly assumed that this role was a form of institutional homosexuality. This is incorrect, of course, because what anthropologists called the berdache was in reality a nonbinary gender: a berdache could partner with men, women, or both. Furthermore, abundant data confirms that indigenous people can participate in homosexual behavior without being berdache.[19]

Many early anthropologists also assumed that only anatomical males could become berdache. Some believed that cross-dressing behavior was by choice, while others believed that it was forced upon those who displayed cowardice in warfare.[20] These are also incorrect assumptions: both anatomical males and females can be berdache, and their manner of dress should not be referred to as "cross-dressing" since they are simply dressing appropriately for their gender.

In the late 1960s, anthropologists studying the berdache began to publish less prejudicial accounts. Research began to be undertaken on a larger scale, so ethnographic data became more complex and cross-cultural syntheses were developed.[21] Researchers realized that what they called the berdache was an alternative gender role; that it was widespread; that a person became a berdache either due to childhood interests or a vision experience; and that berdaches were respected and held a special social and often religious role in their communities.[22]

Because the person anthropologists called berdache occupied a special, liminal space between and combining male and female, they had special gifts: not only were they spiritual intermediaries, but they were also especially skilled and productive with their creative work.[23] For example, We'wha, a Zuni *lhamana* (tribally specific term for the Zuni third gender role), was an expert in both weaving (a men's activity) and pottery (a women's activity). We'wha had a prominent role on the tribal council as well as an important ceremonial role in the kachina society. We'wha's status was not in spite of their[24] gender, but because of it: the Zuni origin myth teaches that the lhamana unifies society.[25]

Many early anthropologists believed that the violence of the colonial binary gender project had eradicated nearly all of the berdache people, and that tribal cultures no longer respected them. While it is true that colonialism enforced (and continues to enforce) cultural assimilation, Native peoples' cultures persist. Like any cultural practice, gender behaviors and roles change over time. Additionally, the prejudice of early anthropologists likely taught indigenous people to distrust ethnographers and hide evidence of gender diversity.[26]

FIGURE 3.2
Portrait of We'Wha Holding Clay Ceremonial Prayer-Meal Basket 1900. NAA INV 02440800, National Anthropological Archives, Smithsonian Institution. Reprinted with permission of Smithsonian Institution.

Criticism, Sovereignty, and Decolonization

Many First Nations and Native American people have criticized the term "berdache" and the colonial mentality that accompanies it. The word "berdache," with its meaning rooted in masculinity, coercion, and specific sexual activity (captive male; male prostitute; passive homosexual intercourse), is offensive and inaccurate. And the ways in which it has been applied to various indigenous identities is derogatory and indicative of a vast ignorance of specific tribal understandings of gender. First colonial soldiers and missionaries, then Anglo and European ethnographers, applied this term to describe cross-gender behaviors and sexual practices as being specifically debased, because in the Anglo-European worldview, femininity is inferior to masculinity. For non-Natives to continue to use this term is an act of violence and erasure of Native identities.[27]

Indigenous people have also criticized the research methodologies of "berdache studies." The large-scale surveys that were used to draw conclusions about the berdache role cross-culturally were inherently flawed: producing a universal berdache is bad methodology because there is no such thing as a Pan-Indian identity.[28] A number of indigenous scholars began producing their own scholarship to counter these misconceptions. For example, Navajo scholar Carolyn Epple produced robust scholarship on the nádleehí, privileging Navajo understandings of interconnectedness and fluidity. She asserted that "the synthesis of nádleehí and others into a single category has often ignored the variability across native American cultures and left unexamined the relevance of gender and sexuality."[29] Indeed, any culturally specific concept must be analyzed by using the appropriate cultural frameworks.

Categorizing and analyzing indigenous concepts through an Anglo-European lens is not only Eurocentric but also produces misinformation. Indigenous scholars and activists have firmly contested the Eurocentric lens, insisting that researchers must privilege indigenous understandings of identity, family, and community in order to accurately describe indigenous identities. In most First Nations and Native American cultures, children are accorded much more autonomy than Anglo children typically are. Parenting emphasizes self-determination and autonomy; children are highly valued and their identity development is respected. In addition, gender differences are complementary rather than hierarchical. Because femininity is not subordinated, gender diversity is not only accepted but celebrated.[30] Finally,

indigenous worldviews generally position the individual as being intercon-
nected with their family, community, and the world as a whole. Within this
framework, each person is valued for their own unique gifts.[31]

Looking through this indigenous lens, gender diversity is not shocking or
confusing. Children are fully expected to determine their own identities and
the idea of guiding them to conform to parental expectations would be insulting and wrong. Women, men, and other genders each have social, religious,
and economic roles that work together in harmony.

In 1990, at a gathering of gay and lesbian First Nations and Native American people in Winnipeg, a group of people coined the term "Two-Spirit"[32] as
an intertribal umbrella term for indigenous gender and sexual identities outside the European binaries. This term signifies direct resistance to colonial in-
terpretations of tribally specific identities, in particular the term "berdache."
At the same time, because it is an umbrella term, it resists rigid definition; it
is slippery, complex, and fluid, intended to be used and defined by indigenous
people from different cultural backgrounds. Two-Spirit contests colonial labels, including the White LGBTQ community's identity categories.[33]

Because Two-Spirit identity is an intersection of indigenous identity and
specifically indigenous gender and sexuality, non-Natives should not use this
term to describe themselves. Yet, some White admirers are doing just that.
To be clear, appropriation of an indigenous identity term is an act of colonial
violence. Indigenous identity is not a costume that can be worn for pleasure
and then discarded. Two-Spirit is "an expression of [indigenous] sexual and
gender identities as sovereign from those of white GLBT movements."[34]

GENDER SYSTEMS IN THE AMERICAS

Many, but not all, indigenous societies in the Americas recognize more than
two genders. In Canada and the United States alone, more than 150 tribes
are represented in the "berdache" literature. This does not take into account
tribes that were not surveyed or tribes that were not forthcoming with the
ethnographers who visited them. In Central and South America, scholars
generally used the term "third gender" or "third sex" to refer to gender diversity. Research in these regions has been more general (i.e., often by country
rather than by village or tribe), but far less pejorative than the early "berdache" studies.

First Nations and Native Americans

In the First Nations (Canada) and Native American (United States) tribes that recognize more than two genders, there are tribally specific names for these identities. For example, among the Osage, there is a third gender identity called *mixu'ga* ("moon instructed"). In the Lakota language, the third gender is referred to as *winkte* ("would-be woman") and the fourth gender is referred to as *lila witkowin* ("crazy woman"). The Quinault call their third gender *keknatsa'nxwix*^W ("part woman") and their fourth gender *tawkxwa'nsix*^W ("man-acting").[35]

It is important to recognize that tribally specific genders are distinct and unique, even though some similarities exist across some cultures. There is no universal "berdache," despite the prevalence of anthropological literature making this claim. Gender diversity in First Nations and Native American tribes can involve crossing from one gender role to another, mixing masculine and feminine components, or moving back and forth between gender roles over time.[36] Individuals occupying these alternate gender roles can partner with or marry members of either sex, just as binary gender has no impact on sexual orientation. In many, but not all, tribes, these individuals were historically respected as healers and medicine persons, and were embodied in oral narratives as culture heroes, tricksters, and other supernatural beings.[37]

While the ethnographic literature and oral traditions of First Nations and Native American tribes reveal respect and reverence for gender diversity, colonialism has had a negative impact on Native attitudes today:

> Native American Queer Communities have to deal with unique issues as a result of our history, cultural status, and perceptions as Natives. We come out of a history of genocide, our people have been persecuted, killed, kidnapped, forced into residential schools and assimilated for hundreds of years, and we still face lingering aspects of genocide. We face homophobia and sexism from our own people, racism from lesbians and gays, and racism, homophobia, and sexism from the dominant society, not to mention the classism many Native Americans have to deal with. It is important to remember that we Natives today are not the same as the Natives that lived before the arrival of the white man.[38]

However, many indigenous people demonstrate survivance—resilience in the face of colonialism and assimilation tactics—and proudly identify as

FIGURE 3.3
Spirit Wildcat (L) and Landa Lakes (R) at the 2015 Bay Area American Indian Two-Spirit Powwow; photograph copyright Alana Perino. Reprinted with permission of Alana Perino.

Two-Spirit today. In February 2015, for example, San Francisco hosted the nation's first Two-Spirit powwow, the Bay Area American Indian Two-Spirit Powwow, which enjoyed high attendance and media attention.[39]

Native Mexico

In Oaxaca, Mexico, two Zapotec communities have multiple gender relations and roles. In the city of Juchitán de Zaragoza, located on the Isthmus of Tehuantepec, some biological males identify as *muxe*. Muxe have both feminine and masculine characteristics and are not perceived as men or women. They have a unique aesthetic and social role and are spoken of highly by female relatives and friends. Muxe may marry women and have children, or partner with men. They are categorized separately from homosexual men, who are men but not muxe.[40]

In the village of Teotitlán del Valle, located on the edge of the Oaxaca Valley and a short bus ride to the capital city, another alternate gender identity exists: *biza'ah*. Biza'ah are biologically male and fill a third gender role, with both masculine and feminine components. Like the muxe, they have a distinct aesthetic and are differentiated from homosexuals.[41]

Because most indigenous communities in present-day Mexico were first colonized by the Aztec people before the arrival of the Spanish, there is very little ethnographic information about traditional gender roles in preconquest times. While it's quite possible that other communities in Mexico recognize more than two genders, this information is not currently published.[42]

Central and South America

The Spanish colonial project extended throughout Central and South America as well as present-day Mexico and the southwest United States. Just like in North America, missionaries and soldiers observed and were horrified by multiple gender systems and sexual relations in these regions. Cross-gender regalia, work, and status were all remarked upon in florid reports; conquistadors were particularly aggrieved by the sexual behavior of these individuals.[43] Unfortunately, there is little contemporary data about alternate genders in these regions, with the exception of Brazil.

Gender and sexual classification in Brazil has been influenced by colonial-era slavery and Catholic instruction. Rigid class and racial systems enforced the idea that White men held absolute power over African and indigenous people; rigid sex and gender systems likewise enforced the idea that White men held absolute power over anyone not classified as a man. Because these systems were implemented through violence, a new model of sexual and gender relations developed: those who penetrate are considered active and masculine, and those who are penetrated are considered passive and feminine. These forms of masculinity and femininity do not rely on biological sex; a man who is penetrated by another man is considered feminine, while the penetrating partner is considered masculine. In this system, the penetrating partner retains his masculinity and heterosexual subjectivity, while the penetrated partner is feminized and perceived to be homosexual.[44]

While some "passive" homosexuals remain closeted in order to preserve their masculine status, others accept their feminine status and emerge publicly as *travesti*. Travesti dress like women, speak and walk like women, and transform their bodies with hormones and silicone implants and injections. They occupy a feminine sexual role, living as a housewife with a macho boyfriend or engaging in prostitution. Despite having feminine names and using feminine pronouns, though, travesti do not claim to be women. They are *like* women, but they have no desire to remove their penises. But they are not men, either, because they enjoy the "passive" sexual role.[45]

POLYNESIAN GENDER ROLES

Polynesia is a subregion of Oceana and includes the Cook Islands, Fiji, Hawaii, New Zealand, Samoa, Tahiti, Tonga, and Tuvalu. Historically, the peoples of this region share certain cultural patterns, including kinship and hierarchy systems, gender complementarity, and respect relationships between siblings.[46] Non-heteronormative sexual relations and nonbinary gender roles and relations continue to be quite common. Reports stemming from European contact in the late eighteenth century and anthropological research in the ensuing years focused heavily on what reporters perceived as "casual" sexual relationships and nonrestrictive child-rearing, but curiously, made little note of gender variance. Therefore it is difficult to theorize about the history of gender diversity in this region,[47] although creation stories involving androgynous or intersex deities are widespread.[48]

FIGURE 3.4
Hinaleimoana Wong-Kalu, from the 2015 film *Kumu Hina*, reprinted with permission of Dean Hamer and Joe Wilson, Qwaves.

Today, however, abundant data confirms the existence of multiple gender relations and roles in Polynesia.[49] In Tahiti and Hawaii, an alternate gender identity called *māhū* is available for both sexes, though it is more common for biological males. Māhū are considered to be good caregivers and are often adoptive parents to child relatives, filling an important familial and cultural role. In addition, many are prominent in performing arts. Aesthetically, most māhū blend traditional masculine and feminine dress, either in the same outfit or changing from one to the other when transitioning from work to home. Very few alter their bodies with hormones or surgeries.[50]

In Samoa, biological males may identify as *fa'afafine*; literally, "like a woman." Similar to the māhū, fa'afafine have an important familial role, acting as caregivers to young relatives, aging parents, and younger fa'afafine. In terms of sartorial choices, fa'afafine may dress in masculine clothing, feminine clothing, or a mixture of the two. They are often involved in performing arts, particularly as part of a music or dance group. Fa'afafine in Samoa form a tight-knit community, working together, playing netball together, and performing together; still, they remain intimately connected with their families of origin.[51]

THIRD GENDER IN INDIA

India is perhaps the best-known country for having a large population of third gender individuals. This third gender is called *hijra* and has been recognized in written records since at least the eighth century BCE. Hijra can be translated as "eunuch" or "intersex," indicating a focus on ambiguous or transformed genitals. Hijras are assigned male at birth (or, rarely, intersex), and dress and behave as women do. However, despite using female names, kinship terms, and pronouns, hijras do not identify as women. They are culturally recognized as neither man nor woman but a third gender.[52]

Hijras have special cultural and social roles and ways of behaving that neither men nor women have. They have an important ritual role in weddings and at the birth of a child: they sing, dance, and bless the family in the name of their goddess, the Bahuchara Mata. This goddess and other deities and ancestors are androgynous or intersexual, indicating that third gender is not just accepted but is institutionalized through the Hindu religion. In order to gain favor with their goddess, hijras must undergo ritual castration. This surgery removes the penis and testicles in order to rid the hijra of her maleness and allow her to become a vehicle for the goddess.[53]

Despite having an important cultural role and religious status, hijras are treated with ambivalence. Many people fear and are disgusted by them because of their loss of virility; yet their emasculation is precisely the source of their religious potency, which is respected and necessary. In addition, because they leave their families of origin to join the hijra community, hijras operate outside the normal caste and kinship systems, a transition that is alarming because it upsets social structure. Hijra communities are composed of houses or subgroups with fictive kin relationships and social hierarchies. Within these networks, hijras care for one another.[54]

There are two less frequent and lesser-known gender alternatives available to those assigned female at birth: *sādhin* and *devadasi*. The sādhin is a voluntary role that a biological female enters into around puberty. She wears men's clothing, cuts her hair in the traditional masculine style, and renounces sexuality. While she retains her feminine name and pronouns, a sādhin is perceived to be free of gender entirely. She may work in traditionally male or female occupations and can participate in traditional male or female ritual behaviors.[55]

In contrast, a biological female becomes a devadasi when her parents dedicate her to the goddess Yellamma. Parents give a child to Yellamma for a variety of reasons: previous generations gave a child and the kinship line must persist; the child is extremely ill and a promise is made upon the condition that the child recovers; or, most frequently, desperate poverty. Once a child is given, she is dedicated to the goddess in a ritual marriage and then trained as a priest in an apprenticeship system. Devadasis perform temple and festival rituals for their communities and mediate between devotees and the goddess. Their sacred marriage also transforms them socially; while they are still perceived as girls and women, they also become sons, and access gendered male privileges including land ownership and inheritance.[56]

GENDER DIVERSITY IN SOUTHEAST ASIA

In Indonesia, the Philippines, and Thailand, gender relations and roles are based on sexual practices and genital configuration. The active, penetrating partner is considered to be masculine and heterosexual. The passive, receptive partner is considered to be feminine, and may be homosexual or heterosexual depending on the biological sex. In other words, there are three possible genders: men, women, and a third gender that is feminine but biologically male.

Indonesia

In Indonesia, this third gender is called *waria*. This term combines *wanita* ("woman") and *pria* ("man"). Waria are differentiated from *banci* ("effeminate men") and *gay* ("gay") men. They dress in women's clothing, wear makeup, and have typical feminine behavior. Yet they do not identify as women: they use the men's toilet, wipe off makeup when they pray, and are said to be even stronger than men. Waria are highly visible in Indonesian society; they own or work in salons, they are well represented in Indonesian television shows and commercials, and they participate in popular *playback* (lip-synching) performances.[57]

Philippines

In the Philippines, the third gender is referred to as *bayot, bantut,* or *bakla,* depending on the specific region. Gender diversity has a long history in this region; third gender deities and ancestral figures are prevalent in traditional narratives, and mediate between humans and the divine. However, multiple colonial presences—Arab, Spanish, and American—have impacted traditional understandings of gender and sexual diversity. Today, third gender Filipinos have a poor public perception, because femininity is associated with weakness and anal intercourse with sin. Furthermore, the influx of Western identities and activisms has led some bakla to identify as gay men. In this region, like in many others, conflicting ideologies and worldviews have made gender and sexuality systems slippery and complex.[58]

Thailand

Thailand's third gender is called *kathoey*. In Thai oral tradition, there were three original genders: males/men, females/women, and intersex/kathoey. Kathoey could be medically intersex or biologically male or female, and they occupied a gender role separate from either men or women. Today, kathoey seems to be exclusively applied to biological males, who self-identify as *phu-ying praphet sorng* ("a second type of woman") or *nang-fa jam-laeng* ("a transformed goddess"). Biological females who exhibit cross-gender behavior are called *toms* (from tomboy), and there is conflicting research on whether they identify as men or third gender.[59]

Kathoeys today tend to be quite feminine: they dress and speak like women, sometimes pursue hormone therapy or plastic surgery, and partner with masculine heterosexual men. Many have no desire to remove their penises; they remain pleasurable and perhaps even considered an exciting extra to their partners. That said, some kathoeys do wish for genital surgery, and some of these immigrate to the United States or other places with more rigid gender binaries, where they identify as women rather than kathoeys.[60] Like all culturally specific cases, gender roles and relations are culture bound; they are difficult to understand and summarize using language that doesn't quite fit.

NOTES

1. Explore the excellent map available at Independent Lens, "A Map of Gender-Diverse Cultures," PBS, August 11, 2015, http://www.pbs.org/independentlens/content/two-spirits_map-html.

2. Jeff Matthews, "The Femminiello in Neapolitan Culture," Naples: Life, Death & Miracles, December 2011, http://www.naplesldm.com/femm.html. Or, if you can

read Italian, see the original source at Abele de Blasio, *Usi e Costumi dei Camorristi; Gambella, Naples* (1897; repr., Naples, Italy: Edizioni del Delfino, 1975).

3. Antonia Young, *Women Who Become Men: Albanian Sworn Virgins* (Oxford: Berg, 2000).

4. See chapter 2 of Judith/Jack Halberstam, *Female Masculinity* (Durham, NC: Duke University Press, 1998).

5. Per the Australian Passport Office, "Sex and Gender Diverse Passport Applicants," https://www.passports.gov.au/passportsexplained/ theapplicationprocess/eligibilityoverview/Pages/changeofsexdoborpob.aspx.

6. Senior Correspondent, "'Third Gender' Gets State Recognition," *BD News*, November 11, 2013, http://bdnews24.com/bangladesh/2013/11/11/third-gender-gets-state-recognition.

7. "Denmark: X in Passports and New Trans Law Works," Transgender Europe, September 12, 2014, http://tgeu.org/denmark-x-in-passports-and-new-trans-law-work.

8. Harmeet Shah Singh, "India's Third Gender Gets Own Identity in Voter Rolls," CNN, November 12, 2009, http://edition.cnn.com/2009/WORLD/asiapcf/11/12/ india.gender.voting.

9. Yogita Limaye, "India Court Recognises Transgender People as Third Gender," BBC, April 15, 2014, http://www.bbc.com/news/world-asia-india-27031180.

10. Clarissa-Jan Lim, "New 'Third Gender' Option on Nepal Passports Finally Protects the Rights of LGBT Community," *Bustle*, January 8, 2015, http://www .bustle.com/articles/57466-new-third-gender-option-on-nepal-passports-finally-protects-the-rights-of-lgbt-community.

11. Simon Collins, "X Marks the Spot on Passport for Transgender Travellers," *New Zealand Herald*, December 5, 2012, http://www.nzherald.co.nz/nz/news/article .cfm?c_id=1&objectid=10852012.

12. John Godfrey, "Kiwis First to Officially Recognize Third Gender," *Nonprofit Quarterly*, July 20, 2015, https://nonprofitquarterly.org/2015/07/20/kiwis-first-to -officially-recognize-third-gender.

13. Anuja Jaiswal, "US Grants Visa to Chhattisgarh Transgender," *Times of India*, May 7, 2015, http://timesofindia.indiatimes.com/city/raipur/US-grants-visa-to -Chhattisgarh-transgender/articleshow/47190053.cms.

14. Robert Fulton and Steven W. Anderson, "The Amerindian 'Man-Woman': Gender, Liminality, and Cultural Continuity," *Current Anthropology* 33, no. 5 (December 1992): 603–4.

15. Richard C. Trexler, "Making the American Berdache: Choice or Constraint?" *Journal of Social History* (Spring 2002): 615–18.

16. Brian T. McCormack, "Conjugal Violence, Sex, Sin, and Murder in the Mission Communities of Alta California," *Journal of the History of Sexuality* 16, no. 3 (September 2007): 395.

17. María Lugones, "Heterosexualism and the Colonial/Modern Gender System." *Hypatia* 22, no. 1 (Winter 2007): 206.

18. I say this as a trained anthropologist myself. The history of anthropology is rooted in racism, sexism, and homophobia; and while current best practices call for cultural sensitivity and advocacy, it is important to remember our history in order to continue to work toward social justice in research.

19. Charles Callender et al., "The North American Berdache [and Comments and Reply]," *Current Anthropology* 24, no. 4 (August–October 1983): 444.

20. Callender et al., "The North American Berdache," 443.

21. For a particularly robust example, see Will Roscoe's excellent "Bibliography of Berdache and Alternative Gender Roles among North American Indians," *Journal of Homosexuality* 14, no. 3/4 (1987): 81–171.

22. Callender et al., "The North American Berdache," 443–56.

23. Fulton and Anderson, "The Amerindian 'Man-Woman,'" 609.

24. Some sources use "she" pronouns; others use "he" pronouns. Because I do not know which pronoun We'wha used, I choose to use the gender-neutral "they" to avoid misgendering them.

25. For more details of We'wha's life, see Will Roscoe's "We'wha and Klah: The American Indian Berdache as Artist and Priest," *American Indian Quarterly* (Spring 1988): 127–50. For a longer read, see Will Roscoe's *The Zuni Man-Woman* (Albuquerque: University of New Mexico Press, 1991).

26. For a glimpse of these cultural adaptations, see Walter L. Williams's "Persistence and Change in the Berdache Tradition among Contemporary Lakota Indians," *Anthropology and Homosexual Behavior* (1986): 191–200.

27. And yet, some anthropologists continue to use the term "berdache" when teaching the upcoming generation of anthropologists.

28. Imagine how ridiculous it would be if an anthropologist observed a rock concert and concluded that all Anglo males played electric guitar and wore denim jackets. In producing a universal identity, most actual identities are erased.

29. Carolyn Epple, "Coming to Terms with Navajo *Nádleehí*: A Critique of *Berdache*, 'Gay,' 'Alternate Gender,' and 'Two-Spirit,'" *American Ethnologist* 25, no. 2 (1998): 268.

30. It is important to note, though, that forced assimilation into a violently sexist colonial culture has diminished gender egalitarianism in some indigenous communities.

31. Andrew Gilden, "Preserving the Seeds of Gender Fluidity: Tribal Courts and the Berdache Tradition," *Michigan Journal of Gender & Law* 13 (2007): 242–46.

32. Also two-spirit, two spirit, two spirited, 2 spirit, and other variants.

33. Qwo-Li Driskill, "Doubleweaving Two-Spirit Critiques: Building Alliances between Native and Queer Studies," *GLQ: A Journal of Lesbian and Gay Studies* 16, no. 1–2 (2010): 72–73.

34. Qwo-Li Driskill, "Stolen from Our Bodies: First Nations Two-Spirits/Queers and the Journey to a Sovereign Erotic," *Studies in American Indian Literatures* 16, no. 2 (Summer 2004): 52.

35. See the glossary for an exhaustive list of indigenous gender terms.

36. Sabine Lang, *Men as Women, Women as Men: Changing Gender in Native American Cultures* (Austin: University of Texas Press, 1998), 342–43.

37. Walter L. Williams, *The Spirit and the Flesh: Sexual Diversity in American Indian Culture* (Boston: Beacon, 1986), 18–43.

38. Sandra Laframboise and Michael Anhorn, "The Way of the Two Spirited People," Dancing to Eagle Spirit Society, 2008, http://www .dancingtoeaglespiritsociety.org/twospirit.php.

39. Jorge Rivas, "Native Americans Talk Gender at a 'Two-Spirit' Powwow," Fusion, February 9, 2015, http://fusion.net/story/46014/native-americans-talk-gender -identity-at-a-two-spirit-powwow.

40. Beverly N. Chiñas, "Isthmus Zapotec Attitudes toward Sex and Gender Anomalies," in *Latin American Male Homosexualities*, ed. Stephen O. Murray (Albuquerque: University of New Mexico Press, 1995), 293–301. See also Lynn Stephen's excellent "Sexualities and Genders in Zapotec Oaxaca," *Latin American Perspectives* 29, no. 2 (March 2002): 41–59; and Alfredo Mirandé, "Hombres Mujeres: An Indigenous Third Gender," *Men and Masculinities*, September 6, 2015, doi:10.1177/1097184X15602746.

41. Stephen, "Sexualities and Genders in Zapotec Oaxaca," 46.

42. Or I haven't been able to locate it if it has.

43. Amara Das Wilhelm, *Tritiya-Prakriti: People of the Third Sex; Understanding Homosexuality, Transgender Identity, and Intersex Conditions through Hinduism* (Philadelphia: Xlibris, 2003), 189.

44. Serena Nanda, *Gender Diversity: Crosscultural Variations* (Long Grove, IL: Waveland, 2000), 43–45.

45. Don Kulick, *Travesti: Sex, Gender, and Culture among Brazilian Transgendered Prostitutes* (Chicago: University of Chicago Press, 1998), 191–238.

46. Nanda, *Gender Diversity*, 57–58.

47. Kalissa Alexeyeff and Niko Besnier, "Gender on the Edge: Identities, Politics, Transformations," in *Gender on the Edge: Transgender, Gay, and Other Pacific Islanders*, ed. Kalissa Alexeyeff and Niko Besnier (Honolulu: University of Hawaii Press, 2014), 10–11.

48. Nanda, *Gender Diversity*, 59.

49. For the sake of brevity, I discuss only two examples. Explore more in Kalissa Alexeyeff and Niko Besnier's edited volume *Gender on the Edge: Transgender, Gay, and Other Pacific Islanders* (Honolulu: University of Hawaii Press, 2014).

50. Makiko Kuwahara, "Living as and Living with *Māhū* and *Raerae*: Geopolitics, Sex, and Gender in the Society Islands," in Alexeyeff and Besnier, *Gender on the Edge*, 93–114.

51. Reevan Dolgoy, "'Hollywood' and the Emergence of a *Fa'afafine* Social Movement in Samoa, 1960–1980," in Alexeyeff and Besnier, *Gender on the Edge*, 56–72.

52. Serena Nanda, *Neither Man nor Woman: The Hijras of India* (Belmont, CA: Wadsworth, 1990), 13–19.

53. Nanda, *Neither Man nor Woman*, 24–37.

54. Nanda, *Neither Man nor Woman*, 38–48.

55. Nanda, *Gender Diversity*, 40–41.

56. Lucinda Ramberg, "Troubling Kinship: Sacred Marriage and Gender Configuration in South India," *American Ethnologist* 40, no. 4 (2013): 661–63.

57. Tom Boellstorff, "Playing Back the Nation: *Waria*, Indonesian Transvestites," *Cultural Anthropology* 19, no. 2 (2004): 160–73.

58. Nanda, *Gender Diversity*, 78–85.

59. LeeRay Costa and Andrew Matzner, *Male Bodies, Women's Souls: Personal Narratives of Thailand's Transgendered Youth* (New York: Haworth, 2007), 17–24.

60. Han ten Brummelhuis, "Transformations of Transgender: The Case of the Thai *Kathoey*," in *Lady Boys, Tom Boys, Rent Boys: Male and Female Homosexualities in Contemporary Thailand*, ed. Peter A. Jackson and Gerard Sullivan (New York: Haworth, 1999), 121–39.

4

Nonbinary Genders in Popular Culture

In recent years, nonbinary gender identities and expressions have enjoyed heightened popularity and visibility in popular culture. This is likely due to three factors: First, the Internet and social media in particular have extended the reach and impact of content dissemination. Second, greater numbers of nonbinary people are coming out, and in many cases, they are coming out at younger ages than previous generations. Finally, several celebrities have allied themselves with nonbinary politics or come out as nonbinary themselves.

This chapter will discuss nonbinary visibility in popular culture, specifically in film and television, music, fashion, and the Internet. For the purposes of this chapter, popular culture is defined as globally accessible mass media consumer content that is reviewed, discussed, argued, and shared online. Print media is not included, because it is generally consumed in solitary and not collaboratively discussed to the same extent. Nonbinary visibility includes self-identified nonbinary people and content as well as media actors and content that are "read" as nonbinary by nonbinary fans and communities.

FILM, TELEVISION, AND ACTORS

The general (cisgender) public seems to be fascinated by gender fluidity and androgyny, as evidenced by the large number of films and television shows that include gender-nonconforming characters. The Star Trek franchise, for example, has featured nonbinary story lines in *Enterprise*, *Deep Space 9*, *Next*

Generation, and *Voyager.*[1] Visibility is by no means limited to science fiction, though: gender-nonconforming characters have appeared in children's animation, police procedurals, romantic comedy, surrealist art, pornography, and nearly every other genre. For an exhaustive list of film and television shows with nonbinary characters, see chapter 13.

Ruby Rose

Australian model and actor Ruby Rose gained worldwide fame—and an enormous number of queer fans—after she costarred in seasons three and four of the Netflix original series *Orange Is the New Black.* Her short, partially shaved hair, slender yet muscular build, and heavy tattoos had many viewers guessing about her gender identity.[2] Rose's gender fluidity was confirmed when she released a short film, *Break Free,* in which she transitions from high femme to masculine, cutting her hair, removing makeup, binding her breasts and packing a dildo.[3] Shortly afterward, she stated in an interview that with regard to gender, "I feel like I'm neither."[4]

Jaden Smith

The son of Will Smith and Jada Pinkett-Smith, Jaden has been a celebrity since childhood, when he costarred with his father in *The Pursuit of Happyness.* In addition to being an accomplished actor, Jaden is also well known for his sartorial choices: At sixteen, he went to his high school prom in a dress.[5] At seventeen, he was modeling womenswear for Louis Vuitton.[6] Now, freshly eighteen, he's starting his own clothing line.[7] Smith is well aware of the implications of his gender nonconformity, as well as the insulation he receives due to his celebrity. In an interview with *Nylon* magazine, he muses, "In five years when a kid goes to school wearing a skirt, he won't get beat up and kids won't get mad at him."[8]

Tilda Swinton

British actor Tilda Swinton is frequently lauded for her androgyny, which has allowed her to play both male and female roles. In addition to film, she is also a fashion icon whose inspirations include David Bowie and 1920s androgynous artist Claude Cahun.[9] Swinton's film career began when director Derek Jarman cast her in his film *Caravaggio;* she was his muse for eight years, appearing in seven of his queer art films. In 1992, she starred in her first Hollywood movie, *Orlando*, based on the Virginia Woolf novel of the same name. *Orlando* is one of the most significant representations of gender fluidity in cinema, telling the story of a noble who changes sex throughout several lifetimes. Swinton took the role in part to explore the idea of transformative gender; when queried about her own gender in an interview, she responded, "I don't know if I could ever really say that I was a girl—I was kind of a boy for a long time. I don't know, who knows? It changes."[10]

MUSIC AND MUSICIANS

Gender nonconformity is common in music, where musicians are often expected to push the cultural envelope. Worth specific mention is the prevalence of androgyny and cross-dressing in Japanese pop music performance. In the late 1980s, a new genre emerged from the J-rock culture: visual kei, a style marked by elaborate, often androgynous, cross-dressing incorporating elements of goth and punk as well as manga and anime cosplay.[11] Visual kei fans often dress as their favorite band members or cosplay androgynous or cross-dressed characters from manga or anime; performances are thus marked by the audience as well as the band engaging in extravagant gender-fluid displays.[12] For a comprehensive list of musicians who identify as nonbinary, see chapter 13.

David Bowie

David Bowie was an accomplished actor and musician, as well as an androgynous style icon. His style changed over several incarnations, with elements of glam, punk, goth, and otherworldly fantasy. He wore makeup, leather, and lace. His hair was always perfectly coiffed. In 1972, he publicly announced that he was gay, later amending that to bisexual.[13] His gender, it seems, was just as slippery: in various personas, he was male, female, both, and neither. He often positioned himself as Other, as Alien. Although he never made a public statement about his gender, he clearly played with gender performance throughout his career. In one of his last music videos, *The Stars (Are Out Tonight)*, released in 2013, Bowie shrewdly commented on his history of transgressing gender, with four other androgynous actors cross-dressing as various Bowie personas.[14]

Miley Cyrus

Singer-songwriter and former *Hannah Montana* star Miley Cyrus transformed from a parent-safe tween favorite to an aggressively explicit boundary pusher when she came of age. While much of her controversial public behavior may be an intentionally curated persona, she has also engaged in extensive philanthropy and recently created a foundation to support LGBTQ and homeless youth. Soon after she launched the Happy Hippie Foundation,[15] Cyrus told *Out* magazine, "I don't relate to what people would say defines a girl or a boy."[16]

Prince

Like Bowie, Prince was an exceptionally gifted musician, an actor, and an androgynous style favorite. Prince wore velvet, lace, brocade, and feathers, merging High Victorian fashion with a glam-punk aesthetic. His outfits incorporated feminine and masculine components: pocket squares with belly shirts, high-heeled boots with purple suits, heavy eyeliner with oversized lapels. He had a guitar to match every outfit. Prince alluded to gender fluidity in songs including 1984's "I Would Die 4 U."[17] And in 1993, when he created the "Love Symbol," he incorporated elements of both the Mars (male) and Venus (female) symbols.[18]

FASHION AND MODELS

In high fashion, a very specific kind of body is particularly valued: tall, slender, toned musculature, an absence of facial and body hair on men and minimal breast tissue and hips on women. This kind of body is often read as androgynous, and when a male can look fabulous in womenswear and vice versa, this is especially celebrated. Some of these models, of course, do identify as nonbinary; others may be read as such by the public or by nonbinary fans and communities.

Of course, many nonbinary people do not have this kind of body, and many are contesting the idealization of a singular body type. Nonbinary bodies are curvy, and not; hairy, and not; disabled or chronically ill, and not. Nonbinary people dress in every imaginable style and groom in every imaginable way. Not every nonbinary person identifies as androgynous and not every nonbinary person wishes to combine traditional masculine and feminine clothing articles.

A small but growing number of bespoke clothing stores have emerged to serve nonbinary clients. Some offer tailoring of masculine clothing to people assigned female at birth;[19] some offer traditionally feminine clothing in appropriate sizes for people assigned male at birth.[20] Others reject the ideas of masculine and feminine entirely and offer interesting patterns and styles to fit every kind of body.[21] To explore more nonbinary styles, see chapter 13 for multimedia representation.

Alok Vaid-Menon

Alok Vaid-Menon performs poetry at universities and other venues worldwide. They focus on issues of gender, diaspora, race and racism, and self- and Othering representations. They are also known for their aesthetics; on their Facebook and Instagram pages, they often share carefully posed portraits. These photographs challenge cisnormative and Eurocentric standards of beauty, sending the message that nonbinary bodies can be hairy and brown and are worthy of self-love and media dissemination.

In a September 2016 Instagram post, Vaid-Menon shared a selfie of themself wearing a gorgeous pink floral ensemble, throat and upper chest coquettishly revealed, lush chest hair peeking out. Vaid-Menon stares directly at the camera, lips slightly open with perfectly matched lipstick. The quote below is a poignant statement about self-love and comfort being challenged by trans-antagonism.

> what selfies allow me to do is to remember who i am, what i am fighting for, and what the world i want to create looks like. a selfie is an earnest invitation into the world i am making for myself.[22]

Jacob Tobia

Jacob Tobia is an outspoken genderqueer change maker. They are the host of NBC OUT's web series *Queer 2.0*; have written for the *Guardian*, *Huffington Post*, the *New York Times*, and many other publications; and speak regularly at universities, conferences, corporations, and other venues. Their message is one of gender education and empowerment and social change.[23] In addition to writing and speaking, Tobia is a bit of a fashion maven; in media appearances, they are always impeccably dressed, with

FIGURE 4.1
Photograph by Alok Vaid-Menon; originally appeared at https://www.instagram.com/p/BJ52jGphgRQ/ on September 3, 2016. Reprinted with permission of Alok Vaid-Menon.

lovely nails and perfectly coiffed hair to go with their vintage and high-fashion accessories. In portraits and snapshots, Tobia resists the idealized "androgynous" image, choosing not only to keep but to flaunt their facial and body hair, demonstrating that there are countless ways to be gender-queer and beautiful.

On Instagram, Tobia frequently shares selfies that range from exquisitely dressed-up, carefully curated self-portraits to casual, often humorous snapshots of themself with friends or on various adventures. Captions describe

FIGURE 4.2
Photograph by Jacob Tobia; originally appeared at https://www.instagram.com/p/BJ JGcl6jOPi/ on August 15, 2016. Reprinted with permission of Jacob Tobia.

locations, moods, and activities. In an August 2016 post, Tobia gazes directly into the camera in a close-up. A double string of chunky costume pearls adorn their neck, resting on a bright blue dress garment. Their red manicured nails rest lightly under their parted lips. Their chin-length hair curls playfully around their face. The caption reads, "Feelin cute and pensive in Asheville."[24] Proud statements of self-love like this one are part of Tobia's overall message of gender empowerment.

INTERNET

While film and television, music, and fashion can all be disseminated on the Internet, some popular culture media are Internet specific. Social media platforms and web forums are used by nonbinary people in distinctive ways. Web comics have also emerged as a vibrant new medium. Finally, the Internet is used for education and activism, in the creation of resource sites. For a full list of nonbinary resources on the Internet, see chapter 12.

Social Media

Social media are those that are participatory, meaning that users can create profiles to represent aspects of themselves; can follow or befriend other users and vice versa; and can share and comment on content. Social media include photo-sharing sites such as Instagram, microblogging sites such as Twitter, chat-based sites such as Snapchat, and video-sharing sites such as Vine. Many sites combine two or more of these features; Facebook, for example, allows users to post text and multimedia. Social media sites tend to attract certain kinds of users and gradually form distinct cultures and subcultures, complete with community-specific language, posting conventions, and memes.

Almost all of the nonbinary celebrities mentioned earlier in this chapter have multiple social media profiles. Noncelebrity individuals often have social media profiles, as well: some grow in popularity until the individual achieves a form of celebrity; others remain relatively quiet, interacting only with "in real life" friends. Groups also have profiles: nonprofit organizations, political groups, artist collaborations, and even corporations create social media personas in order to market themselves and form relationships with fans.

In the world of nonbinary social media, individuals and groups create profiles in order to share their art, their work, and their ideas, as well as to create new relationships and nurture old ones. Several nonbinary-specific conventions have emerged. On Facebook, groups like Gender Dysphoria Memes pair surreal images with text that slyly exposes transphobia where the punch line is cispatriarchy.[25] On Tumblr, a host of sites titled "Fuck Yeah _" have sprung up to celebrate various ways of being nonbinary or otherwise queer. Users share photos intended to capture the full range of whatever the particular topic is: femmes, androgynes, fat genderqueer people, and so forth.[26]

Web Forums

Web forums are online discussion sites that focus on particular topics. They often require registration in order to make posts and comment on others' posts; they generally have moderators who make sure that participants are following rules; and they generally archive posts in a structured way for users to easily locate threads. Nonbinary communities have created forums on several platforms, including LiveJournal, Reddit, and Google Groups. These groups function as asynchronous support groups, where users can ask questions, share anecdotes, and receive advice and feedback.[27]

In the nonbinary community, popular topics include transition experiences (and often photographs), coming-out stories, dating and sex, legal rights, and fashion. Although some forums, particularly LiveJournal, have been largely abandoned by the majority of users in favor of newer blogging platforms, they are still highly relevant to the nonbinary and larger trans community because of the ability to make posts (and even the entire group) secret from cisgender users. This relative anonymity is vital for safety and comfort.

Web Comics

Web comics are ongoing comic strips that are shared online, often both on the creator's website and through social media. Some web comics are also printed as zines or bound books for fans to purchase. Arguably one of the most popular and well-known web comics featuring nonbinary characters is *Robot Hugs*.[28] This comic is semiautobiographical, sharing snippets of its anonymous nonbinary creator's life in a humorous way. As a slice-of-life comic, topics include transition, dating and sexuality, family, and transphobia both overt and in the form of microaggressions. See appendix B for a reprint of a *Robot Hugs* comic about gender pronouns.

Another excellent web comic is *Assigned Male*, written by Sophie Labelle.[29] This comic focuses on the life of a young trans girl in elementary school. The main character, Stephie, came out to her parents and transitioned very young. Her mother and friends are very supportive; her father and some of her schoolmates are not so understanding and require education. One of Stephie's best friends is a child named Ciel who is nonbinary. Ciel is not featured in every comic, but is a strong secondary character.

Education and Activism

The Internet has also become a primary medium for education and activism. Nonbinary activists have created a plethora of resource sites for fellow nonbinary people as well as for allies; these sites may include glossaries, information about pronoun usage, transition timelines and resources, coming out strategies, medical and legal advice, and more. Particularly popular posts and pages are often reblogged or disseminated on web publications with greater reach, such as news sites and more general social justice sites.

Besides sharing resources, activism also includes political campaigns. Frequent topics are gender-inclusive restrooms, pronouns and honorifics, and hate crime legislation. Again, posts and pages are disseminated widely in an effort to gain more allies to the cause. Another form of education is the relatively new genre of transition memoirs, which are generally a series of blogs, photographs, or videos that follow a person through their transition journey, sharing thoughts, feelings, and strategies as well as physical changes. These are immensely helpful to fellow nonbinary people earlier in transition to get an idea of what to expect; they are also interesting to allies, for anticipating changes in their loved ones and gaining knowledge of how to best support them.

Marilyn Roxie and Genderqueer and Non-Binary Identities

Marilyn Roxie's aptly named Genderqueer and Non-Binary Identities website is a treasure trove of resources for nonbinary people and allies.[30] The site features a very friendly FAQ section with accessible 101-type information; recommended resources, including books, articles, organizations, and Internet sources; Roxie's own highly detailed story of their gender identification journey; information about academic research, including data from two large surveys; and an ongoing blog, which features resources and articles on various nonbinary-related topics. Of particular interest is Roxie's research article on genderqueer history, which was originally written for a college history class and includes an excellent bibliography.[31]

Micah and Neutrois Nonsense

Micah is a published writer and educator who works as a consultant on transgender health issues. Neutrois Nonsense began as a transition memoir, with several years of documentation of medical, surgical, and social transition. Because nonbinary transition has historically had so little visibility,

FIGURE 4.3
Still of Marilyn Roxie from 2015 documentary *Three to Infinity: Beyond Two Genders*, copyright Lonny Shavelson. Reprinted with permission of Lonny Shavelson.

FIGURE 4.4
Photograph of Micah Rajunov, 2015. Reprinted with permission of Micah Rajunov.

this blog became immensely popular with nonbinary people curious about transition options. Micah shared journaling about and photographs of their top surgery and hysterectomy, musings and video about their testosterone journey, and their evolving strategies for coming out, pronouns, and navigating family and work. In early 2016, Micah launched "Featured Voices," where nonbinary guest posters blog about a monthly theme. Neutrois Nonsense has thus expanded from individual chronicle to community history.[32]

NOTES

1. Stephen Kerry, "'There's Genderqueers on the Starboard Bow': The Pregnant Male in *Star Trek*," *Journal of Popular Culture* 42, no. 4 (2009): 704–7.

2. It couldn't have just been me.

3. Ruby Rose (Producer) and Phillip Lopez (Director), *Break Free* (short film), YouTube, July 14, 2014, https://youtu.be/EFjsSSDLl8w.

4. Erika Jarvis, "Ruby Rose: 'I Used to Pray to God That I Wouldn't Get Breasts,'" *Guardian*, July 25, 2014, https://www.theguardian.com/world/2014/jul/25/ruby -rose-video-break-free-gender.

5. Maria Mercedes Lara, "Jaden Smith Wears a Dress to Prom with *The Hunger Games*'s Amandla Stenberg," *People*, May 30, 2015, http://www.people.com/article/ jaden-smith-prom-hunger-games-rue-dress.

6. Matt Donnelly, "Jaden Smith's Adventures in Gender Fluidity: What It Means, Who Profits," The Wrap, February 11, 2016, http://www.thewrap.com/jaden -smiths-adventures-in-gender-fluidity-what-it-means-who-profits/.

7. https://msftsrep.com.

8. Melissa Giannini, "Hollywood's Most Famous Progeny Is Entering Adulthood as the Key Progenitor of a Boundless Mode of Existence," *Nylon*, July 6, 2016, http:// www.nylon.com/articles/jaden-smith-nylon-august-cover.

9. Diane Solway, "Planet Tilda: When It Comes to Acting—and Dressing—Tilda Swinton, the Star of the Harrowing New Film *We Need to Talk about Kevin*, Is Literally Out of this World," *W Magazine*, August 2011, http://www.wmagazine .com/fashion/2011/08/tilda-swinton-cover-story-fashion.

10. Vera von Kreutzbruck, "Interview with Actress Tilda Swinton: 'I Am Probably a Woman,'" The WIP, March 20, 2009, http://thewip.net/2009/03/20/interview-with-actress-tilda-swinton-i-am-probably-a-woman.

11. Costume role-playing; dressing up as a character from popular culture fandoms.

12. Ken McLeod, "Visual Kei: Hybridity and Gender in Japanese Popular Culture," Young 21, no. 4 (2013): 309–14.

13. Barry Walters, "David Bowie, Sexuality and Gender: A Rebel Who Changed the Face of Music," Billboard, January 14, 2016, http://www.billboard.com/articles/news/magazine-feature/6843021/david-bowie-sexuality-gender-rebellion-changing-music.

14. Lisa Perrott, "Gender Transgression: How Bowie Blurred the Lines," CNN, January 11, 2016 (originally published July 14, 2015), http://www.cnn.com/2016/01/11/fashion/david-bowie-gender-drag.

15. http://www.happyhippies.org.

16. Shana Naomi Krochmal, "Exclusive: Miley Cyrus Launches Anti-homelessness, Pro-LGBT 'Happy Hippie Foundation,'" Out, May 5, 2015, http://www.out.com/music/2015/5/05/exclusive-miley-cyrus-launches-anti-homelessness-pro-lgbt-happy-hippie-foundation.

17. Nathan Smith, "The Queer Legacy of Prince," Out, June 7, 2016, http://www.out.com/music/2016/4/22/queer-legacy-prince.

18. Christina Cauterucci, "How Prince Led the Way to Our Gender Fluid Present," Slate, April 21, 2016, http://www.slate.com/blogs/outward/2016/04/21/prince_dead_at_57_embraced_gender_fluidity_ahead_of_his_time.html.

19. http://www.bindleandkeep.com.

20. http://www.tillyandwilliam.com.

21. http://www.flavnt.com.

22. Alok Vaid-Menon (DarkMatter), Instagram post, September 3, 2016, https://www.instagram.com/p/BJ52jGphgRQ.

23. Jacob Tobia, Jacob Tobia: Speaker—Writer—Advocate, http://www.jacobtobia.com.

24. Jacob Tobia (jacobtobia), "Feelin cute and pensive in Asheville," Instagram post, August 15, 2016, https://www.instagram.com/p/BJJGcI6jOPi.

25. https://www.facebook.com/Gender-Dysphoria-Memes-316076561895174.

26. See, for example, http://fyeahgenderqueers.tumblr.com.

27. See, for example, http://non-binary.livejournal.com.

28. http://www.robot-hugs.com.

29. http://www.assignedmale.com.

30. http://genderqueerid.com.

31. http://genderqueerid.com/gqhistory.

32. https://neutrois.me.

5

Notable Nonbinary People

While nonbinary representation in popular culture has only recently begun to proliferate, pioneers in the community have been engaging in scholarship, activism, and art since the 1970s. This chapter provides brief biographies and cultural contributions of six notable nonbinary people in the United States: Vaginal Davis, Kate Bornstein, Leslie Feinberg, Justin Vivian Bond, Riki Wilchins, and Qwo-Li Driskill. Entries are organized according to the date of the earliest contribution to nonbinary culture. A range of gender pronouns are used in accordance with each person's personal use.

VAGINAL DAVIS

Vaginal "Crème" Davis was a pioneer of the queercore movement[1] of 1970s Los Angeles, producing zines, music, art videos, and installations. Her[2] work engages with queerness and racialized identities, mixing sex, humor, and politics into a scandalous pastiche that defies easy categorization.

Early Life

Dr. Davis describes herself as "a strange hybrid creature,"[3] being intersex, genderqueer, and multiracial. She was born and raised in Los Angeles, California. Her date of birth is not publicly known, as her biographies are self-created and legendary,[4] but she was born sometime in the early 1960s. As a child, she was drawn to ephemeral art and communication. She began writing

FIGURE 5.1
Vaginal Davis, Beware the Holy Retarded Whore by John Vlautin, 2002. Reprinted with
permission of John Vlautin.

letters at the age of seven or eight, amassing an international group of pen pals with which to explore intercultural exchange and collaboration.[5] Later, still in elementary school, she created her first zine, *Dowager* (1972–1975), secretly using the school's mimeograph machine.[6] These early creative urges were the beginnings of a long career in subversive experimental art.

Queercore Punk Movement

Dr. Davis emerged in the Los Angeles punk scene and developed a cult following through her zine *Fertile La Toyah Jackson* (1982–1991) and punk performances with her backup singers, the Afro Sisters. Her first shows were "performative skits" sung a cappella; only after her fan base grew did she add instrumentals.[7] The Afro Sisters released eight albums between 1978 and 1986. Then, Dr. Davis quickly moved on to create ¡Cholita! The Female Menudo, which released three albums between 1987 and 1996; Black Fag, which released four albums between 1992 and 1995; and Pedro, Muriel, & Esther, which released two albums in 1991 and 1998.[8]

Besides *Fertile La Toyah Jackson*, which was both a print and video zine, Dr. Davis created several other zines between the 1970s and late 1990s.[9] Her work preceded the term "zine" and was one of the primary originators of queer zine culture. In addition to music and zine creation, Dr. Davis has been very active in video and film production, writing and starring in experimental and art productions ranging from satirical fake commercials to talk show parodies to dance performance.[10]

Much of Dr. Davis's art practice engages with Black and Chicana identity, gender and sexuality, and class struggle. Straight, cisgender, White audiences often don't understand her work. She muses:

> Only a few people got those influences, or that there was a political concept to things, because I wasn't being dogmatic, I was being humorous. It wasn't tackling politics in the way that a white liberal would've tackled it, so of course it got dismissed.[11]

White, nonqueer audiences are left out of the joke purposely; Dr. Davis performs for queer consumption and doesn't dumb down her work to make it palatable or easy to understand for those who do not share her intersecting identities. Indeed, her work is antagonistic rather than commercial; theorist José Esteban Muñoz characterizes her style as "terrorist drag," commenting

that "the fantasies she acts out involve cultural anxieties around miscegena-
tion, communities of color, and the queer body."[12]

Dr. Davis moved to Berlin in 2005, where she has continued to create
performance art as well as visual art exhibitions, lecturing and teaching, and
writing.

KATE BORNSTEIN

Kate Bornstein was born on March 15, 1948. She[13] is a playwright, performer,
and gender theorist whose work has been translated and taught in more than
two hundred high schools and universities.

Early Life

Bornstein grew up in Neptune City, New Jersey, in a conservative, middle-
class Jewish family. Growing up, she knew that she wasn't a boy, but she was
really good at acting like one. After graduating from Brown University with a
degree in theatre arts in 1969, Bornstein joined the Church of Scientology, got
married, and had children. Over time, she became frustrated with Scientology, and left the movement in 1981. This choice cost Bornstein her daughter,
but allowed her to finally explore her gender more fully.[14]

Because medical and psychiatric understandings of transsexuality were
rigidly binary in the 1980s, Bornstein was forced to settle for a binary transition. Soon after, though, she began questioning binary gender oppression,
likening it to the cultic religion she had fled. "The trouble is, we're living in a
world that insists we be one or the other—a world that doesn't bother to tell
us exactly what one or the other *is*."[15] This line of questioning led to a burst
of creative production in order to make nonnormative genders visible and
encourage others to contest gender assumptions.

Theatre and Performance

In 1989, Bornstein collaborated with Noreen Barnes to produce her play
Hidden: A Gender, a witty and poignant exploration of the life of historical
intersex person Herculine Barbin intertwined with Bornstein's own life. This
performance was also a metanarrative of how identities in general and gender
identity in particular are performative. Bornstein has used theatre throughout
her career to express and play with identity/ies.

FIGURE 5.2
Photograph of Kate Bornstein in 2013; copyright Danielle Levitt/AUGUST and re-printed with permission of Danielle Levitt/AUGUST.

In addition to a variety of stage performances, Bornstein has also appeared on television and film. She has appeared on daytime television talk shows including *Geraldo* (1989); she has been featured on the *Melissa Harris-Perry* show (2012); she was the subject of Sam Feder's documentary *Kate Bornstein Is a Queer and Pleasant Danger* (2014); and she was a regular cast member on season two of *I Am Cait* (2016).[16]

Writing

Bornstein's radical gender politics have also been disseminated in print, and, like her performance art, are imbued with humor, warmth, and hope. Her first text, *Gender Outlaw: On Men, Women, and the Rest of Us* (1994), is a (fittingly) transgenre work that combines gender theory, tongue-in-cheek Q&A, her own coming-of-age story, and a treatise on queer theatre. This was quickly followed up with Bornstein's sole fiction novel, *Nearly Roadkill: An Infobahn Gender Adventure* (1996), cowritten with Caitlin Sullivan. Written when the Internet was in its infancy, the novel follows two genderless folks as they create different Internet personas to fight the government.

In 1998, Bornstein published *My Gender Workbook: How to Become a Real Man, a Real Woman, the Real You, or Something Else Entirely*, a hands-on workbook designed to gently aid in the reader's exploration of their unique gender. This book was updated in 2013 to provide an intersectional lens. In 2006, Bornstein expanded her focus to depressed adolescents, publishing *Hello Cruel World: 101 Alternatives to Suicide for Teens, Freaks, & Other Outlaws*, providing encouragement and support without denying the very real suicidal urge that many depressed teens experience.

Next, Bornstein ventured into anthology: *Gender Outlaws: The Next Generation* (2010), coedited with S. Bear Bergman, offers essays, art, poems, and comics by transgender and gender-nonconforming contributors. Bornstein's latest book is a memoir, *A Queer and Pleasant Danger* (2012), which is a fascinating and very frank account of her life from childhood to post-transition adulthood.

In between writing, theatre, and television appearances, Bornstein keeps busy with workshops, lectures, and advocacy. She has struggled with lymphocytic leukemia and lung cancer and is currently in remission. She lives in New York City with her partner, Barbara Carrellas, and their menagerie of pets.[17]

LESLIE FEINBERG

Leslie Feinberg was born September 1, 1949, and died on November 15, 2014. Sie[18] was a socialist, transgender activist, and author whose work has been widely taught in gender studies and related classes around the world.

Early Life

Feinberg grew up in Buffalo, New York, in a working-class Jewish family. Sie was forced to move out and seek work as an adolescent, due to hir family's queerantagonism. Because of rampant transgender-exclusive discrimination, Feinberg had difficulty finding steady work throughout hir life.[19]

Political Activism

In hir twenties, Feinberg joined the Workers World Party and became heavily involved in antiwar, antiracism, anti-imperialism, pro-labor, pro-choice, and LGBTQ politics—including rallies, marches, community self-defense, and

FIGURE 5.3
Leslie Feinberg speaking at Boston Pride in 2006; photograph © 2006 Marilyn Humphries and reprinted with permission of Marilyn Humphries.

other direct action organizing. Sie also took a position as managing editor for the *Workers World* newspaper, and wrote a long-running series on socialism and LGBTQ politics.[20]

Feinberg experienced health issues that were exacerbated by transphobic medical personnel. In 1996, sie was fighting bacterial endocarditis, a heart infection. At the emergency room, when the physician discovered hir anatomy, Feinberg was refused care for being "a very troubled person."[21] A few weeks later, at a Catholic hospital where patients are placed on wards according to their birth sex, Feinberg was openly humiliated by staff, who demanded "it" be placed elsewhere.[22] These and many similar experiences inspired Feinberg to write a passionate essay on the desperate need for transcompetent health care.[23]

Writing

Feinberg was equally accomplished in fiction and theory. Hir first published book was the award-winning novel *Stone Butch Blues* (1993), a semiautobiographical story of a genderqueer lesbian's experience with police brutality and bar raids. Next came *Transgender Warriors: Making History from Joan of Arc to Dennis Rodman* (1996), a broad and extensively researched history of transgender and gender-nonconforming people. The decision to write a history book after a novel was strategic; fiction was meant to be a stepping-stone for readers to grow the capacity to take a broader view. Feinberg stated:

> As I read the sort of gender theory that was coming out of academia at the time, I felt that gender theory had to be put back onto the soil of race, class, and sexuality in order to have meaning in people's lives. It couldn't be an abstraction because we were living gender theory.[24]

Another nonfiction book, *Trans Liberation: Beyond Pink or Blue* (1998) followed. This book took a decidedly theoretical bent, combining personal anecdotes with theoretical essays.

In 2006, Feinberg wrote another novel, *Drag King Dreams*, in which a young transgender person becomes friends with two Muslim men; this book is a direct call for solidarity between marginalized communities. Feinberg firmly believed that racism and police brutality are relevant to queer communities despite the whitewashing that takes place in the mainstream gay movement.[25] Feinberg's final book, *Rainbow Solidarity in Defense of Cuba* (2009), is a collection of Feinberg's *Workers World* essays.

Feinberg died after a long battle with multiple tick-borne coinfections. Hir last words were "Remember me as a revolutionary communist." Sie is survived by hir spouse of twenty-two years, Minnie Bruce Pratt, and a large family of choice.[26]

JUSTIN VIVIAN BOND

Justin Vivian Bond was born on May 9, 1963. They[27] are a singer-songwriter, author, actor, and performance artist who has been described as "the best cabaret artist of [their] generation."[28]

Early Life

Mx[29] Viv was born in Hagerstown, Maryland, and raised Christian. They identified with Lucille Ball and other beautiful, funny women they saw on television and began singing and dancing in an effort to emulate them.[30] After exploring structured vocal and acting lessons via church and community theatre, Mx Viv attended Adelphi University to study theatre, graduating in 1985. After college, they moved to San Francisco, changed their name, and began developing their career as a queer performer. In 1989, they played the role of Herculine Barbin in Bornstein's *Hidden: A Gender* to great acclaim. This performance launched their career and initiated a flurry of creative work.[31]

Performance Art

While in San Francisco, Mx Viv became interested in cabaret. When they met pianist Kenny Mellman, the two hit it off and began collaborating. Their act, Kiki and Herb, was an instant sensation when they debuted on Gay Pride Day 1993. Mx Viv played Kiki DuRane, an aging lounge singer with an alcohol problem who rambled about her shocking past and interjected terribly politically incorrect jokes between songs. Queer audiences, exhausted by the steadily climbing AIDS toll, loved her for her life-affirming scandalousness.[32] Kiki and Herb soon moved to New York City and continued to gather fans from seedy back rooms to Broadway, until 2008, when Mx Viv retired Kiki in order to focus on their solo cabaret career.[33]

FIGURE 5.4
Photograph of Justin Vivian Bond by Michael Hart, January 2013; reprinted with permission of Justin Vivian Bond.

Between Kiki and Herb performances, Mx Viv obtained a master's degree in scenography at Central Saint Martin's in London, with the goal of directing. They also appeared on-screen, playing an erotic salon host in John Cameron Mitchell's 2006 film *Shortbus*. Post-Kiki, Mx Viv has had several other film appearances as well as visual art exhibitions, and released several musical albums.[34] Of their role in the trans community, Mx Viv says, "I think of myself first and foremost as an artist. . . . Any impact I've made in that way is sort of a side effect of my being an artist, not driven by my activism."[35]

Memoir

In 2011, Mx Viv published a memoir of their childhood, titled *Tango: My Childhood, Backwards and in High Heels*. Just like their various cabaret personas, the writing is witty and utterly charming, with moments of breathtaking poignancy. In an early scene, Mx Viv describes the delicious discovery of lipstick—and the distressing moment when their mother takes it away. With a matter-of-fact tone, they recount the many instances of bullying from peers and family. And with equal frankness, they describe the sexual encounters that took place with one of those same bullies.[36] In this vivid, entertaining memoir, audiences are invited to reflect on the nature of "normalcy" and the ways in which it impacts gender-nonnormative children.[37]

RIKI WILCHINS

Riki Wilchins was born in 1952 and is a longtime activist. Hir[38] work melds gender theory, direct action, and political and educational advocacy.

Early Life

Wilchins grew up in Cincinnati in a family hostile to gender nonconformity. S/he was a successful student and was the valedictorian of hir high school class. S/he attended Cleveland State University where s/he transitioned and graduated in 1980 with a bachelor's in psychology and communication. Hir transition led to a seven-year romantic relationship dissolving and the estrangement of hir family. Wilchins moved to New York in 1981 to work as a computer consultant on Wall Street and pursue a graduate program in clinical psychology.[39]

FIGURE 5.5
Photograph of Riki Wilchins, 2013. Reprinted with permission of Riki Wilchins.

Direct Action and Advocacy

In 1994, as a result of hir own experiences with transphobia as well as the violent interactions s/he observed within hir community as a whole, Wilchins cofounded Transexual Menace, a direct action group that grew to more than forty chapters throughout the United States. These groups wore black T-shirts emblazoned with "Transexual Menace" and groups arranged vigils for victims of transphobic murder and held peaceful demonstrations at court hearings for their murderers.[40] Wilchins also published a Transexual Menace newsletter in which s/he coined the term "genderqueer":

> It's about all of us who are genderqueer: diesel dykes and stone butches, leath-erqueens and radical fairies, nelly fags, crossdressers, intersexed, transsexuals, transvestites, transgendered, transgressively gendered, and those of us whose gender expressions are so complex they haven't even been named yet.[41]

In 1995, Wilchins cofounded Camp Trans in response to the Michigan Womyn's Music Festival's eviction of trans woman Nancy Jean Burkholder and retroactive enunciation of a trans-exclusionary policy. This educational event was held across the road from the festival every year until the festival closed in 2015. Transgender women and men, genderqueer and gender-nonconforming people, and cisgender allies attended to protest transgender discrimination and educate festival attendees on transgender lives and issues. While the festival founders never changed their policy, Camp Trans raised public awareness, educated new allies, and provided safety and community for the trans community.[42]

Also in 1995, feeling that the street activism of Transexual Menace had limits in terms of shifting social attitudes and the ongoing political disem-powerment of trans people, Wilchins founded the Gender Public Advocacy Coalition (GenderPAC). This national organization developed from hir ear-lier street activism as a mechanism to pursue long-term organizing and ad-vocacy for gender rights. GenderPAC focused on workplace discrimination, hate crimes, media visibility, and psychiatric diagnostic categories. While much of GenderPAC's work concentrated on trans rights, they also assisted cisgender people who were victims of gender norms—including a butch les-bian allegedly fired for looking "too masculine."[43]

Some members of the transgender community criticized GenderPAC for not focusing solely on transgender issues; Wilchins responded that it was the principle of gender discrimination that was at issue, rather than excluding people politically based on their identity. "At one time or another almost all of us have been harassed, attacked, isolated, or shamed because we didn't fit someone's ideal of a 'real man' or a 'real woman.'"[44] GenderPAC had many successes and was disbanded in 2009.

Writing

In addition to hir tireless activism and advocacy, Wilchins is also a scholar. S/he published the influential *Read My Lips: Sexual Subversion and the End of Gender* (1997), an accessible and entertaining blend of gender theory and personal experience. Some chapters are acerbically witty ("17 Things You DON'T Say to a Transexual"); others offer historical insight ("The Menace Statement to Janice Raymond"); some are unflinchingly personal ("Our Cunts Are NOT the Same"); and others are tongue-in-cheek hilarious ("A Subversive Glossary"). Throughout the text, humor is woven with a fierce struggle against gender oppression.

In 2002, Wilchins followed up with *GenderQueer: Voices from beyond the Sexual Binary*, coedited with Joan Nestle and Clare Howell. Part theoretical text and part literary anthology, this book includes several essays by Wilchins as well as thirty contributed pieces engaging with nonbinary identity through short stories, anecdotes, interviews, and histories. Wilchins then published *Queer Theory, Gender Theory: An Instant Primer* (2004), which aimed to make theory—often coached in obscure, academic language—accessible to the average gender-nonconforming person, by combining postmodern sex and gender theory, queer history and politics, and the ways in which queer youth engage with theory and politics in their personal lives.

Wilchins continues to advocate for marginalized genders through hir activism, political advocacy, and writing for a number of anthologies and news publications.

QWO-LI DRISKILL

Qwo-Li Driskill was born in 1975 and is a (noncitizen) Cherokee Two-Spirit and queer writer, activist, and performer also of African, Irish, Lenape, Lumbee, and Osage ascent.

FIGURE 5.6
Photograph of Qwo-Li Driskill, 2014, reprinted with hir permission.

Early Life

Born in Glenwood Springs, Colorado, Dr. Driskill came from a poor mixed family in a primarily White, middle- to upper-class town. S/he[45] obtained hir bachelor's in social transformation and the arts at University of Northern Colorado in 1998. In 2001, s/he received hir master's in whole systems design: Native writing, theatre, story and resistance at Antioch University. Then in 2008, s/he graduated from Michigan State University with a PhD in rhetoric and writing.

Performance and Poetry

Dr. Driskill began publishing hir poetry and creative nonfiction in 2001, in literary journals, zines, anthologies, magazines, and the web. Themes include genocide, land theft, decolonization, sexuality, gender, and disability, among others. In 2002, s/he published two books of poetry: *Book of Memory: Honor Poems* (2002), created for the Hate Crimes Remembrance Project; and *Burning Upward Flight* (2002). In 2005, s/he published another book of poetry titled *Walking with Ghosts*. Dr. Driskill's creative work is highly intersectional—tying together themes of gender, sexuality, and colonialism—because Two-Spirit identity is itself an intersectional identity. As s/he states in one piece, "Two-Spirit liberation is part of a larger process of decolonization."[46]

In addition to the written word, Dr. Driskill's creativity extends to live performance, both onstage and in film and video. S/he has performed many of hir poetry pieces at poetry slams, conferences, universities, bookstores, and other venues. S/he has also participated in theatre workshops and performances, as performer, playwright, director, and facilitator. S/he has been particularly active in facilitating Theatre of the Oppressed workshops for fellow First Nations participants.

Scholarship

Dr. Driskill's scholarly activity has been similarly intersectional, focusing on decolonization, gender, and sexuality. S/he coedited *Queer Indigenous Studies: Critical Interventions in Theory, Politics, and Literature* (2002) with Chris Finley, Brian Joseph Gilley, and Scott Lauria Morgensen. This groundbreaking collection incorporates indigenous methodologies and histories with queer and Two-Spirit studies, combining scholarship and activism. Dr. Driskill also contributed an essay, "Asegi Ayetl: Cherokee Two-Spirit People Reimagining Nation." In the same year, Dr. Driskill coedited *Sovereign Erotics: A Collection of Two-Spirit Literature* with Daniel Heath Justice, Deborah Miranda, and Lisa Tatonetti. This landmark literary collection includes fiction, nonfiction, poetry, and essay, including five poems contributed by Dr. Driskill.

In 2016, Dr. Driskill authored a scholarly book, *Asegi Stories: Cherokee Queer and Two-Spirit Memory*, the first full-length scholarly Two-Spirit critique. This text explores asegi stories, those that involve people who are Two-Spirit. Through the vehicle of narrative, Dr. Driskill analyzes the histories of colonial gender regulation. Besides book projects, Dr. Driskill has also produced extensive scholarly articles focusing on colonized genders and sexualities[47] and decolonizing queer studies.[48]

Dr. Driskill is an assistant professor and the director of graduate studies in the Women, Gender, and Sexuality Studies program at Oregon State University. S/he continues to produce scholarship, poetry, and creative nonfiction;

s/he facilitates Theatre of the Oppressed and other social justice workshops; and s/he serves on graduate supervisory committees.

NOTES

1. A postpunk subgenre of music and associated DIY cultural production.

2. Vaginal Davis uses she/her pronouns, per her website: http://vaginaldavis.com.

3. Hili Perlson, "Vaginal Davis Speaks," *Sleek*, September 30, 2011, http://www.sleek-mag.com/2011/09/30/vaginal-davis-interview.

4. In her long-running blog (http://blog.vaginaldavis.com), Dr. Davis cheerfully celebrates her birthday each February, announcing that she is several hundred years old.

5. Vaginal Davis and Lewis Church, "My Womanly Story: Vaginal Davis in Conversation with Lewis Church," *PAJ: A Journal of Performance and Art* 38, no. 2 (May 2016): 81.

6. Davis and Church, "My Womanly Story," 86.

7. Davis and Church, "My Womanly Story," 84.

8. For a full discography, see her website, http://www.vaginaldavis.com.

9. See her website, http://www.vaginaldavis.com, for a full zineography.

10. Again, see her website, http://www.vaginaldavis.com, for a full filmography.

11. Davis and Church, "My Womanly Story," 85–86.

12. José Esteban Muñoz, "'The White to Be Angry': Vaginal Davis's Terrorist Drag." *Social Text* 52/53 (Autumn–Winter 1997): 91.

13. Kate Bornstein uses she/her pronouns, per her website: http://katebornstein.com.

14. For the full story, see Kate Bornstein, *A Queer and Pleasant Danger: A Memoir* (Boston: Beacon, 2012).

15. Kate Bornstein, *Gender Outlaw: On Men, Women, and the Rest of Us* (New York: Routledge, 1994), 8.

16. Visit her website, http://katebornstein.com, to stay updated on upcoming performances.

17. Keep current on life events through her blog, http://katebornstein.typepad.com.

18. Leslie Feinberg used sie/hir pronouns: "I am a human being who would rather not be addressed as Ms. or Mr., ma'am or sir. I prefer to use gender-neutral pronouns like *sie* (pronounced like "*see*") and *hir* (pronounced like "*here*") to describe myself." Leslie Feinberg, *Trans Liberation: Beyond Pink or Blue* (Boston: Beacon, 1998), 1.

19. Leslie Feinberg and Minnie Bruce Pratt, "Leslie Feinberg: 1949–2014," 2014, http://www.lesliefeinberg.net/self.

20. Martha E. Stone, "Leslie Feinberg Beheld a World without Gender," *Gay & Lesbian Review Worldwide* 22, no. 2 (March–April 2015): 7.

21. Leslie Feinberg, "Trans Health Crisis: For Us It's Life or Death," *American Journal of Public Health* 91, no. 6 (June 2001): 897.

22. Feinberg, "Trans Health Crisis," 898.

23. Feinberg, "Trans Health Crisis," 897–900.

24. Gary Bowen, "Transgendered Warriors: An Interview with Leslie Feinberg," *Lambda Book Report* 6, no. 6 (January 1998): 19.

25. Michele Spring-Moore, "Leslie Feinberg," *Lambda Book Report* 14, no. 2 (Summer 2006): 16.

26. Feinberg and Pratt, "Leslie Feinberg."

27. After several years using v as a pronoun, Bond now uses they/them pronouns, per an e-mail exchange with the author.

28. Hilton Als, "Life Is a Cabaret," *New Yorker*, January 10, 2011.

29. Justin Vivian Bond uses Mx as an honorific, rather than Mr., Mrs., or Ms.

30. For the whole story, see Justin Vivian Bond, *Tango: My Childhood, Backwards and in High Heels* (New York: Feminist Press, 2011).

31. Carl Swanson, "The Story of V," *New York*, May 16, 2011.

32. Als, "Life Is a Cabaret."

33. Swanson, "The Story of V."

34. See their website, http://www.justinvivianbond.com, for performance updates and merchandise.

35. Adam Feldman, "Justin Vivian Bond on Art, Gender, NYC and the Future of Kiki and Herb," *TimeOut*, September 16, 2015, https://www.timeout.com/newyork/music/justin-vivian-bond-on-art-gender-nyc-and-the-future-of-kiki-and-herb.

36. Bond, *Tango*.

37. Z. Nicolazzo, "'Couldn't I be Both Fred and Ginger?': Teaching about Nonbinary Identities through Memoir," *Journal of LGBT Youth* 11 (2014): 171–75.

38. Riki Wilchins uses s/he/hir pronouns, per hir books and an e-mail exchange.

39. Carey Goldberg, "Public Lives: Issues of Gender, from Pronouns to Murder," *New York Times*, June 11, 1999, http://www.nytimes.com/1999/06/11/nyregion/public-lives-issues-of-gender-from-pronouns-to-murder.html.

40. Carey Goldberg, "Shunning 'He' and 'She,' They Fight for Respect," *New York Times*, September 8, 1996, http://www.nytimes.com/1996/09/08/us/shunning-he-and-she-they-fight-for-respect.html.

41. Riki Anne Wilchins, *In Your Face*, Transexual Menace newsletter, Spring 1995.

42. Riki Anne Wilchins, *In Your Face*, Transexual Menace newsletter, Summer 1999.

43. Jack Drescher, "An Interview with GenderPAC's Riki Wilchins," *Journal of Gay & Lesbian Psychotherapy* 6, no. 2 (2002): 67–72.

44. Riki Anne Wilchins, "Time for Gender Rights," *GLQ: A Journal of Lesbian and Gay Studies* 10, no. 2 (2004): 266–67.

45. Dr. Driskill uses both s/he/hir and they/them pronouns, per an e-mail exchange with the author.

46. Qwo-Li Driskill, "Shaking Our Shells: Cherokee Two-Spirits Rebalancing the World," in *Beyond Masculinity: Essays by Queer Men on Gender & Politics*, ed. Trevor Hoppe (Ann Arbor, MI: Self-published, 2008), 125, http://www.beyondmasculinity.com.

47. See especially Qwo-Li Driskill, "Stolen from Our Bodies: First Nations Two-Spirits/Queers and the Journey to a Sovereign Erotic," *Studies in American Indian Literatures* 16, no. 2 (Summer 2004): 50–64.

48. See especially Qwo-Li Driskill, "Doubleweaving Two-Spirit Critiques: Building Alliances between Native and Queer Studies," *GLQ: A Journal of Lesbian and Gay Studies* 16, no. 1–2 (2010): 69–92.

II

RESOURCES

Archives and
Special Collections

Archives are organizations that preserve, organize, and make accessible historical materials. Collections of historical materials generally are focused on, or come from, a specific community: a corporation, university, city, or affinity group. Historical materials in these collections are referred to as primary sources, that is, documentation of history without analysis. Primary sources include journals and diaries, photographs and scrapbooks, business ledgers, legal transactions, meetings notes, correspondence, and ephemera such as concert flyers and political signage. Some archives and libraries also hold special collections that are not necessarily primary source materials. An organization's or individual's book collection, for example, may be of note for its intentional focus, even if some or all of the books are available elsewhere.

Archives are important because they preserve community history and thus aid collective memory. Collections may enable researchers to construct lineages, verify legal rights such as land claims, and strengthen community identity. That said, neither archives nor archivists are entirely neutral or objective. The decision to collect and preserve some materials and not others is inherently political and subject to bias, whether intentional or not. Marginalized groups are consequently severely underrepresented in many repositories.[1] Furthermore, when marginalized groups are represented in archives, the materials are not always discoverable. Finding aids, descriptive guides to archival collections, are created by archivists who may not be aware of community terminology or have the time to sift through the materials to figure it out. And archivists must decide which details are most significant, a tall order for somebody who might not be familiar with the community.[2]

Even in repositories devoted to queer and transgender materials, researchers may have difficulty locating specific materials. Sexual and gender minorities may have been closeted and their materials are heavily coded. Sexual and gender identities have a long and difficult history with the medical and legal establishment; historical materials may be described with terminology like "deviant," "pervert," or "mentally ill." And queer communities themselves rapidly evolve their own identity terms and definitions.[3] The term "nonbinary" is quite new; researchers may need to use terms such as "genderqueer" or search for clues in broader transgender materials.

This chapter provides a list of archives and special collections that may be fruitful for researchers seeking nonbinary materials. In some cases, materials pertaining to nonbinary gender will be immediately obvious. In most cases, however, this particular segment of LGBTQ heritage will have to be teased out of the materials with creative search terms and a knowledge of how nonbinary history has emerged from the wider transgender narrative.

The first section, "Discovery Tools," lists tools for locating queer and transgender archival materials. Discovery tools include maps, repository lists, research portals, and databases. Entries are arranged alphabetically by the entity responsible for creating the resource. The second section, "Repositories and Collections," showcases repositories and collections that vary widely in terms of size and content. Repositories include college and university libraries, historical societies, public libraries, and community organizations, some of which are located in private homes. Some repositories focus solely on queer and transgender materials; others have a wider collection scope. In these cases, specific collections are listed. In terms of collections, some are complete while others are actively collecting. Entries are arranged alphabetically by state and country. For repositories devoted to queer and transgender materials, the repository name appears first, followed by the address and URL. For queer- and transgender-focused collections residing within more general repositories, the collection name appears first, followed by the repository, address, and URL.

DISCOVERY TOOLS

Bailey, Erin, and Nicole Robert. Queering the Museum Project. https://
queeringthemuseum.org.
    A project exploring queer representation in museums.

Bowman, Mark (Project Coordinator). Lesbian, Gay, Bisexual and Transgender
Religious Archives Network (LGBT-RAN). https://www.lgbtran.org.
    An organization that helps religious archives preserve their holdings, and
directs researchers to those holdings.

Brown, Elspeth (Principal Investigator). LGBTQ History Digital Collaboratory Oral
History Hub. http://lgbtqdigitalcollaboratory.org/oral-history-hub.
    A collaborative project collecting LGBTQ oral history resources.

Gale Cengage. Archives of Human Sexuality and Identity (Subscription Database).
2016. http://www.gale.com/primary-sources/archives-of-sexuality-and-gender.
    Database providing access to queer primary sources.

Gay, Lesbian, Bisexual and Transgender Round Table, American Library
Association. "GLBTQ Libraries and Archives." http://www.ala.org/glbtrt/tools/
glbtq-libraries-and-archives.
    A list of queer libraries and archives.

Lesbian and Gay Archives Roundtable, Society of American Archivists. "Lavender
Legacies: Guide to Sources in North America." Last updated 2012. http://www2
.archivists.org/groups/lesbian-and-gay-archives-roundtable-lagar/lavender
-legacies-guide.
    A guide to queer archival resources.

Rawson, K. J. (Director). Digital Transgender Archive. https://www
.digitaltransgenderarchive.net.
    An online hub for digitized queer archival materials.

REPOSITORIES AND COLLECTIONS

Repositories and Collections in the United States

Arizona

Arizona Queer Archives. University of Arizona, Institute for LGBT Studies. 1731 E.
2nd St., #201, Tucson, AZ 85721. http://www.azqueerarchives.org.
    The state of Arizona's Lesbian, Gay, Bisexual, Transgender, Queer, Intersex
(LGBTQI) collecting archives of the Institute for LGBT Studies at the University
of Arizona.

California

The Center for Sex & Culture Library and Archive. 1349 Mission St., San Francisco, CA 94103. http://www.sexandculture.org/libary.

The Center for Sex & Culture Library and Archive was born from, and is sustained by, donated collections of books, magazines, journals, zines, comics, dissertations, works of art, videos, memorabilia, and the personal papers of key members of the community. The collection is unique in its dedication to collecting and preserving information about sex as we have known it, do know it, and continue to learn about it, worldwide.

Fresno LGBT Community Center Lending Library & Media Room. 1067 N Fulton Ave., Fresno, CA 93728. http://www.fresnolgbtcenter.org/?page_id=138.

A book, DVD, and magazine lending library, focusing on queer titles.

Gay, Lesbian, Bisexual and Transgender Periodicals Collection (1968–2003). Collection number MSS.2005.05. San Jose State University, Special Collections & Archives. One Washington Square, San Jose, CA 95192. http://www.oac.cdlib.org/findaid/ark:/13030/kt1h4nc63m.

The Gay, Lesbian, Bisexual and Transgender Periodicals Collection (1968–2003) contains a variety of periodicals that document the gay, lesbian, bisexual and transgender (GLBT) movement. The place of origin for a majority of these periodicals is California, with the remainder originating from other states in the western United States.

GLBT Historical Society Archives & Museum. 989 Market St., Lower Level, San Francisco, CA 94103. http://www.glbthistory.org.

The GLBT Historical Society collects, preserves, and interprets the history of GLBT people and the communities that support them.

Human Sexuality Collection. California State University, Northridge Special Collections & Archives. 18111 Nordhoff St., Northridge, CA 91330. http://library.csun.edu/SCA.

The collection is maintained for research and educational purposes, and is composed of books, periodicals, manuscripts, and archival materials covering such topics as cross-dressing, gender roles in various time periods, the homosexual community in Los Angeles, prostitution, the transgendered community, children and gender, nudism, gender and medicine, fetishism, and pornography.

Lambda Archives of San Diego. 4545 Park Blvd., Suite 104, San Diego, CA 92116. http://www.lambdaarchives.us.

The mission of the Lambda Archives of San Diego is to collect, preserve, and teach the history of lesbian, gay, bisexual, and transgender people in the San Diego and northern Baja California region.

Lavender Library Archives + Cultural Exchange. 1414 21st St., Sacramento, CA 95811. http://www.lavenderlibrary.com.
 The Lavender Library is a lending library and archive housing lesbian, gay, bisexual, transgender, queer, and intersex (LGBTQI) books and magazines, various media, and archival materials.

LGBT Center Long Beach LGBTQ Library. 2017 E. 4th St., Long Beach, CA 90814. https://www.centerlb.org/lgbtq-library.
 The Center's LGBTQ lending library contains a variety of fiction and nonfiction literature spanning decades.

LGBT History Collection. Oakland Museum of California. 1000 Oak St., Oakland, CA 94607. http://museumca.org.
 Collection exploring the legacy of early LGBT leaders in San Francisco such as José Sarria and recent California issues such as Proposition 8 and its overturning.

LGBT Interest Collection. San Francisco Public Library, Eureka Valley/Harvey Milk Memorial Branch. 1 Jose Sarria Ct., San Francisco, CA 94114. http://sfpl.org/index.php?pg=0100002301.
 LGBT Interest Collection includes materials on the culture, history, and life experience of the LGBT community: lesbians, gay men, bisexuals, transgender, queer, questioning, intersex people, and other sexual minorities.

LGBTQIA Collections. James C. Hormel LGBTQIA Center. San Francisco Public Library. 100 Larkin St., San Francisco, CA 94102. http://sfpl.org/index.php?pg=0200002401.
 Collections documenting lesbian, gay, bisexual, transgender, queer, questioning, intersex, and allies' history and culture, with a special emphasis on the San Francisco Bay Area.

ONE National Gay & Lesbian Archives. University of Southern California Libraries. 909 W. Adams Blvd., Los Angeles, CA 90007. http://one.usc.edu.
 ONE National Gay & Lesbian Archives at the USC Libraries is the largest repository of lesbian, gay, bisexual, transgender, queer (LGBTQ) materials in the world. Founded in 1952, ONE Archives currently houses more than two million archival items including periodicals, books, film, video and audio recordings, photographs, artworks, organizational records, and personal papers.

Queer Nation Archive. Chicano Studies Research Center, University of California, Los Angeles. 193 Haines Hall, Los Angeles, CA 90095. http://www.chicano.ucla. edu/library.

Queer Nation was a lesbian, gay, bisexual, and transgender (LGBT) grassroots local organization first established in New York, which then proliferated into many other chapters across the country including Chicago, Los Angeles, San Francisco, and Houston. The collection encompasses correspondence, budgets, propaganda materials, press contact information, membership lists, newsletters, and photographs.

Rae Lee Siporin Library. University of California, Los Angeles. 220 Westwood Plaza B36, Los Angeles, CA 90095. http://www.lgbt.ucla.edu/Rae-Lee-Siporin-Library.

The Rae Lee Siporin Library is one of the largest libraries of its kind at a college or university with nearly four thousand books and periodicals written for and about LGBTQ people.

Colorado

Denver Zine Library. 2400 Curtis St., Denver, CO 80205. https://denverzinelibrary .org.

The Denver Zine Library currently houses one of the largest zine collections in North America with a preserved collection of more than fifteen thousand independent and alternative zines.

LGBTQ Student Resource Center Library. Metropolitan State University of Denver. Tivoli Student Union 213, 900 Auraria Pkwy., Denver, CO 80204. http://www .msudenver.edu/glbtss/library.

The LGBTQ SRC Library contains more than 1,600 items, including fiction and nonfiction books, documentary videos, and feature films.

Terry Mangan Memorial Library. The Center: Advancing LGBT Colorado. 1301 E. Colfax Ave., Denver, CO 80218. http://www.glbtcolorado.org/home/terry -mangan-memorial-library.

The Terry Mangan Memorial Library is home to more than three thousand volumes of LGBT texts, making it the largest lending library of its kind in the state.

Connecticut

Alternative Press Collection. University of Connecticut Archives & Special Collections. 405 Babbidge Rd., Unit 1205, Storrs, CT 060269. http://archives.lib .uconn.edu.

The Alternative Press Collection was founded in the late 1960s as a repository for publications emanating from activist movements for social, cultural, and political change. The collection contains thousands of newspapers, serials, books, pamphlets, ephemera, and artifacts documenting activist themes and organizations.

Gender and Sexuality Collections. Yale University Library Manuscripts and Archives. Yale University, 128 Wall St., New Haven, CT 06520. http://guides .library.yale.edu/mssa_subjects_sexuality.

The Manuscripts and Archives Sexuality Subject Guide is an annotated list of personal papers and organization records in Manuscripts and Archives related to gender, sexuality, and lesbian, gay, bisexual, and transgender lives and culture.

LGBT Collections. Wesleyan University Special Collections & Archives. 252 Church St., Middletown, CT 06459. http://www.wesleyan.edu/libr/schome/index.html.

The Queer Periodicals Collection contains more than 490 different gay, lesbian, bisexual, and transgender periodicals published between 1966 and 1998. Special Collections also includes vertical files on queer subjects.

LGBTQI Collections. Beinecke Rare Book and Manuscript Library. Yale University, 121 Wall St., New Haven, CT 06511. http://guides.library.yale.edu/LGBTQI.

Includes the papers of writers and artists such as Gertrude Stein and Alice B. Toklas, Larry Kramer, Glenway Wescott and Monroe Wheeler, among many others. Also includes books, magazines and other serials, and digitized archival materials.

Queer Zines, Magazines, and Newspapers Collection (MS 1847). Yale University Library Manuscripts and Archives. Yale University, 128 Wall St., New Haven, CT 06520. http://hdl.handle.net/10079/fa/mssa.ms.1847.

The Queer Zines, Magazines, and Newspapers Collection includes printed ephemera and publications documenting the development of lesbian, gay, bisexual, transgender, and queer communities in their own voices. Includes mass circulation and small-press publications.

Florida

LGBT Collections. University of South Florida Libraries. 4202 E. Fowler Ave., Tampa, FL 33620. http://www.lib.usf.edu/special-collections/lgbt-collections.

The USF Libraries' focus is on collecting materials that document LGBT history, culture, politics, community relations, and public health. While the Tampa Bay region remains an important focus, these collections are international in scope.

Stonewall National Museum & Archives. 1300 E. Sunrise Blvd., Fort Lauderdale, FL
    33304. http://www.stonewallnationalmuseum.org.
    Stonewall National Museum & Archives promotes understanding through
    preserving and sharing the proud culture of lesbian, gay, bisexual, and
    transgender people and their significant role in American society.

Georgia

LGBT Resource Center Library. University of Georgia. 221 Memorial Hall, Athens,
    GA 30602. https://lgbtcenter.uga.edu/students/library.html.
    The LGBT Resource Center provides many resources for UGA students,
    faculty, and staff through the library. The resources include books, videos,
    journals, magazines, and a variety of brochures.

PFLAG Atlanta Library. http://www.pflagatl.org/library.
    Lending library open to PFLAG members; includes material on transgender
    and gender-nonconforming people.

Illinois

Gerber/Hart Library and Archives. 6500 N. Clark St., Chicago, IL 60626. http://
    www.gerberhart.org.
    Gerber/Hart Library and Archives was founded in 1981 to be a depository
    for the records of lesbian-, gay-, bisexual-, transgender-, and queer-identified
    (LGBTQ) individuals and organizations, and for other resources bearing upon
    their lives and experiences in American society.

Queer Oral History Project. Gender and Sexuality Center, University of Illinois,
    Chicago. Chicago, IL. http://genderandsexuality.uic.edu/programs_events/queer
    -oral-history-project.
    The GSC and the Department of Gender and Women's Studies are collecting
    oral histories around the life experiences of LGBTQ people who have engaged
    with and passed through UIC over the years.

Teri Rose Memorial Library. Leather Archives & Museum. 6418 N. Greenview Ave.,
    Chicago, IL 60626. http://www.leatherarchives.org.
    The Leather Archives & Museum is dedicated to the compilation, preservation,
    and maintenance of leather, kink, and fetish lifestyles.

Transgender Resource Collection. Oak Park Public Library. 834 Lake St., Oak Park,
    IL 60301. http://oppl.org/collections-download/transgender-resource-collection.

The Oak Park Public Library has created a unique collection to serve transgender people and everyone seeking information, including employers, medical providers, allies, friends, and family.

Indiana

Chris Gonzalez Library & Archives. Indy Pride. 429 E. Vermont St., Indianapolis, IN 46202. http://www.indypride.org/library.
  The Library & Archives contain items of interest to the community: back issues of LGBT publications, videotapes of local LGBT events, T-shirts, memorabilia, photos, and artwork.

Helmke Library. Northeast Indiana Diversity Library. Indiana University–Purdue University. PO Box 5537, Fort Wayne, IN 46895. http://www.nidl.info.
  This library houses the oldest GLBT collection in Indiana. More than 6,600 items are in the NIDL circulating collection of books and videotapes. The archives hold local and regional GLBT history that ranges from articles and newsletters to pictures, T-shirts, buttons, and more.

Kinsey Institute Library & Archives. Indiana University. 1165 E. 3rd St., Bloomington, IN 47405. https://www.kinseyinstitute.org/collections/library/index .php.
  The Kinsey Institute's Library maintains a research collection of unrivaled scope with manuscripts, data, materials, and papers from some of the world's most influential sex researchers.

LGBTQ Collection. Indiana University South Bend Archives. 1700 Mishawaka Ave., South Bend, IN 46615. https://www.iusb.edu/library/about/collection/archives/ index.php.
  The Indiana University South Bend Civil Rights Heritage Center LGBTQ Collection contains materials relating to the experience of people in and around South Bend, Indiana, who describe their sexual and/or gender identity as lesbian, gay, bisexual, transgendered, or queer, as well as people who consider themselves allies to the LGBTQ rights cause.

Iowa

ATCA (Alternative Traditions in the Contemporary Arts) Periodicals and Zines Collection. Collection number MSC0779. University of Iowa Special Collections. University of Iowa Libraries, Iowa City, IA 52242. http://collguides.lib.uiowa .edu/?MSC0779.

This ATCA collection brings together journals, newspapers, zines, and similar formal and informal periodicals that are art related or have artistic merit. The range of subjects is broad and includes political and cultural issues, gender and sexuality questions, as well as music, film, poetry, and religion.

Des Moines Pride Center Library. 1620 Pleasant St., Ste. 244, Des Moines, IA 50314. http://www.dsmpridecenter.org/index.php/library.
    The library contains nearly two thousand GSM-(gender and sexual minority) based books and videos.

Kansas

Under the Rainbow: Oral Histories of Gay, Lesbian, Transgender, Intersex and Queer People in Kansas. University of Kansas Libraries. 1425 Jayhawk Blvd., Lawrence, Kansas 66045. https://kuscholarworks.ku.edu/handle/1808/5330.
    An oral history project focusing on queer people in Kansas.

Kentucky

Queer Appalachia Oral History Collection. Collection number OHQUAPP. Louie B. Nunn Center for Oral History, University of Kentucky Libraries. Margaret I. King Building, Lexington, KY 40506. https://kentuckyoralhistory.org/catalog/xt7prr1pk41j.
    The Queer Appalachia Oral History Project captures the diverse stories of gay, lesbian, transgender, bisexual, and questioning individuals who grew up and/or currently live in the Appalachian Regional Commission (ARC) designated central Appalachian region, especially eastern Kentucky.

Williams-Nichols Archive. University of Louisville Special Collections and Archives. Ekstrom Library Lower Level, Louisville, Kentucky 40292. http://special.library.louisville.edu/display-collection.asp?ID=884.
    Established in 1982 by the donor, Louisville activist David Williams, the collection holds more than 3,500 books, three thousand issues of journals and periodicals, nearly twenty-five linear feet of manuscripts, hundreds of video- and audiotapes, and nearly 1,500 items of memorabilia and ephemera on the LGBT experience.

Louisiana

Newcomb Archives & Vorhoff Library Special Collections. Tulane University. 62 Newcomb Pl., New Orleans, LA 70118. http://www2.tulane.edu/newcomb/archives-library.cfm.

The Newcomb Archives collects, preserves, and makes available records that document the legacy of Newcomb College and the history of women and gender in the Gulf South. It is home to approximately three hundred unique collections. The Vorhoff Library is a noncirculating special collections library devoted to women's education, prescriptive literature, culinary history, Newcomb authors, gender and sexuality, third-wave feminist zines, and other topics.

Maine

LGBTQ+ Collection. University of Southern Maine Special Collections. University of Southern Maine. 314 Forest Ave., Portland, ME 04103. http://usm.maine.edu/ library/specialcollections/lgbt-collection.

This collection contains LGBT periodicals, organization papers, photographs, ephemera, and more.

Maryland

Lesbian, Gay, Bisexual, and Transgender Equity Center Library. University of Maryland. 2218 Marie Mount Hall, College Park, MD 20740. http://www.umd .edu/lgbt/library.html.

The library provides material that develops and empowers agents of social justice for lesbian, gay, bisexual, transgender, and queer people.

Massachusetts

ACT UP Oral History Project Archive. Harvard University. Widener Library, Cambridge, MA 02138. http://id.lib.harvard.edu/aleph/013527824/catalog.

The ACT UP Oral History Project is a collection of interviews with surviving members of the AIDS Coalition to Unleash Power, New York.

GLBTQA Special Collections. Northeastern University Archives and Special Collections. 92 Snell Library, 360 Huntington Ave., Boston, MA 02115. http:// library.northeastern.edu/archives-special-collections/find-collections/finding -aids#glbtqa.

Collections include ACT UP, Lesbian, Gay, Bisexual and Transgender Political Alliance of Massachusetts, and Theater Offensive.

The History Project Special Collections. 29 Stanhope St., Boston, MA 02116. http:// www.historyproject.org/resources/boston_resources.php.

The History Project maintains research files or organizational files on Boston LGBT history from the colonial period to the present.

Papercut Zine Library. 10 Ward St., Somerville, MA. http://www.papercutzinelib
rary.org/wordpress.
    Papercut is a fully functioning lending library, with a focus on handmade and
independently produced materials. The collection includes everything from
the all-familiar photocopied punk rock zines from the eighties to handcrafted
personal zines bound together with yarn.

Queer Resource Center Library. Brandeis University. Usdan G105, 415 South
St., Waltham, MA 02453. https://sites.google.com/site/qrcbrandeis/resources/
oncampus/library.
    Lending library with queer materials including DVDs and books, with a sizable
transgender collection.

Sexual Minorities Archives. PO Box 6579, Holyoke, MA 01041. https://
sexualminoritiesarchives.wordpress.com.
    Sexual Minorities Archives (SMA) is a project of the Sexual Minorities
Educational Foundation Inc., and one of the oldest and largest collections of
LGBTQIA+ historical documents, media, and artifacts in the world.

Stonewall Center Library. University of Massachusetts Amherst. Crampton Hall, 56
Sunset Ave., Amherst, MA 01003. http://www.umass.edu/stonewall/resources/
library.
    Resource center with a lending library with lesbian, gay, bisexual, trans, queer,
intersex, and asexual materials.

Michigan

Bayard Rustin Library. Affirmations Media Center. 290 W. Nine Mile Rd. Ferndale,
MI 48220. http://www.goaffirmations.org.
    The Bayard Rustin Library houses one of the largest collections of LGBTQ-
specific books and movies in the state.

Gay, Lesbian, Bisexual and Transgender Collections. University of Michigan Bentley
Historical Library. 1150 Beal Ave., Ann Arbor, MI 48109. http://bentley.umich
.edu/legacy-support/gaylesbian.
    The Bentley Historical Library has a large number of materials on the topic of
gender and sexuality, particularly at the local and state levels.

Grand Rapids Pride Center LGBTQ Library. 343 Atlas Ave. SE, Grand Rapids, MI
49506. http://www.grpride.org/learning-center.
    Collection of LGBTQ fiction and nonfiction books.

James B. Knox Resource Library. Kalamazoo Gay Lesbian Resource Center. 629
Pioneer St. #102, Kalamazoo, MI 49008. http://www.kglrc.org/resources/resource
-library.
   The James B. Knox Resource Library, a component of the Kalamazoo Gay
Lesbian Resource Center, supports the mission of the center by collecting,
preserving, and making available to the public a variety of media that promote
knowledge and understanding of bisexual, gay, lesbian, and transgender issues.

Jim Toy Library. Spectrum Center, University of Michigan. 3200 Michigan
Union, 530 S. State St., Ann Arbor, MI 48109. https://spectrumcenter.umich.
edu/JimToy.
   The Jim Toy Library (JTL) supports LGBTQA student development by
exposing students to, and engaging them in, the rich cultural, social, historical,
psychological, political, and relational aspects of LGBTQ people, identities,
experiences, and communities.

Joseph A. Labadie Collection. University of Michigan Special Collections. 913
S. University Ave., Ann Arbor, MI 48109. http://www.lib.umich.edu/labadie-
collection.
   A collection documenting the history of social protest movements and
marginalized political communities from the nineteenth century to the present.

National Transgender Library and Archives. University of Michigan Special
Collections. 913 S. University Ave., Ann Arbor, MI 48109. http://guides.lib
.umich.edu/LGBTQ.
   Believed to be the largest cataloged collection of books, magazines, films,
videotapes, journals and newspaper articles, unpublished papers, photographs,
artwork, letters, personal papers, and memorabilia transgender-related materials.

Minnesota

GLBT Movement Collections. Minnesota Historical Society Library. 345 W. Kellogg
Blvd., St. Paul, MN 55102. http://libguides.mnhs.org/glbt.
   Includes organizational records, ephemera, photographs, periodicals, and
secondary sources pertaining to GLBT social movements.

Jean-Nickolaus Tretter Collection in Gay, Lesbian, Bisexual and Transgender Studies.
University of Minnesota Libraries Special Collections, Rare Books, and Manuscripts.
222 21st Ave. S, Minneapolis, MN 55455. https://www.lib.umn.edu/tretter.
   The Tretter Collection houses more than three thousand linear feet of material
about the GLBT experience. It includes published material, organizational

records, personal manuscripts, informational files, films, music, textiles, posters, and other items.

Quatrefoil Library. 1220 E. Lake St., Minneapolis, MN. https://www.qlibrary.org.
    The Quatrefoil Library's mission is to provide a welcoming place to foster GLBT community, culture, and camaraderie through literature and media.

Missouri

Gay and Lesbian Archive of Mid-America (GLAMA). University of Missouri, Miller Nichols Library. 800 E. 51st St., Kansas City, MO 64110. http://library.umkc.edu/ spec-col/glama/index.htm.
    The mission of GLAMA is to collect, preserve, and make accessible the materials that reflect the histories of the LGBT communities of the Kansas City region.

Ozarks Lesbian and Gay Archives (OLGA). Missouri State University Libraries Special Collections and University Archives. 850 S. John Q. Hammons Pkwy., Springfield, MO 65897. http://purl.missouristate.edu/library/archives/ FindingAids/M018.
    The collection was established as a cooperative project with the Missouri State University Libraries, Lambda Alliance, and BiGALA.

Ozarks Lesbian and Gay Archives (OLGA) Oral History Project. Missouri State University Libraries Special Collections and University Archives. 850 S. John Q. Hammons Pkwy., Springfield, MO 65897. http://purl.missouristate.edu/library/ archives/FindingAids/M019.
    The Oral History Project was initiated in 2004 and has grown to include more than 150 interviews with members of the region's LGBT community.

St. Louis LGBT History Project. St. Louis, MO. http://www.stlouislgbthistory .com.
    The St. Louis LGBT History Project's mission is to preserve and promote the diverse and dynamic history of the lesbian, gay, bisexual, transgender, and queer community of greater St. Louis.

Montana

Western Montana Gay and Lesbian Community Center Library. 127 N. Higgins Ave. #202, Missoula, MT 59802. http://www.librarything.com/profile/wmglcc.
    A collection of LGBTQ fiction and nonfiction books.

Nebraska

Queer Omaha Archives. University of Nebraska Criss Library Archives & Special Collections. 6001 Dodge St., Omaha, NE 68182. http://queeromahaarchives. omeka.net.

The Queer Omaha Archives preserves Omaha's LGBTQIA+ history as part of the UNO Libraries' Archives & Special Collections. Historical materials documenting Omaha's diverse LGBTQIA+ communities are collected and made available to the public by archivists and librarians to more widely share Omaha's stories.

Nevada

Gay and Lesbian Community Center of Southern Nevada Library. 401 S. Maryland Pkwy., Las Vegas, NV 89101. http://www.librarything.com/profile/thecenter. Collection of LGBTQ fiction and nonfiction books and videos.

New Jersey

Queer Newark Oral History Project. Rutgers University, Department of History. 323 Conklin Hall, 175 University Ave., Newark, NJ 07102. http://queer.newark .rutgers.edu.

An initiative to collect and preserve the history of LGBTQ and gender -nonconforming communities in Newark.

New Mexico

LGBT Educational Archives Project. PO Box 25881, Albuquerque, NM 87125. http://www.hammerarchives.com.

The LGBT Educational Archives Project includes more than 150,000 items and is an educational project devoted to preserving its LGBT collective history one archive at a time.

LGBTQ Resource Library. University of New Mexico LGBTQ Resource Center. 608 Buena Vista Dr. NE, Albuquerque, NM 87131. http://lgbtqrc.unm.edu/ services/lgbtq-library.html.

The LGBTQ Resource Library is a collection of books, magazines, and movies pertaining to LGBTQ individuals and the community.

New York

ABC No Rio Zine Library. 107 Suffolk St., Rm. 305, New York, NY. http://www .abcnorio.org/facilities/zine_library.html.

The ABC No Rio Zine Library contains more than thirteen thousand publications. The collection includes independent, underground, and marginal publications on subjects such as music, culture, politics, personal experience, and travel.

ACT UP Oral History Project. New York Public Library Manuscripts & Archives Division. 476 5th Ave., 3rd Floor, Rm. 328, New York, NY 10018. http://www .actuporalhistory.org.
    The ACT UP Oral History Project is a collection of interviews with surviving members of the AIDS Coalition to Unleash Power, New York.

Barnard Zine Library. Barnard College. 3009 Broadway, New York, NY 10027. http://zines.barnard.edu.
    Barnard collects zines on feminism and femme identity by people of all genders. The zines are personal and political publications on activism, anarchism, body image, third-wave feminism, gender, parenting, queer community, riot grrrl, sexual assault, trans experience, and other topics.

Black Gay & Lesbian Archive. New York Public Library, Schomburg Center for Research in Black Culture. 515 Malcolm X Blvd., New York, NY 10037. https:// www.nypl.org/locations/schomburg.
    Collections pertaining to Black LGBTQ history and culture.

Capital District Transgender Community Archive Collection, 1970–2004. Collection number APAP-185. University at Albany, SUNY, M.E. Grenander Department of Special Collections and Archives. 1400 Washington Ave., Albany, NY 12222. http://library.albany.edu/speccoll/findaids/apap185.htm.
    The Capital District Transgender Community Archive Collection contains material pertaining to local transgender history.

Downtown Collection. Fales Library & Special Collections. New York University. 70 Washington Square S., 3rd Floor, New York, NY 10012. http://guides.nyu.edu/ downtown-collection.
    The Downtown Collection includes the personal papers of artists, filmmakers, writers, and performers; archives of art galleries, theatre groups, and art collectives; and collections relating to AIDS activism, music, and off-off-Broadway theatre.

Gay Alliance Library & Archives. The Gay Alliance of the Genesee Valley. 875 E. Main St., Rochester, NY 14605. http://www.gayalliance.org/programs/library-archives.

The Gay Alliance Library is a circulating and reference collection of more than six thousand fiction and nonfiction books, and eight hundred magazine and journal titles, as well as video and audio recordings related to gay and lesbian, bisexual, transgender, and queer issues. The Gay Alliance Archives house a historic collection of copies of the *Empty Closet* newspaper, as well as vital paper records and ephemera of the events, organizations, and people important to the Rochester LGBTQ community.

Human Sexuality Collection. Carl A. Kroch Library Division of Rare and Manuscript Collections. Cornell University. Ithaca, NY 14853. https://rare.library.cornell.edu/collections/HSC.

The Human Sexuality Collection seeks to preserve and make accessible primary sources that document historical shifts in the social construction of sexuality, with a focus on U.S. lesbian and gay history and the politics of pornography.

Interference Archive. 131 8th St. #4, Brooklyn, NY 11215. http://interferencearchive.org.

The mission of Interference Archive is to explore the relationship between cultural production and social movements. This work manifests in an open stacks archival collection, publications, a study center, and public programs.

Lesbian, Gay, Bisexual and Transgender Periodical Collection. New York Public Library, Manuscripts and Archives Division. Stephen A. Schwarzman Building, 5th Ave. & 42nd St., Rm. 324, New York, NY 10018. https://www.nypl.org/sites/default/files/archivalcollections/pdf/lgbtperi.pdf.

The Lesbian, Gay, Bisexual and Transgender (LGBT) Periodical Collection was initially composed of periodicals collected by the International Gay Information Center (IGIC) and were made available to the public by the New York Public Library in 2006.

Leslie-Lohman Museum of Gay and Lesbian Art. 26 Wooster St., New York, NY 10013. https://www.leslielohman.org.

The Leslie-Lohman Museum of Gay and Lesbian Art is the first dedicated LGBTQ art museum in the world with a mission to exhibit and preserve LGBTQ art, and foster the artists who create it. Also, it houses a library of more than 1,600 volumes that is one of the most comprehensive collection of published books, catalogs, and pamphlets on LGBTQ art.

LGBT Community Center National History Archive. 208 W. 13th St., New York, NY 10011. https://gaycenter.org/archives.

The LGBT Community Center National History Archive serves to preserve the history of its community and its rich heritage. Founded in 1990 by volunteer archivist Rich Wandel, the archive provides a look into the lives and experiences of LGBT people throughout the years.

The Madeline Davis Gay, Lesbian, Bisexual, Transgender Archives of Western New York. Buffalo State University, E. H. Butler Library. 1300 Elmwood Ave., Buffalo, NY 14222. http://digitalcommons.buffalostate.edu/mdaviscollection.
     The Madeline Davis Gay, Lesbian, Bisexual, Transgender Archives of Western New York was founded in 2001 to collect, safeguard, and provide access to archive and manuscript materials that document the gay, lesbian, bisexual, and transgender communities of western New York and southern Ontario.

New York City Trans Oral History Project. New York Public Library. 476 5th Ave., New York, NY 10018. http://oralhistory.nypl.org/neighborhoods/trans-history.
     A collective, community archive working to document transgender resistance and resilience in New York City.

NYU LGBTQ Student Center Library. New York University, 60 Washington Square S. #602, New York, NY 10012. http://www.nyu.edu/students/communities-and-groups/student-diversity/lesbian-gay-bisexual-transgender-and-queer-student-center/about-us/resources-services.html.
     Lending library collection of LGBTQ fiction and nonfiction.

Pat Parker/Vito Russo Center Library. 208 W. 13th St., New York, NY 10011. https://gaycenter.org/community/library.
     Founded in 1991 to encourage and facilitate the reading and research of LGBT literature, the Pat Parker/Vito Russo Center Library is named in honor of individuals who championed LGBT causes in their professional and personal lives.

The Pop-Up Museum of Queer History. New York. http://www.queermuseum.com.
     The Pop-Up Museum of Queer History is a grassroots organization that transforms spaces into temporary installations dedicated to celebrating the rich, long, and largely unknown histories of lesbian, gay, bisexual, and transgender people.

The Riot Grrrl Collection. Fales Library & Special Collections. New York University. 70 Washington Square S., Third Floor, New York, NY 10012. http://www.nyu.edu/library/bobst/research/fales/riotgrrrltest.html.

The Riot Grrrl Collection documents the evolution of the feminist, punk youth movement riot grrrl in the 1990s, as well as adjacent queer and feminist activism and performance emerging from or inspired by riot grrrl.

North Carolina

Donaldson King, Sue Henry, Blake Brockington Community Archive. University of North Carolina J. Murrey Atkins Library Special Collections. 9201 University City Blvd., Charlotte, NC 28223. https://mrc.uncc.edu/lgbtq-archive.

In 2013, the Multicultural Resource Center and the J. Murrey Atkins Library partnered to establish a local LGBTQ archive focusing specifically on Charlotte and the surrounding community.

LGBT Center of Raleigh Library. 324 S. Harrington St., Raleigh, NC 27601. https://lgbtcenterofraleigh.com/library.html.

Since the library opened in October 2011, the collection has approximately three thousand volumes focused on and celebrating LGBT life. The library's collection development priorities are aimed at supporting the resource and information needs of the center's vital outreach programs such as SAGE Raleigh, Youth Coffeehouse, Affirming Faith Forum, and Transgender Initiative.

LGBT Collections. Duke University Rare Book, Manuscript, and Special Collections Library. 103 Perkins Library, Durham, NC 27708. http://library.duke.edu/rubenstein.

The Rubenstein Library collects rare print and manuscript material documenting LGBTQ history and culture, primarily in the American South in the twentieth century, with a particular emphasis on literature, political activism, and publishing.

Ohio

Lesbian, Gay, Bisexual and Transgender Archives. Western Reserve Historical Society Research Library. 825 East Blvd., Cleveland, OH 44108. http://www.wrhs.org/research/library/significant-collections/lgbt-archives.

The mission of the Lesbian, Gay, Bisexual and Transgender Archives is to foster greater understanding of the region's LGBT history by documenting the lives of northeast Ohio's LGBT residents and organizations and their contributions to its community.

Popular Culture Library. Bowling Green State University. Jerome Library, 4th Floor, Bowling Green, OH 43403. http://www.bgsu.edu/library/pcl.html.

The Browne Popular Culture Library (BPCL), founded in 1969, is the most comprehensive archive of its kind in the United States. Its focus and mission is to acquire and preserve research materials on American popular culture (post-1876) for curricular and research use. Includes a large collection of alternative and underground press publications.

Oklahoma

LGBT History Project. Oklahomans for Equality. 621 E. 4th St., Tulsa, OK 74120. http://www.okeq.org/lgbt-history-project.html.
   Launched by OkEq in 2002, the Tulsa Lesbian, Gay, Bisexual, Transgender (LGBT) History Project uncovers, preserves, and presents the rich contributions of lesbian, gay, bisexual, and transgender people within the state of Oklahoma, with a particular emphasis on Tulsa and the northeast Oklahoma area.

Nancy & Joe McDonald Rainbow Library. Dennis R. Neill Equality Center. 621 E. 4th St., Tulsa, OK 74120. http://www.okeq.org/rainbow-library.html.
   The Nancy & Joe McDonald Rainbow Library houses more than 3,500 LGBT-related titles.

Oregon

Bitch Community Lending Library. Bitch Media. 4930 NE 29th Ave., Portland OR 97211. https://bitchmedia.org/library.
   The library holds more than 2,500 books, zines, magazines, and DVDs that explore feminism, media studies, pop culture, queer studies, race studies, sex and sexuality, body image, and much more. The library also holds rare issues of *ROCKRGRL* and *Sassy* magazines.

Cascade AIDS Project Archives. 208 SW 5th Ave., Ste. 800, Portland, OR 97204. http://www.caparchives.org.
   A record of the far-reaching effects of HIV and AIDS in Portland, and the strength, love, and community that have rallied to fight the virus.

Gay & Lesbian Archives of the Pacific Northwest. 1200 SW Park Ave., Portland, OR 97205. http://www.glapn.org.
   Since 1994, GLAPN has been working to discover and publicize the history of sexual minorities in the Pacific Northwest.

Independent Publishing Resource Center (IPRC) Zine Library. 1001 SE Division St., Portland, OR 97202. http://www.iprc.org/about/our-facility/library.

The IPRC maintains a library of more than nine thousand self-published and independently produced materials. Located on the shelves are comics, chapbooks, novels, catalogs, zines, artists' books, and more.

McNabb Archives. Salem, OR. https://mcnabbarchives.wordpress.com.
A small DIY archives with a zine collection, a nonbinary collection, and a queer menarche collection.

OSU Queer Archives. Oregon State University. 201 SW Waldo Pl., Rm. 5069, Corvallis, OR 97331. http://wpmu.library.oregonstate.edu/oregon-multicultural-archives/2015/05/09/osqa.
The mission of the OSU Queer Archives (OSQA) is to preserve and share the stories, histories, and experiences of LGBTQ+ people within the OSU and Corvallis communities.

Transgender Reference Library. Q Center. 4115 N. Mississippi Ave., Portland, OR 97217. http://www.pdxqcenter.org/programs/education-training/library.
An extensive collection of transgender materials.

Pennsylvania

Barbara Gittings GLBTQ Collection. Free Library of Philadelphia, Independence Branch. 18 S. 7th St., Philadelphia, PA 19106. https://libwww.freelibrary.org/locations/independence-library.
The Barbara Gittings Collection is the largest dedicated GLBT public library collection east of the San Francisco Public Library. The collection is a circulating one, with fiction and nonfiction books in a range of genres from romance to biography to graphic novels.

Carter/Johnson Leather Library. PO Box 65, Willow Grove, PA 19090. http://www.leatherlibrary.org/home.html.
The library collection includes thousands of leather, fetish, S/M, kink and alternate sexuality books, magazines, posters, art, newspapers, ephemera, and memorabilia dating back to the 1700s.

Gay and Lesbian Community Center Library. 210 Grant St., Pittsburgh, PA 15219. http://www.librarything.com/profile/GLCC.
Circulating collection of queer and trans fiction and nonfiction books, audio recordings, videos, periodicals, and more.

John J. Wilcox Jr. GLBT Archives of Philadelphia. William Way Community Center. 1315 Spruce St., Philadelphia, PA 19107. http://waygay40.org/archives.

The John J. Wilcox Jr. Archives are Philadelphia's most extensive collection
of personal papers, organizations records, periodicals, audiovisual material, and
ephemera documenting the rich history of its LGBT community.

Reading Room at the LGBT Center. University of Pennsylvania. 3907 Spruce St.,
Philadelphia, PA 19104. http://www.vpul.upenn.edu/lgbtc.
A library and study space with hundreds of queer books.

Rhode Island

Library at the Center for Sexual Pleasure and Health. 250 Main St. #1, Pawtucket, RI
02860. http://www.thecsph.org/the-csph-resources/resources-in-the-csph/library.
The Sexuality Library includes curricula, teaching tools, books, and media
pertaining to sexuality and LGBTQ issues.

Texas

Black Queer Studies Collection. University of Texas Libraries. http://guides.lib
.utexas.edu/bqsc.
The Black Queer Studies Collection, which is designated digitally through
notes in library catalog records, is meant to feature, promote, and increase the
discoverability of the UT Libraries' unique holdings in the area of African and
African diasporic lesbian, gay, bisexual, transgender, and queer studies.

Gender and Sexuality Center Library. University of Texas. 2201 Speedway, Austin,
TX 78712. http://www.librarything.com/profile/UT_GSC.
The Gender and Sexuality Center provides opportunities for all members of the
UT Austin community to explore, organize, and promote learning around issues
of gender and sexuality. They have a large collection of literature in the GSC,
including books, magazines, videotapes, and DVDs.

Gulf Coast Archive and Museum of Gay, Lesbian, Bisexual and Transgender History
Inc. 5326 Dora St., Houston, TX 77005. http://gcam.org.
The Gulf Coast Archive and Museum of Gay, Lesbian, Bisexual and
Transgender History Inc. is a 501(c)(3) organization that was formed in Houston,
Texas, by a group of concerned activists so that its collective histories could be
saved—as well as be available for educational uses.

Lesbian, Gay, Bisexual and Transgender Archive. University of North Texas, Willis
Library. 1506 Highland St., Denton, TX 76203. http://www.library.unt.edu/
collections/special-collections/lgbt-archive.

The Lesbian, Gay, Bisexual and Transgender (LGBT) Archive at UNT is a repository for records documenting the history and culture of the LGBT communities in the South and the Southwest. This major collecting initiative documents people, places, and events through primary source materials, including letters, photographs, newspapers and magazines, scrapbooks, diaries, audiovisual materials, organizational records, posters, flyers, and objects.

Lesbian, Gay, Bisexual, Transgender, and Queer (LGBTQ) Collections. University of Texas, Harry Ransom Center, Austin, TX 78713. http://www.hrc.utexas.edu/collections/guide/lgtbq.

The Ransom Center holds various collections containing materials that document, in fact and fiction, the lives of LGBTQ people, and the study of sexuality more broadly.

LGBTQ Manuscript Collections. University of Texas John Peace Library. 1 UTSA Cir., San Antonio, TX 78236. http://lib.utsa.edu/specialcollections.

Includes business and organization records, activist papers, and community publications.

Transgender Archives. Transgender Foundation of America. 604 Pacific St., Houston, TX 77006. http://tgarchive.org.

Currently, the archives holds transgender magazines dating back to 1750, transgender statuaries from diverse cultures such as China, Africa, and Europe; original newspapers recording transgender history dating back to the early 1700s; rare transgender books dating back to the 1600s; original transgender photos dating back to before the Civil War; and other transgender artifacts dating back as far as the Roman Empire.

Vermont

Pride Center Vermont Lending Library. 255 S. Champlain St. #12, Burlington, VT 05401. http://www.pridecentervt.org/about-us/center-space/library.

Circulating fiction and nonfiction collection with sizable queer theory and trans materials.

Vermont Queer Archives. 255 S. Champlain St. #12, Burlington, VT 05401. http://vermontqueerarchives.org.

A collection encompassing the experiences of LGBTIQA (Lesbian, Gay, Bisexual, Transgender, Intersexed, Questioning individuals and their Allies) Vermonters, both past and present.

Virginia

Ricketson-Harris-Verkruisen LGBT Memorial Library. Metropolitan Community
    Church of the Blue Ridge. 806 Jamison Ave. SE, Roanoke, VA 24013. http://www
    .mccblueridge.org/outreach/lgbt-library.
    The Ricketson-Harris-Verkruisen LGBT Library (with a three-thousand-plus-
    volume collection) is unique in southwest Virginia and includes both rare and
    new volumes of LGBT literature.

Washington

GLBTQ Special Collections & Archival Resources. University of Washington Allen
    Library. 482 Allen Library, Seattle, WA 98195. http://guides.lib.uw.edu/research/
    GLBTQ.
    This guide highlights archival and printed materials, archived websites, and
    photographs available in Special Collections that relate to the lesbian, gay,
    bisexual, transgender, and queer community in the Pacific Northwest.

LGBT Northwest Serials and Related Ephemera Collection, 1966–2013. Collection
    number 5792. University of Washington Allen Library. 482 Allen Library, Seattle,
    WA 98195. http://archiveswest.orbiscascade.org/ark:/80444/xv57742.
    A large collection of Northwest lesbian/gay/bisexual/transgender materials
    from organizations, groups, and other collectors.

Michael C. Weidemann LGBT Library. Gay City Health Project. 517 E. Pike St.,
    Seattle, WA 98122. https://www.gaycity.org/library.
    In 2009, the Gay City Health Project began to house and staff the LGBT lending
    library after the closing of the Seattle LGBT Community Center. Since then, the
    Michael C. Weidemann LGBT Library at Gay City has grown to a collection of
    more than seven thousand books that cover a wide range of LGBT topics.

Northwest Lesbian and Gay History Museum Project. 1122 E. Pike St., Seattle, WA
    98122. Founded 1994. http://lgbthistorynw.org.
    The Northwest Lesbian and Gay History Museum Project, founded in 1994,
    is an organization that researches, interprets, and communicates the history of
    lesbian, gay, bisexual, and transgender people in the Pacific Northwest for the
    purposes of study, education, and enjoyment.

Northwest Lesbian and Gay History Museum Project Oral Histories, 1995–2015.
    Collection number 5929. University of Washington Allen Library. 482 Allen
    Library, Seattle, WA 98195. http://archiveswest.orbiscascade.org/ark:/80444/
    xv01058.

Oral history collection of gay, lesbian, bisexual, transgender, and heterosexual narrators focusing on the conditions the narrators experienced before the activist period, the early homophile movement in Seattle, the founding or early days of activist and service organizations, and ongoing activism since those times.

Olympia Zine Library. 211 E. 4th Ave., Olympia, WA 98501. http://zinelibrary .blogspot.com.
A large collection of self-published zines as well as a zine creation station.

Pride Foundation Ephemera Collection, 1987–2004. Collection number 5664. University of Washington Allen Library. 482 Allen Library, Seattle, WA 98195. http://archiveswest.orbiscascade.org/ark:/80444/xv91601.
Materials from organizations funded by the Pride Foundation or associated with the GLBTQ community.

Robert Ashworth Collection on the Union of Sexual Minorities Center of Western Washington University, 1975–1984. Collection number XOE_ CPNWS0081ashworth. Western Washington University, Western Libraries Heritage Resources. 516 High St., Bellingham, WA 98225. http://archiveswest .orbiscascade.org/ark:/80444/xv19512.
Robert Ashworth is a politically active member of the gay and lesbian community in Bellingham, Washington. During the 1970s and 1980s he compiled a collection of papers documenting the activities of the Union of Sexual Minorities Center (USMC) of Western Washington University. The collection consists of the administrative records, program and activity materials, and publications.

UW Bothell Social Justice & Diversity Archive. University of Washington, Bothell. 18225 Campus Way NE, Bothell, WA 98011. http://digitalcollections.lib. washington.edu/cdm/landingpage/collection/p16786coll12.
The UW Bothell Social Justice and Diversity Archive documents and preserves the work and history of social justice organizations in Bothell and the Puget Sound region. With the guidance and instruction of UW Bothell faculty, UW Bothell student researchers conduct interviews and record oral histories with activists and organization members and founders, collect documents and media important to the organizations' formation and actions, and record organization events.

Washington, District of Columbia

Gender & Sexuality Collection. American University Library. 4400 Massachusetts Ave. NW, Washington, DC 20016. http://www.american.edu/library/news/cdi _collection_move.cfm.

Since 1994, the Gender and Sexuality Library has provided members of the AU community with access to a diverse collection of fiction and nonfiction books, as well as various TV series and movies.

Latino GLBT History Project Archival Collection. 2000 14th St. NW, Ste. 105, Washington, DC 20009. http://www.latinoglbthistory.org/about-the -archive.

The Latino GLBT History Project's Archival Collection is among a handful of repositories entirely dedicated to documenting the unique intersection of Latino activism and queer identity. It has the largest collection of materials covering more than twenty-five years of Latino activism in the Washington area's LGBT community.

Lesbian, Gay, Bisexual, and Transgender Collection. Collection number 1146. National Museum of American History, Smithsonian Institution. Archives Center, MRC 601, Washington, DC 20013. http://americanhistory.si.edu/ archives.

This series contains a variety of periodicals, newsletters, and newspapers produced by and for the LGBT community.

LGBT Collections and Resources. Library of Congress. 101 Independence Ave. SE, Washington, DC 20540. http://www.loc.gov/lgbt/resources.html.

A group of collections pertaining to LGBT culture, politics, and history.

Rainbow History Project Archive. 801 K St. NW, Washington, DC 20001. http:// rainbowhistory.org.

The Rainbow History Project Archive's mission is to collect, preserve, and promote an active knowledge of the history, arts, and culture relevant to sexually diverse communities in metropolitan Washington DC.

Wisconsin

Earl Greely Memorial Library. OutReach Community Center. 2701 International Ln., Ste. 101, Madison, WI 53704. http://www.lgbtoutreach.org/?q=node/4.

The Earl Greely Memorial Library, housed at OutReach, is one of the largest and most extensive LGBT libraries in the Midwest. The transgender collection covers transitioning, SRS, coming out, and appearance.

Jack H. Smith Library. Milwaukee LGBT Community Center. 1110 N. Market St. #2, Milwaukee, WI 53202. http://www.mkelgbt.org/services/jack-smith-library.

The Jack H. Smith Lending Library is one of the largest LGBT libraries in Wisconsin and encourages and facilitates the reading and research of LGBT literature.

LGBT Campus Center Library. University of Wisconsin, Madison. 716 Langdon St.,
    Madison, WI 53706. https://lgbt.wisc.edu/library.htm.
    Circulating collection of queer fiction and nonfiction books and DVDs.

Madison LGBT History Project. University of Wisconsin, Madison, Archives &
    Records Management Services. 430 Steenbock Memorial Library, 550 Babcock
    Dr., Madison, WI 53706. https://www.library.wisc.edu/archives.
    The LGBTQ archive contains oral histories, personal papers, photographs,
    ephemera, and organizational records related to LGBTQ life in Madison and
    Dane Counties from the 1940s to today. Since 2007, this ongoing collection has
    documented the stories and memories of politicians, professors, students, and
    activists.

Wyoming

Rainbow Resource Center Library. University of Wyoming. 106 Wyoming Union,
    Dept. 3135, 1000 E. University Ave., Laramie, WY 82071. http://www.uwyo.edu/
    rrc/services-and-sponsors.
    Contains GLBTQ publications, magazines, videos, and newsletters.

International Repositories and Collections
Australia

Australian Lesbian and Gay Archives. 6 Claremont Str., South Yarra, Melbourne.
    http://alga.org.au.
    The collections include material of national or international scope, but the
    heart of the archives' work is the collection and preservation of the historical life
    of the lesbian, gay, bisexual, and transgender communities of Australia.

Austria

Archives of the Women's & Lesbians' Movement. Stichwort Archives & Library.
    Gusshausstraße 20/1A+B, 1040 Wien. http://www.stichwort.or.at.
    Stichwort collects all kinds of documentation pertaining to the women's and
    lesbians' movements and provides access to a broad range of literature relevant to
    feminist research.

Belgium

Suzan Daniel Fund: Gay/Lesbian Archives and Documentation Centre. P/A Hubert
    Frère-Orbanlaan 510, 9000 Gent. http://www.fondssuzandaniel.be/fsd/en/
    welcome.html.

The archives documents the activities of people, groups, organizations, and companies, and is the most important source collection for postwar gay and lesbian life in Belgium.

Canada

Anchor Archive Zine Library. Roberts Street Social Centre. 6050 Almon St., Halifax, NS. http://www.robertsstreet.org.
   The Anchor Archive Zine Library has a collection of more than five thousand zines from the local area and around the world.

Canadian Lesbian & Gay Archives. 34 Isabella St., Toronto, ON. http://www.clga.ca.
   The Canadian Lesbian and Gay Archives is the largest independent LGBTQ+ archives in the world. With a focus on Canadian content, the CLGA acquires, preserves, and provides public access to information and archival materials in any medium.

EXILE Infoshop Library. 256 Bank St., Ste. 200, Ottawa, ON. http://exilebooks.org/en/library_new/index.html.
   The EXILE Infoshop opened May Day 2007 as Ottawa's first-ever infoshop with an actual, physical space. It is a radical and activist resource center, library, and bookstore.

Lesbian, Gay, Bisexual and Transgender Collection. Toronto Public Library, Yorkville Branch. 22 Yorkville Ave., Toronto, ON M4W 1L4. http://www.torontopubliclibrary.ca/books-video-music/specialized-collections/gay-lesbian.jsp.
   The Lesbian, Gay, Bisexual and Transgender (LGBT) Collection at the Yorkville branch includes books, magazines, and DVDs. The collection is of particular interest to the lesbian, gay, bisexual, and transgendered communities and contains works of a more popular nature as well as selected scholarly titles.

Manitoba Gay and Lesbian Archives. University of Manitoba Archives & Special Collections. 330 Elizabeth Dafoe Library, University of Manitoba, Winnipeg, MB R3T 2N2. http://umanitoba.ca/libraries/units/archives/digital/gay_lesbian.
   The formation of the Manitoba Gay and Lesbian Archives is a symbolic culmination of lesbian, gay, bisexual, transgendered, Two-Spirited, and queer individuals and organizations recording people's history.

Media Queer. Queer Media Database Canada-Quebec Project. Montreal, QC. http://www.mediaqueer.ca.

The goal of the Queer Media Database Canada-Québec Project is to maintain a dynamic online catalog of LGBTQ Canadian film, video, and digital works; their makers; and related institutions.

Open Book Library. Community Centre for Gays and Lesbians of Montreal (CCGLM). 2075 Rue Plessis #110, Montréal, QC H2L 2Y4. http://www.ccglm.org/ biblio.php?langue=en.

The Open Book Library (OBL) is the only specialized documentation center on issues related to sexual diversity in Quebec and one of the largest in French-speaking nations and Canada.

Pride Library. University of Western Ontario, D. B. Weldon Library. 1151 Richmond St., London, ON N6A 5B7. http://www.uwo.ca/pridelib.

The Pride Library's mission is to acquire and provide public access to materials by and about the lesbian, gay, bisexual, trans and queer community.

Quebec Gay Archives/Les Archives Gaies du Québec. 103-1000 Amherst St., Montreal, QC. http://www.agq.qc.ca.

The Quebec Gay Archives is a nonprofit, community-based organization that is mandated to preserve all handwritten, printed, visual, audio, and other documents that bear witness to the history of gays and lesbians in Quebec.

Toronto Zine Library. 292 Brunswick Ave., Toronto, ON. http://www .torontozinelibrary.org.

The Toronto Zine Library is run by a collective of zine readers, zine makers. and librarians who are looking to make zines more accessible in Toronto.

Transgender Archives. University of Victoria. 3800 Finnerty Rd., Victoria, BC V8P 5C2. http://www.uvic.ca/transgenderarchives.

The Transgender Archives are actively acquiring documents, rare publications, and memorabilia of persons and organizations that have worked for the betterment of trans and gender-nonconforming people.

Two-Spirited Collection. University of Winnipeg Archives and Records Centre. 515 Portage Ave., Winnipeg, MB R3B 2E9. https://main.lib.umanitoba.ca/two -spirited-collection.

Collection of Two-Spirit materials, including published materials, ephemera, art, organizational records, films, and more.

France

Conservatory of LGBT Archives and Memories. Académie Gay & Lesbienne, Boîte Postale n° 28, 94402 Vitry sur Seine Cedex. http://archiveshomo.info/english.htm.

Collections include periodicals, fiction and nonfiction books, event
documentation, ephemera, and other archival materials relating to LGBT history.

Germany

Haeberle-Hirschfeld Archive of Sexology. Universitätsbibliothek der Humboldt-
Universität zu Berlin, Wagner-Régeny-Str. 81, 12489 Berlin. https://www
.ub.hu-berlin.de/en/literature-search/historical-collections/historical-and-special
-collections-of-the-library/overview-of-the-historical-and-special-collections-of
-the-library/haeberle-hirschfeld-archive-of-sexology/haeberle-hirschfeld-archive
-of-sexology.
  The Haeberle-Hirschfeld Archive of Sexology is part of the University
Library's special collections and contains literature on sexology in the
sociological context.

Netherlands

LGBT Heritage Collections. IHLIA. Oosterdokskade 143, 6e verdieping 1011 DL
Amsterdam. http://www.ihlia.nl.
  Archival materials and information about gay men, lesbians, bisexuals, and
transgender people, and their history, environment, and culture.

New Zealand

Lesbian and Gay Archives of New Zealand/Te Pūranga Takatāpui o Aotearoa.
Alexander Turnbull Library. PO Box 11-695, Manners St., Wellington 6142.
http://www.laganz.org.nz.
  Collections include manuscript collections, books, periodicals, photographs,
memorabilia, ephemera, and other materials pertaining to queer history and
culture.

South Africa

Cooper-Sparks Queer Community Library and Resource Centre. GALA: Gay
and Lesbian Memory in Action. 7th Floor, University Corner, University of
the Witwatersrand, Braamfontein. http://www.gala.co.za/archives_research/
community_library.htm.
  The Cooper-Sparks Queer Community Library and Resource Centre began
more than twenty-five years ago as a very special library hidden in someone's
closet. LGBTI people in Johannesburg used to meet there from time to time to

borrow books and spend time together. Today, out and proud and in the care of GALA, the library has more than four thousand books and several hundred movies available for loan.

GALA Archives. GALA: Gay and Lesbian Memory in Action. 7th Floor, University Corner, University of the Witwatersrand, Braamfontein. http://www.gala.co.za/archives_research.htm.

GALA's archive and research facility was set up to serve the needs of rigorous academic research on LGBTI issues in Africa, while also maintaining a dual role as a repository of community histories and cultural artifacts.

Spain

Centre de Documentació Armand de Fluvià. Casal Lambda, Carrer Verdaguer i Callís, 10, Barcelona. http://www.lambda.cat/index.php/centre-de-documentacio/informacio-practica.

Library and archive focusing on queer history in Spain.

Thailand

Thai Rainbow Archive. http://thairainbowarchive.anu.edu.au.

A digitized collection of Thai gay, lesbian, and transgender publications.

United Kingdom

GayKitschCamp. 70 Golden Knowes Rd., Frampton on Severn, GL2 7WY. http://www.gaykitschcamp.com.

A resource and research center focusing on documentation of queer life.

Hall-Carpenter Archives. London School of Economics Library, Houghton St., London WC2A 2AE. http://www.lse.ac.uk/library/collections/featuredcollections/lgbtcollections.aspx.

This collection contains primary source material mainly relating to gay and lesbian rights.

Irish Queer Archive/Cartlann Aerach na hÉireann. National Library of Ireland. 7-8 Kildare St., Dublin 2, D02 P638. http://www.irishqueerarchive.com.

A collection of material pertaining to LGBT history and studies.

Lesbian and Gay Newsmedia Archive. Bishopsgate Institute. 230 Bishopsgate, London EC2M 4QH. http://www.lagna.org.uk/archive.

The Lesbian and Gay Newsmedia Archive (LAGNA) is an archive of an estimated two hundred thousand cuttings from the nongay press. It is the only collection of its kind in the United Kingdom.

rukus! Black LGBT Cultural Archive. Collection number 4571. London Metropolitan Archives. 40 Northampton Rd., Clerkenwell, London EC1R 0HB. http://www.cityoflondon.gov.uk/things-to-do/london-metropolitan-archives/the-collections/Pages/migration-settlement-and-activities-of-new-communities.aspx.
    The rukus! Black LGBT Archive, launched in 2005, generates, collects, preserves, and makes available to the public historical, cultural, and artistic materials relating to its lived experience in the UK. The work of the archive makes a unique and significant contribution to the development and celebration of the Black LGBT Community.

Untold Stories: The Leicester LGBT Centre Oral History Project. 15 Wellington St., Leicester LE1 6HH. http://www.lgbt-stories.org.
    An oral history project focusing on LGBT people in Leicester.

Primarily Online Collections

Alder, David "Scratch" (Founder). Queer Oral History Project. http://qohp.org.
    The Queer Oral History Project celebrates and commemorates the diversity of lived experiences in the queer community and is dedicated to preserving those experiences for future generations, through making digital recordings of queer people's life stories on video.

Fors Szuba, Eleonora (Chairman of the Board). The Unstraight Museum. http://www.unstraight.org.
    The Unstraight Museum is an online space and museum dedicated to LGBTQI history in all its forms.

Garringer, Rachel. Country Queers. https://countryqueers.com.
    Country Queers is a multimedia oral history project documenting the diverse experiences of rural, small-town, and country LGBTQIA folks in the United States through audio recordings, transcriptions, and photographs.

Gonzaba, Eric (Founder). Wearing Gay History. http://wearinggayhistory.com.
    Digitized T-shirt collections of numerous lesbian, gay, bisexual, and transgender archives across the United States.

Isay, Dave (Founder). StoryCorps OutLoud. https://storycorps.org/outloud.

StoryCorps OutLoud launched in 2014 on the forty-fifth anniversary of the Stonewall uprising and is dedicated to documenting and sharing stories from lesbian, gay, bisexual, transgender, and queer people from across the United States.

Katz, Jonathan Ned (Founder). OutHistory. http://outhistory.org.
OutHistory.org was founded in October 2008 by Jonathan Ned Katz, in order to archive, establish LGBTQ chronologies, and highlight new discoveries.

Manske, Nathan (Founder). I'm from Driftwood: The LGBTQ Story Archive. http://imfromdriftwood.com.
I'm From Driftwood aims to help LGBTQ people learn more about their community, straight people learn more about their neighbors, and everyone learn more about themselves through the power of storytelling and story sharing.

Miller, Milo, and Christopher Wilde (Founders). QZAP: Queer Zine Archive Project. http://www.qzap.org/v8.
The primary function of QZAP is to provide a free online searchable database of the collection with links allowing users to download electronic copies of zines. By providing access to the historical canon of queer zines, they hope to make them more accessible to diverse communities and reach wider audiences.

Oral Histories. Queer in Brighton. http://www.queerinbrighton.co.uk/category/stories/oral-histories.
Through the themes of place, family, politics, and language, this inspiring intergenerational heritage learning project uses oral histories, photography, performance, and creative writing as tools to explore, uncover, and share real-life stories and experiences of LGBT people in Brighton and Hove, past and present.

Pérez, André (Founder). Transgender Oral History Project. http://transoralhistory.com.
The Transgender Oral History Project is a community-driven effort to collect and share a diverse range of stories from within the transgender and gender-variant communities.

NOTES

1. Randall C. Jimerson, *Archives Power: Memory, Accountability, and Social Justice* (Chicago: Society of American Archivists, 2009), 267.

2. Jimerson, *Archives Power*, 310–11.

3. Alana Kumbier, *Ephemeral Material: Queering the Archive* (Sacramento, CA: Litwin Books, 2014), 113–14.

7

Nonfiction Books

This chapter provides an annotated bibliography of nonfiction books relevant to nonbinary gender identities. Books are organized according to the following genres: art books, biography and memoir, creative nonfiction, essay, ethnography, history, reference, religious text, and theory. Books that span multiple genres are located under the primary genre, determined by Library of Congress subject headings and classification. Both adult and juvenile nonfiction are represented.

ART

Allen, Mariette Pathy. *The Gender Frontier*. Heidelberg: Kehrer Verlag, 2003.
   A collection of photographs documenting transgender and genderqueer communities. Includes essays by Riki Wilchins and others. Text in German and English.

Graham, F. Lanier. *Duchamp & Androgyny: Art, Gender, and Metaphysics*. Berkeley, CA: No-Thing, 2003.
   Discussion and criticism of Marcel Duchamp's art, much of which explored androgyny. Includes color reproductions.

Roos, Daïjna. *Miroir Aux Androgynes*. Tübingen: Konkursbuchverl, 1997.
   Portraits of androgynous individuals, with text in German, French, and English.

Swan, Rebecca. *Assume Nothing*. Berkeley, CA: Soft Skull, 2010.
Photographs exploring nontraditional gender identities.

Von Unwerth, Ellen. *Omahyra & Boyd*. Paris: Kamel Mennour, 2005.
Exhibition book to accompany an exhibit of erotic androgynous portraits.

BIOGRAPHY AND MEMOIR

Bond, Justin Vivian. *Tango: My Childhood, Backwards and in High Heels*. New York: Feminist, 2011.
In this candid and moving memoir, musical, visual, and theatrical artist Mx Justin Vivian Bond tells the story of their childhood and early adolescence as a transgender youth. The very first paragraph describes their memory of dancing and having their grandfather ask, "Where's Ginger?" Justin Vivian wondered why they couldn't be both Fred *and* Ginger. While they don't explicitly mention the term "nonbinary" in this book, it's quite clear in their narrative, as well as other media and public speaking.

Bornstein, Kate. *Gender Outlaw: On Men, Women, and the Rest of Us*. New York: Routledge, 1994.
This book is genre defying: Bornstein combines and alternates between a coming-of-age story, serious gender theory, and a theatrical piece based on the life of intersex historical individual Herculine Barbin. This book was groundbreaking in terms of theorizing about genderqueer identities.

———. *A Queer and Pleasant Danger: A Memoir*. Boston: Beacon, 2012.
This autobiography covers Kate Bornstein's early childhood through the present. Bornstein was born into a middle-class conservative Jewish family and assigned male at birth. Bornstein studied theatre and became a Scientologist, before leaving the church and having sexual reassignment surgery. Despite not identifying as male, though, Kate soon realized that "woman" didn't fit, either. Kate now identifies as a gender outlaw and is a performance artist, gender theorist, and author.

Clare, Eli. *Exile and Pride: Disability, Queerness, and Liberation*. Cambridge, MA: SouthEnd, 1999.
Memoir of a disabled genderqueer person.

Costa, LeeRay, and Andrew Matzner. *Male Bodies, Women's Souls: Personal Narratives of Thailand's Transgendered Youth*. New York: Haworth, 2007.
Presents the life stories of *sao braphet song* ("second type of women") Thai youth in their own words. The authors also describe and analyze the contemporary Thai sex/gender system.

Feinberg, Leslie. *Journal of a Transsexual*. Atlanta: World View, 1980.
     Brief, heartbreaking autobiographical essays describing the transphobic
harassment that Feinberg experienced in hir daily life.

Krieger, Nick. *Nina Here nor There: My Journey beyond Gender*. Boston: Beacon,
2011.
     Nick, née Nina, was a lesbian for years until moving to the Castro and meeting
gender-variant people who initially made her feel uncomfortable. Gradually, she
played with gender expression, using binders and packers, exploring the limits
and possibilities of language, and experimenting with sexuality. By the end of
this compelling memoir, Nick has moved beyond traditional gender, choosing
to navigate the binary system by taking a male name and pronoun, but resisting
binary definition.

Kuklin, Susan. *Beyond Magenta: Transgender Teens Speak Out*. Somerville, MA:
Candlewick, 2014.
     Six transgender and genderqueer youth are interviewed and photographed in this
gorgeous book. Susan Kuklin includes portraits and informal candid photographs,
as well as older family photographs to portray her subjects' gender presentations and
family dynamics. Text is respectful, informative, and interesting.

Lind, Earl. *Autobiography of an Androgyne*. New York: Medico-Legal Journal, 1918.
     Earl Lind, the pseudonym for Ralph Werther, also known as Jennie June, was
a self-identified member of the "third sex" and used the term "androgyne." This
diary presents both a life narrative and a fascinating glimpse of turn-of-the-
century queer New York.

———. *The Female Impersonators*. New York: Medico-Legal Journal, 1922.
     In this sequel to *Autobiography of an Androgyne*, Lind presents the life stories
of several androgyne associates.

Lowrey, Sassafras, and Jennifer Clare Burke. *Kicked Out*. Ypsilanti, MI: Homofactus,
2010.
     A collection of autobiographical essays written by gender and sexual minority
youth who were kicked out of their homes as minors.

Nelson, Maggie. *The Argonauts*. London: Melville House, 2016.
     Memoir about a love affair with a genderfluid person.

O'Keefe, Tracie, and Katrina Fox. *Finding the Real Me: True Tales of Sex and Gender
Diversity*. San Francisco: Jossey-Bass, 2003.
     A collection of autobiographical essays written by queer and transgender
people, several of whom identify on the nonbinary spectrum.

Piepzna-Samarasinha, Leah Lakshmi. *Dirty River*. Vancouver, BC: Arsenal Pulp, 2015.
    Memoir of a disabled femme of color.

Pratt, Minnie Bruce. *S/He*. Ithaca, NY: Firebrand Books, 1995.
    Poetic memoir by the partner of the late Leslie Feinberg, with much musing on gender.

Roscoe, Will. *The Zuni Man-Woman*. Albuquerque: University of New Mexico Press, 1991.
    A biographical account of We'wha (1849–1896), a lhamana (Zuni alternate gender role) who was greatly respected for weaving, pottery, and diplomacy.

Schimel, Lawrence, and Richard Labonté. *First Person Queer: Who We Are (So Far)*. Vancouver, BC: Arsenal Pulp, 2007.
    A collection of autobiographical accounts of queer and trans people. Several identify on the nonbinary spectrum.

Spoon, Rae. *First Spring Grass Fire*. Vancouver, BC: Arsenal Pulp, 2012.
    Songwriter Rae Spoon grew up in a Pentecostal family and spent their childhood trying to avoid notice and survive abuse, neglect, and bullying. The storytelling is subtle and emotionally powerful, and the theme of growing up and coming out will resonate for nonbinary people who have navigated similar experiences. Chapters meander through Spoon's childhood and adolescence haphazardly, so the reader gets a series of nonlinear vignettes.

Wilchins, Riki. *Read My Lips: Sexual Subversion and the End of Gender*. Ithaca, NY: Firebrand Books, 1997.
    Transexual Menace cofounder Riki Wilchins combines incisive gender commentary with captivating personal history in this groundbreaking book. Chapters meander between political manifestos, autobiographical storytelling, archival documents from activist activities, and critique of theory. This was one of the first books to explore genderqueer identity, and Riki's comments about gender fluidity and the gender binary as an oppressive system are still radical today.

CREATIVE NONFICTION

Amato, Toni, and Mary Davies. *Pinned Down by Pronouns*. Jamaica Plain, MA: Conviction Books, 2004.
    This literary anthology is described as being a "community conversation" among Boston transgender, genderqueer, and queer communities. Poets,

activists, and scholars critique and push back against gender theory in favor of gender survival. Pieces include photographs, drawings and paintings, poems, essays, stories, letters, and interviews.

Bornstein, Kate. *My New Gender Workbook: A Step-by-Step Guide to Achieving World Peace through Gender Anarchy and Sex Positivity*. New York: Routledge, 2013.
 In this new edition of the 1997 original text, Bornstein provides quizzes, puzzles, and other exercises in a workbook format to help guide readers through their own gender exploration. This edition is more intersectional, with attention paid to ethnicity, class, and sexuality. Gender is posited as a spectrum and readers are encouraged to consider it from all angles.

Bornstein, Kate, and S. Bear Bergman. *Gender Outlaws: The Next Generation*. Berkeley, CA: Seal, 2010.
 Fifteen years after Bornstein's *Gender Outlaw*, she collaborated with S. Bear Bergman on this anthology of essays, comic art, poetry, and interviews by trans-spectrum folks, including several genderqueer contributors.

Broadhead, Talcott. *Meet Polkadot*. Olympia, WA: Dangerdot, 2013.
 Polkadot, together with their big sister Gladiola and friend Norma Alicia, explains the nuances, challenges, and joys of being nonbinary. Although this is a picture book, it is very text heavy and introduces complex concepts. Young children will enjoy the pictures and gradually understand the text over time with the help of adults.

Bunnell, J. T, and Irit Reinheimer. *Girls Will Be Boys Will Be Girls Will Be . . .: A Coloring Book*. Brooklyn, NY: Soft Skull, 2004.
 A coloring book for children and adults that playfully deconstructs binary gender roles.

Clare, Eli. *The Marrow's Telling: Words in Motion*. Ypsilanti, MI: Homofactus, 2007.
 Poetry by a disabled genderqueer person.

Clemmer, Cass. *The Adventures of Toni the Tampon: A Period Coloring Book*. N.p.: Bloody Queer, 2016.
 A coloring book with anthropomorphized menstrual management supplies, several of whom are queer.

Coyote, Ivan E., and Zena Sharman. *Persistence: All Ways Butch and Femme*. Vancouver, BC: Arsenal Pulp, 2011.
 Butch genderqueer spoken word performer Ivan E. Coyote and their femme partner Zena Sharman collaborated on this anthology of essays, poems, personal

stories, short fiction, and manifestos from amazing queer writers on the topics of butch and femme. Several contributors are genderqueer, gender variant, or otherwise nonbinary.

Cronn-Mills, Kirstin. *Transgender Lives: Complex Stories, Complex Voices.* Minneapolis: Twenty-First Century Books, 2015.

Using color photograph portraits, quotes and journalistic information, and snippets of gender theory, Cronn-Mills provides a highly accessible introduction to the transgender spectrum. Featured individuals identify as transgender and transsexual men and women, genderqueer and genderfluid, drag performers, and intersex. Brief, easy-to-read chapters introduce the concepts of sex and gender spectra, trans issues such as bathrooms and health care, and gender variance across history and cultures.

Diamond, Morty. *From the Inside Out: Radical Gender Transformation, FTM and Beyond.* San Francisco: Manic D, 2004.

Editor Morty Diamond is a gender-variant person who yearned to read about the experiences of other people who were assigned female at birth but do not identify as fully men or women. Having discovered that many books are rigidly binary, he decided to invite FTM and genderqueer people to create this literary collection. Essays and poems explore gender diversity and the many ways in which people transition, from a range of class, race, and sexual orientation backgrounds.

———. *Trans/Love: Radical Sex, Love, and Relationships beyond the Gender Binary.* San Francisco: Manic D, 2011.

This anthology presents the voices of twenty-nine transgender, Two-Spirit, nonbinary, and intersex writers as they explore the intersections between gender identity and sexual and romantic relationships. These are deeply personal and erotic pieces, each with a distinct voice and different take on love and sex.

Driskill, Qwo-Li. *Burning Upward Flight.* Seattle, WA: Dragonfly Rising, 2002.

Poetry chapbook by Cherokee/mixed-race Two-Spirit poet and scholar Qwo-Li Driskill. Includes biographical information.

———. *Walking with Ghosts: Poems.* Cambridge, UK: Salt Pub, 2005.

A collection of poems by Cherokee/mixed-race Two-Spirit poet and scholar Qwo-Li Driskill. Poems explore colonial violence, transphobia, and ethnic and gender identities.

Driskill, Qwo-Li, Daniel Heath Justice, Deborah A. Miranda, and Lisa Tatonetti. *Sovereign Erotics: A Collection of Two-Spirit Literature.* Tucson: University of Arizona Press, 2011.

Despite the title, this anthology is not a collection of erotica. The erotic, in this volume, is a creative force of decolonization, which includes sexuality but also spirituality and empowerment. Native Two-Spirit and queer contributors write their resistance to colonial gender and sexual systems through poetry, fiction, and essay. Themes include history, sexuality, gender, community, and love.

Feinberg, Leslie. *Trans Liberation: Beyond Pink or Blue*. Boston: Beacon, 1998.
  A collection of speeches, essays, and anecdotes about transgender civil rights. Includes autobiographical pieces by gender-variant and intersex people.

Gonzalez, Maya Christina. *Gender Now Coloring Book: A Learning Adventure for Children and Adults*. San Francisco: Reflection, 2010.
  This activity book includes stories, games, and engaging drawings for children to color and learn with. Children of many different ethnicities, shapes, and genders are represented; fully clothed in the "school edition" and occasionally nude in the original. In age-appropriate text, children three years old and up can learn about gender diversity, gender expression, and gender in nature and culture.

———. *I Am Free to Be Me: Gender Now Activity Book*. San Francisco: Reflection, 2011.
  Adapted from the *Gender Now Coloring Book*, this activity book introduces child-appropriate stories, history, and cultural information about gender variance.

Hoffman-Fox, Dara. *You and Your Gender Identity: A Guide to Discovery*. Colorado Springs, CO: DHF, 2016.
  A gentle and accessible guide for self-discovery. Includes self-paced exercises.

Kusinitz, Nathaniel, and Jacinta Bunnell. *Sometimes the Spoon Runs Away with Another Spoon*. Oakland, CA: PM Press, 2010.
  Anecdotes mixed with fairy tales that defy rigid gender expectations.

Levithan, David, and Billy Merrell. *The Full Spectrum: A New Generation of Writing about Gay, Lesbian, Bisexual, Transgender, Questioning, and Other Identities*. New York: Knopf, 2006.
  Young adult fiction author David Levithan and poet Billy Merrell partnered with the Gay, Lesbian and Straight Education Network (GLSEN) to publish this anthology of personal stories, essays, and poems by LGBTQ young adults. Subjects include coming out, first kisses, family, friendship, and religion. Several contributors are outside the gender binary.

Luczak, Raymond. *QDA: A Queer Disability Anthology*. Minneapolis: Squares & Rebels, 2015.

    An anthology of poetry, comics, essays, and more from forty-eight queer, trans, and nonbinary writers with disabilities.

McNamara, Jacks. *Inbetweenland*. Oakland, CA: Deviant Type, 2013.

    Poetry written by genderqueer artist and activist Jacks McNamara. Themes include madness, loss, violence, and queer desire.

Morrigan, Clementine. *Rupture*. Ontario: Demeter, 2012.

    Poetry about trauma by a queer nonbinary artist.

Piepzna-Samarasinha, Leah Lakshmi. *Bodymap*. Toronto: Mawenzi House, 2015.

    Poetry by a disabled femme of color.

———. *Love Cake: Poems*. Toronto: TSAR, 2011.

    Poetry by a disabled femme of color.

Proulx-Turner, Sharron. *She Walks for Days inside a Thousand Eyes: A Two Spirit Story*. Winnipeg: Turnstone, 2008.

    Mixed-genre prose/poetry collection by Two-Spirit Métis poet Sharron Proulx-Turner. Includes first-person narratives from contemporary and historical Two-Spirit people, historical information, and cultural teachings.

Sharman, Zena. *The Remedy: Queer and Trans Voices on Health and Health Care*. Vancouver, BC: Arsenal Pulp, 2016.

    An edited anthology of poems and essays focusing on sexual and gender minority health and health care.

Thom, Kai Cheng. *A Place Called No Homeland*. Vancouver, BC: Arsenal Pulp, 2017.

    Poetry collection focusing on gender, race, sexuality, and violence.

Tolbert, T. C., and Trace Peterson. *Troubling the Line: Trans and Genderqueer Poetry and Poetics*. Callicoon, NY: Nightboat Books, 2013.

    This massive collection features fifty-five transgender and genderqueer poets and includes both poetry and "poetic statements" where each contributor reflects on identity, activism, and the multiple contexts for their work. Editor T. C. Tolbert identifies as genderqueer, and many authors identify as genderqueer, nonbinary, or otherwise gender nonconforming.

ESSAY

Bergman, S. Bear. *Butch Is a Noun*. San Francisco: Suspect Thoughts, 2006.

    S. Bear Bergman is a self-described gender-jammer as well as a marvelous storyteller. This book is nicely structured with chapters that can stand alone, so readers can dive in anywhere they please. The tone is conversational, slipping in gender theory and challenging experiential topics in a very accessible manner. There is discussion of pronouns and public bathrooms, as you'd expect, but also chapters about the pleasures of butch friendships, tensions within the transgender community, and the delights of Calvin Klein boxer briefs.

———. *The Nearest Exit May Be Behind You.* Vancouver, BC: Arsenal Pulp, 2009.
Inspired by an episode of airplane seating homophobia, Bergman returns with a second book of essays, this one focusing on what it's like to be visible as a queer person, an Other, in a heteronormative world. Topics include the ambiguity of being both butch and trans, names and naming, assumptions and the exhaustion of coming out over and over, and reading and misreading fellow queers.

Coyote, Ivan E., and Rae Spoon. *Gender Failure.* Vancouver, BC: Arsenal Pulp, 2014.
Musician and writer Rae Spoon and writer and performer Ivan E. Coyote collaborated on a touring live show to great acclaim. This collaborative book collects visual and textual ephemera from their tour, along with essays exploring their journeys within and beyond the gender binary. Essays are candid, funny, and very moving, as Spoon and Coyote recall early childhood memories; muse about religion, relationships, and the queer community; and celebrate their realizations that they are gender failures because the gender binary doesn't fit everyone.

Lee, Jiz. *Coming Out Like a Porn Star: Essays on Pornography, Protection, and Privacy.* Berkeley, CA: ThreeL Media, 2015.
An edited collection of essays by pornography performers on the various aspects of coming out. Includes several essays by transgender and genderqueer contributors.

Nestle, Joan, Clare Howell, and Riki Wilchins. *GenderQueer: Voices from beyond the Sexual Binary.* Los Angeles: Alyson Books, 2002.
Lesbian archivist Joan Nestle, gender activist Riki Wilchins, and librarian Clare Howell coedited this anthology, which includes thirty personal stories by genderqueer writers. The book begins with an introductory essay by each coeditor, followed by four theoretical essays by Riki Wilchins.

Queen, Carol, and Lawrence Schimel. *PoMoSEXUALS: Challenging Assumptions about Gender and Sexuality.* San Francisco: Cleis, 1997.
This transgressive anthology asks, "What happens to identities based on essentialist thinking when we begin to challenge fixed notions of gender identity, binary thinking, monosexuality?" (p. 21). Postmodern queerness is investigated with this compelling collection of essays from noted queer writers and activists

including Riki Wilchins and Kate Bornstein. Some pieces are theory heavy; others are sexually explicit; all push back against binary assumptions.

Sycamore, Matt/Mattilda Bernstein. *Nobody Passes: Rejecting the Rules of Gender and Conformity*. Emeryville, CA: Seal, 2006.
> An incredibly diverse collection of essays investigate the notion of "passing" in terms of gender, sexuality, ability, and ethnicity. Essays are an accessible mixture of theory, history, and personal experience. Several contributors, including Rocko Bulldagger, Amy André and Sandy Chang, and Stephanie Abraham, explore nonbinary gender identity.

———. *That's Revolting! Queer Strategies for Resisting Assimilation*. Brooklyn, NY: Soft Skull, 2008.
> This fantastic anthology challenges the mainstream gay movement's sanitized, straight-friendly presentation (i.e., striving to be the "Stepford Homosexual") with radical essays about queer identity, struggle, and resistance. Essays are contributed by activists and theorists including Patrick Califia and Kate Bornstein, and edited by Matt/Mattilda Bernstein Sycamore. Nonbinary activists and activism are included; see especially the essay about the importance of gender-neutral restrooms.

ETHNOGRAPHY

Beemyn, Genny, and Sue Rankin. *The Lives of Transgender People*. New York: Columbia University Press, 2011.
> A groundbreaking survey of nearly 3,500 transgender people in the United States, many of whom identify as nonbinary.

Kulick, Don. *Travesti: Sex, Gender, and Culture among Brazilian Transgendered Prostitutes*. Chicago: University of Chicago Press, 1998.
> Rich case studies of Brazilian travesti, some of whom identify as a third sex.

Nanda, Serena. *Gender Diversity: Crosscultural Variations*. Long Grove, IL: Waveland, 2014.
> This slim text is a synthesis of ethnographic research in many different cultures. Each chapter provides a case study of a particular group, including the Mohave alyha, Indian hijras, Thai kathoeys, Balkan sworn virgins, and more.

———. *Neither Man nor Woman: The Hijras of India*. Belmont, CA: Wadsworth, 1990.
> Case studies of several hijras with rich historical and contextual details.

People's Union for Civil Liberties-K. *Human Rights Violations against the Transgender Community: A Study of Kothi and Hijra Sex Workers in Bangalore, India*. Bangalore, India: PUCL-K, 2003.

An in-depth report on structural violence against gender minorities in India. Includes personal narrative testimonies from kothi and hijra sex workers.

Reddy, Gayatri. *With Respect to Sex: Negotiating Hijra Identity in South India*. Chicago: University of Chicago Press, 2005.

An ethnography of the Hyderabad hijra community in the late 1990s. Reddy analyzes multiple sites of identity in this community, including sexuality, gender, dress, religion, kinship, class, and corporeality.

HISTORY

Bell-Metereau, Rebecca Louise. *Hollywood Androgyny*. New York: Columbia University Press, 1993.

Film scholar Bell-Metereau investigates gender variance in more than 250 films, from pre-1960 to the 1990s (second edition).

Besnier, Niko, and Kalissa Alexeyeff. *Gender on the Edge: Transgender, Gay, and Other Pacific Islanders*. Honolulu: University of Hawaii Press, 2014.

In this edited volume, contributors explore non-heteronormative gender and sexual practices and categories in the Pacific Islands. Broad themes include historical representations, gender performance, and global politics.

Brisson, Luc. *Sexual Ambivalence: Androgyny and Hermaphroditism in Graeco-Roman Antiquity*. Berkeley: University of California Press, 2002.

Translation and interpretation of sexual and gender variance in ancient Greek and Roman texts.

Bullough, Bonnie, Vern L. Bullough, and James Elias. *Gender Blending*. Amherst, NY: Prometheus Books, 1997.

Edited volume exploring gender variance through historical case studies. Includes essays on Balkan sworn virgins, androgynous Egyptian pharaoh Akhenaten, and androgyny and the law.

Bullough, Vern L., and Bonnie Bullough. *Cross Dressing, Sex, and Gender*. Philadelphia: University of Pennsylvania Press, 1993.

A broad survey of gender variance throughout history and across cultures.

Epstein, Julia, and Kristina Straub. *Body Guards: The Cultural Politics of Gender Ambiguity*. New York: Routledge, 1991.

In this edited volume, contributors analyze historical gender variance in religion, theatre, law, and science.

Feinberg, Leslie. *Transgender Warriors: Making History from Joan of Arc to Dennis Rodman*. Boston: Beacon, 1996.
A historical survey of gender variance mixed with Feinberg's personal experiences of gender oppression.

Halberstam, Judith. *Female Masculinity*. Durham, NC: Duke University Press, 1998.
A deep examination of female gender variance through history.

———. *In a Queer Time and Place: Transgender Bodies, Subcultural Lives*. New York: New York University Press, 2005.
An exploration of transgender representations in art, film, and news media, with a focus on historical figures and subcultures.

Herdt, Gilbert H. *Third Sex, Third Gender: Beyond Sexual Dimorphism in Culture and History*. New York: Zone Books, 1994.
In this edited anthology, historians and anthropologists explore sexual and gender diversity through time and space.

Lang, Sabine. *Men as Women, Women as Men: Changing Gender in Native American Cultures*. Austin: University of Texas Press, 1998.
A comprehensive survey of Native American gender diversity through history.

Lester, Toni P. *Gender Nonconformity, Race, and Sexuality: Charting the Connections*. Madison: University of Wisconsin Press, 2002.
An edited volume investigating the intersections of racial identities and gender and sexual variance through a historical lens.

MacLeod, Catriona. *Embodying Ambiguity: Androgyny and Aesthetics from Winckelmann to Keller*. Detroit: Wayne State University Press, 1998.
An examination of the androgyny myth in eighteenth- and nineteenth-century German literature.

Meyerowitz, Joanne J. *How Sex Changed: A History of Transsexuality in the United States*. Cambridge, MA: Harvard University Press, 2002.
A comprehensive cultural and medical history of transsexual, transgender, and gender-variant identities in the United States in the twentieth century.

Roscoe, Will. *Changing Ones: Third and Fourth Genders in Native North America*. New York: St. Martin's, 1998.

Case studies of Native American gender diversity through history and across specific cultures.

Simels, Steven. *Gender Chameleons: Androgyny in Rock 'n' Roll*. New York: Arbor House, 1985.
History and discussion of gender variance in rock music and musicians.

Springate, Megan E. *LGBTQ America: A Theme Study of Lesbian, Gay, Bisexual, Transgender, and Queer History*. Washington, DC: National Park Service, 2016.
This two-volume edited collection offers expert discussion of LGBTQ (including gender-variant) history and historical sites.

Stryker, Susan. *Transgender History*. Berkeley, CA: Seal, 2008.
An introductory text exploring transgender history in the United States from the mid-twentieth century to the present.

Williams, Walter L. *The Spirit and the Flesh: Sexual Diversity in American Indian Culture*. Boston: Beacon, 1986.
History of colonial violence against sexual and gender minority Native Americans, as well as a survey of gender and sexual variance in historical and contemporary Native American communities.

REFERENCE

Ehrensaft, Diane. *Gender Born, Gender Made: Raising Healthy Gender-Nonconforming Children*. New York: Experiment, 2011.
An introduction to gender-variant children and guide to parenting them.

Erickson-Schroth, Laura. *Trans Bodies, Trans Selves: A Resource for the Transgender Community*. Oxford: Oxford University Press, 2014.
The transgender community's answer to classic feminist text *Our Bodies, Ourselves* includes terrific resources on transgender health care, coming out, transition, discrimination, employment, and relationships. Nonbinary identities are included in several sections.

Hill, Mel Reiff, and Jay Mays. *The Gender Book*. Houston, TX: Marshall House, 2013.
An engaging introduction to gender diversity. Includes surveys and a glossary.

James, Sandy E., Jody L. Herman, Susan Rankin, Mara Keisling, Lisa Mottet, and Ma'ayan Anafi. *The Report of the 2015 U.S. Transgender Survey*. Washington, DC: National Center for Transgender Equality, 2016.

Data and analysis from the biggest survey of transgender people in the United States; roughly one-third of respondents identified as nonbinary.

Makadon, Harvey J., Kenneth H. Mayer, Jennifer Potter, and Hilary Goldhammer. *The Fenway Guide to Lesbian, Gay, Bisexual, and Transgender Health*. 2nd ed. Philadelphia: American College of Physicians, 2015.
Surveys and case studies regarding LGBTQ demographics and health and social issues, and clinical guidelines for inclusive health care. This second edition includes guidelines for gender-variant patient care.

Shlasko, Davey, and Kai Hofius. *Trans* Ally Workbook: Getting Pronouns Right & What It Teaches Us about Gender*. N.p.: Think Again Training, 2014.
A brief but thorough guide to understanding gender identities and becoming proficient with pronoun use.

Teich, Nicholas M. *Transgender 101: A Simple Guide to a Complex Issue*. New York: Columbia University Press, 2012.
This slim text is exactly what it purports to be: a beginner's guide to understanding transgender identity. Most relevant to this bibliography is chapter 8: "Lesser-Known Types of Transgenderism," which explores genderqueer, gender-variant, gender-nonconforming, and Two-Spirit identities.

World Professional Association for Transgender Health. *Standards of Care for the Health of Transsexual, Transgender, and Gender Nonconforming People*. Minneapolis: WPATH, 2011.
Guidelines for trans-competent health care, including psychiatric, general practice, and transition-related care. In this seventh version, there is an abundance of nonbinary-specific information.

RELIGIOUS TEXT

Conner, Randy P. *Blossom of Bone: Reclaiming the Connections between Homoeroticism and the Sacred*. San Francisco: HarperSanFrancisco, 1993.
Cross-cultural study of gender-variant shamanic practice.

Doniger, Wendy. *Women, Androgynes, and Other Mythical Beasts*. Chicago: University of Chicago Press, 1980.
An exploration of androgyny in Hinduism, with deep reading of Sanskrit texts.

Goldberg, Ellen. *The Lord Who Is Half Woman: Ardhanārīśvara in Indian and Feminist Perspective*. Albany: State University of New York Press, 2002.
An extensive study of dual-gendered Hindu god Ardhanārīśvara, also known as Śiva-Śakti.

Kaldera, Raven. *Hermaphrodeities: The Transgender Spirituality Workbook.*
Philadelphia: Xlibris, 2001.
An exploration of spiritual gender variance through essay and poetry, with
ritual activities to practice.

Mollenkott, Virginia R. *Omnigender: A Trans-Religious Approach.* Cleveland, OH:
Pilgrim, 2001.
Discussion of gender variance in religious traditions, focusing primarily on
Judaism and Christianity.

Pattanaik, Devdutt. *The Man Who Was a Woman and Other Queer Tales from
Hindu Lore.* New York: Harrington Park, 2002.
A collection of sacred Hindu narratives involving sexual and gender diversity.
Includes in-depth introductory text and analysis.

Singer, June. *Androgyny: Toward a New Theory of Sexuality.* Garden City, NY:
Anchor, 1976.
An examination of gender and sexual androgyny in sacred texts, followed by a
suggestion to move toward psychological androgyny for personal growth.

Tanis, Justin Edward. *Trans-Gendered: Theology, Ministry, and Communities of
Faith.* Cleveland, OH: Pilgrim, 2003.
Written by a transgender priest, this book addresses gender variance in
Christian scripture.

Wilhelm, Amara. *Tritiya-Prakriti: People of the Third Sex: Understanding
Homosexuality, Transgender Identity, and Intersex Conditions through Hinduism.*
Philadelphia: Xlibris, 2003.
An examination of third gender identity through Hindu texts and teachings.

Zolla, Elémire. *The Androgyne, Reconciliation of Male and Female.* New York:
Crossroad, 1981.
Cross-cultural study of androgyny in sacred texts.

THEORY

Brown, Lester B. *Two Spirit People: American Indian, Lesbian Women and Gay Men.*
New York: Haworth, 1997.
An edited volume with discussion of Native American gender roles and
implications for social services.

Burke, Phyllis. *Gender Shock: Exploding the Myths of Male and Female.* New York:
Anchor, 1996.

An analysis and critique of binary gender, focusing on gendered behavior, biological sex, and gender aesthetics.

Butler, Judith. *Gender Trouble: Feminism and the Subversion of Identity*. New York: Routledge, 1990.
    A deep exploration of compulsory gender and sexuality. Includes in-depth analysis of key theorists including Foucault, Lacan, and Kristeva.

———. *Undoing Gender*. New York: Routledge, 2004.
    Addresses gender regulation in medicine, policy, kinship, and aesthetics.

Clare, Eli. *Brilliant Imperfections: Grappling with Cure*. Durham, NC: Duke University Press, 2017.
    Critical analysis of cure rhetoric, focusing on disability, gender, and sexuality.

Crawford, Lucas. *Transgender Architectonics: The Shape of Change in Modernist Space*. Farnham, Surrey, UK: Ashgate, 2015.
    Case studies examining the connections between modernist architecture and gender variance and transition.

Driskill, Qwo-Li. *Asegi Stories: Cherokee Queer and Two-Spirit Memory*. Tucson: University of Arizona Press, 2016.
    An exploration and interpretation of Cherokee Two-Spirit and queer histories. Scholar Qwo-Li Driskill provides a tribally specific Two-Spirit lens with which to understand and critique colonial history.

Driskill, Qwo-Li, Chris Finley, Brian Joseph Gilley, and Scott Lauria Morgensen. *Queer Indigenous Studies: Critical Interventions in Theory, Politics, and Literature*. Tucson: University of Arizona Press, 2011.
    An edited collection by scholars and activists centering indigenous queer and Two-Spirit people and theories. These essays push back against White anthropologists' imaginings of indigenous gender variance and sexuality.

Erickson-Schroth, Laura, and Laura A. Jacobs. *"You're in the Wrong Bathroom!": And 20 Other Myths and Misconceptions about Transgender and Gender Nonconforming People*. Boston: Beacon, 2017.
    A psychiatrist and psychologist debunk fallacies about transgender and gender-nonconforming people.

Fausto-Sterling, Anne. *Myths of Gender: Biological Theories about Women and Men*. New York: Basic, 1992.
    A critique of binary gender stereotypes backed up by scientific evidence.

———. *Sex/Gender: Biology in a Social World*. New York: Routledge, 2012.
An overview of the scientific and cultural construction of gender.

———. *Sexing the Body: Gender Politics and the Construction of Sexuality*. New York: Basic, 2000.
An investigation of gender and sexual identities through biological and cultural lenses.

Girshick, Lori B. *Transgender Voices: Beyond Women and Men*. Hanover, NH: University Press of New England, 2008.
As a social constructionist, Lori Girshick believes that human beings create our own social realities, based upon cultural and social training rather than scientific "facts." And as a sociologist, she uses grounded theory to explore gender identity through the experiences of 150 gender-variant people in this scholarly yet thoroughly accessible text. Many study participants identified as male and/or female, but quite a few identified as genderqueer, ungendered, bigendered, and a host of other nonbinary identities. Topics include the social construction of the gender binary, self-definition, coming out, gender policing and discrimination, and relationships and sexual orientation. Participants' words are nicely interwoven with analysis and history.

Haynes, Felicity, and Tarquam McKenna. *Unseen Genders: Beyond the Binaries*. New York: Peter Lang, 2001.
In this edited volume, contributors explore transgender, nonbinary gender, and intersex identities. Of particular relevance is part 3, "Toward Theories of Androgyny."

Jacobs, Sue-Ellen, Wesley Thomas, and Sabine Lang. *Two-Spirit People: Native American Gender Identity, Sexuality, and Spirituality*. Urbana: University of Illinois Press, 1997.
An edited anthology focusing on how Two-Spirit people are treated and interpreted by anthropologists and other Native Americans, with contributions from Two-Spirit people and non-Native anthropologists.

Miller, SJ. *Teaching, Affirming, and Recognizing Trans and Gender Creative Youth: A Queer Literacy Framework*. New York: Palgrave Macmillan, 2016.
An edited volume proposing and articulating a queer literacy framework, with models for prekindergarten through twelfth grade. Contributors include educators and education theorists.

Morgensen, Scott Lauria. *Spaces between Us: Queer Settler Colonialism and Indigenous Decolonization*. Minneapolis: University of Minnesota Press, 2011.

This book examines queerness in Native and non-Native communities, and how "queer" is defined by colonial powers and by Native communities. The author draws from indigenous feminist and queer thought and Native Two-Spirit and queer activism. Chapters explore the anthropological fascination with the "berdache," citizenship and sexual rights, Radical Faeries politics, solidarity and collaboration, and AIDS organizing.

Rothblatt, Martine Aliana. *The Apartheid of Sex: A Manifesto on the Freedom of Gender.* New York: Crown, 1995.
    Argues that assigning binary gender at birth is both oppressive and inaccurate and offers a new model that acknowledges all genders.

Roughgarden, Joan. *Evolution's Rainbow: Diversity, Gender, and Sexuality in Nature and People.* Berkeley: University of California Press, 2004.
    Joan Roughgarden is an evolutionary ecologist and a transgender woman. In this dense yet readable text, she discusses sexual and gender diversity through science-heavy explanations and a series of fascinating and fun examples. The underlying thread throughout the book is the idea that diversity does not equal deviance but is a driving force of evolution as well as a normal part of social life.

Serano, Julia. *Whipping Girl: A Transsexual Woman on Sexism and the Scapegoating of Femininity.* Berkeley, CA: Seal, 2007.
    Very accessible gender analysis and theory focusing on femmephobia, cissexism, fetishization, and binary gender stereotypes.

Wilchins, Riki. *Queer Theory, Gender Theory: An Instant Primer.* Los Angeles: Alyson Books, 2004.
    An introduction to postmodern queer and gender theory and theorists. Wilchins describes the ideas of Derrida, Foucault, and Butler in an accessible and engaging way, and introduces key issues in queer and gender politics.

Zimman, Lal, Jenny Davis, and Joshua Raclaw. *Queer Excursions: Retheorizing Binaries in Language, Gender, and Sexuality.* New York: Oxford University Press, 2014.
    This anthology analyzes cultural dichotomies in terms of language, social meaning, and self-identification. Linguists, anthropologists, and gender theorists offer historical context and analysis of culture-based gender, sex, and sexual orientation binaries. These perspectives make it clear that binary social structures are not the same the world over, and gender and sexual minorities navigate these systems in complex and powerful ways.

8

Journal Literature

Various aspects of nonbinary gender have been studied in academic disciplines, and a great deal of scholarly literature has been produced. This chapter provides a select list of scholarly journal literature. To ensure relevance, only those articles that include nonbinary gender-related terms in subject headings, author-supplied keywords, or abstracts have been included. Resources in this chapter are organized according to disciplinary domain. The "Humanities" section includes history, linguistics and languages, literature, media studies, performing and visual arts, philosophy, and religion. The "Science and Technology" section includes biological psychology, computer science, information science, medicine, and physical anthropology. The "Social Sciences" section includes cultural anthropology, education, political science, social psychology, sociology, and women and gender studies.

HUMANITIES

Allison, Marcia. "Other-Sexed/Other-Gendered: Narrating a Spectrum in a
   Language of Binaries." *Otherness: Essays and Studies* 2, no. 2 (2011): 1–223.
      Literary analysis of Virginia Woolf's *Orlando* and argument for gender-neutral
   pronouns.

Bittner, Robert. "Hey, I Still Can't See Myself! The Difficult Positioning of Two-
   Spirit Identities in YA Literature." *Bookbird: A Journal of International Children's
   Literature* 52, no. 1 (2014): 11–22.

A discussion of the representation of Two-Spirit people in young adult literature, focusing on *The Miseducation of Cameron Post* by Emily Danforth and Celu Amberstone's *The Dreamer's Legacy*.

Breger, Claudia. "Feminine Masculinities: Scientific and Literary Representations of 'Female Inversion' at the Turn of the Twentieth Century." *Journal of the History of Sexuality* 14, no. 1–2 (2005): 76–106.

A historical overview of the categorization of "deviant" gender configurations in female-assigned people, who have sometimes been described as a "third sex" in scientific literature.

Cameron, Michelle. "Two-Spirited Aboriginal People: Continuing Cultural Appropriation by Non-Aboriginal Society." *Canadian Woman Studies* 24, no. 2–3 (2005): 123–27.

Provides historical context of Two-Spirit identities and the harmfulness of appropriation.

Cantor, Libay Linsangan. "To Conform or Not to Conform, That Is the Genderqueer Question: Re-Examining the Lesbian Identity in Bernal's *Manila by Night*." *Kritika Kultura*, no. 19 (2012): 90–114.

An exploration of the lesbian character in Ishmael Bernal's film *Manila by Night* through a genderqueer Philippine cinema studies lens.

Connell, Catherine. "Fashionable Resistance: Queer 'Fa(t)shion' Blogging as Counterdiscourse." *Women's Studies Quarterly* 41, no. 1–2 (2012): 209–24.

An investigation of fat (gender)queer femme fashion blogging as sociopolitical resistance.

Estrada, Gabriel S. "*Two Spirits, Nádleeh*, and LGBTQ2 Navajo Gaze." *American Indian Culture and Research Journal* 35, no. 4 (2011): 167–90.

A critical analysis of Two-Spirit representation in film, with detailed discussion of Two-Spirit identities and activism.

Fink, Marty, and Quinn Miller. "Trans Media Moments: Tumblr, 2011–2013." *Television and New Media* 15, no. 7 (2014): 611–26.

Analysis and discussion of transgender and nonbinary self-representation on social media platform Tumblr.

Halberstam, J. "Global Female Masculinities." *Sexualities* 15, no. 3–4 (2012): 336–54.

A historical overview of the ways in which understandings of gender variance have shifted in the United States and Europe, and how Anglocentric gender concepts have been used to theorize about non-Western gender systems.

Keenan, Deirdre. "Unrestricted Territory: Gender, Two Spirits, and Louise Erdrich's *The Last Report on the Miracles at Little No Horse.*" *American Indian Culture and Research Journal* 30, no. 2 (2006): 1–15.
    An investigation of the character of Father Damien in Louise Erdrich's *The Last Report on the Miracles at Little No Horse* through a Two-Spirit lens.

Kelso, Tony. "Still Trapped in the U.S. Media's Closet: Representations of Gender-Variant, Pre-Adolescent Children." *Journal of Homosexuality* 62, no. 8 (2015): 1058–97.
    An analysis of gender nonconformity in television and other media; reveals a stark absence of gender-variant youth.

Kerry, Stephen. "'There's Genderqueers on the Starboard Bow': The Pregnant Male in *Star Trek.*" *Journal of Popular Culture* 42, no. 4 (2009): 699–714.
    An analysis of genderqueerness in the *Star Trek* universe.

Kronz, Victoria. "Women with Beards and Men in Frocks: Gender Nonconformity in Modern American Film." *Sexuality & Culture: An Interdisciplinary Quarterly* 20, no. 1 (2016): 85–110.
    An analysis of gender nonconformity in thirty-six American films from 2001 to 2011.

Lipton, Shawna. "Trouble Ahead: Pleasure, Possibility and the Future of Queer Porn." *New Cinemas: Journal of Contemporary Film* 10, no. 2 (2012): 197–207.
    An analysis of queer porn, including the claim that queer porn is characterized by body and gender variance.

McLeod, Ken. "Visual Kei: Hybridity and Gender in Japanese Popular Culture." *Young* 21, no. 4 (2013): 309–25.
    An analysis of visual kei, a Japanese pop music genre that employs androgynous imagery.

Muñoz, José Esteban. "'The White to Be Angry': Vaginal Davis's Terrorist Drag." *Social Text*, no. 52–53 (1997): 81–103.
    An analysis of intersections of race and gender in genderqueer performance artist Vaginal Davis's work.

Peletz, Michael G. "Transgenderism and Gender Pluralism in Southeast Asia since Early Modern Times." *Current Anthropology* 47, no. 2 (2006): 309–40.
    Historical analysis of gender systems in Southeast Asia.

Soto, Christopher, ed. *Nepantla: A Journal Dedicated to Queer Poets of Color.* 2014. http://www.lambdaliterary.org/wp-content/uploads/2014/09/nepantla.ajournal.pdf.
    A literary journal focusing on queer poets of color.

Stotko, Elaine M., and Margaret Troyer. "A New Gender-Neutral Pronoun in
Baltimore, Maryland: A Preliminary Study." *American Speech* 82, no. 3 (2007):
262–79.
A case study of a spontaneously coined gender-neutral pronoun being used in
a young Black community in Baltimore.

Summers, Robert. "Queer Archives, Queer Movements: The Visual and Bodily
Archives of Vaginal Davis." *Radical History Review* 122 (2015): 47–54.
An investigation of the ways in which genderqueer performance artist Vaginal
Davis archives queer history and uses her archives to construct her performances.

Wasserstrom, Steven M. "Uses of the Androgyne in the History of Religions."
Studies in Religion/Sciences Religieuses 27, no. 4 (1998): 437–53.
A survey and discussion of the image of the androgyne in religions.

SCIENCE AND TECHNOLOGY

Agarwal, Sabrina C. "The Past of Sex, Gender, and Health: Bioarchaeology of the
Aging Skeleton." *American Anthropologist* 114, no. 2 (2012): 322–35.
A discussion of how assigning biological sex to human remains can obscure
analysis; the concept of gender fluidity is explored.

Beek, Titia F., Baudewijntje P. C. Kreukels, Peggy T. Cohen-Kettenis, and Thomas
D. Steensma. "Partial Treatment Requests and Underlying Motives of Applicants
for Gender Affirming Interventions." *Journal of Sexual Medicine* 12, no. 11
(2015): 2201–5.
Cases studies of binary and nonbinary transgender patients' medical and
surgical transition requests.

Cruz, Taylor M. "Assessing Access to Care for Transgender and Gender
Nonconforming People: A Consideration of Diversity in Combating
Discrimination." *Social Science & Medicine* 110 (2014): 65–73.
A discussion of medical discrimination against gender-variant people and ways
to improve access to biomedicine and health care.

Davies, Shelagh, Viktoria G. Papp, and Christella Antoni. "Voice and Communication
Change for Gender Nonconforming Individuals: Giving Voice to the Person
Inside." *International Journal of Transgenderism* 16, no. 3 (2015): 117–59.
Literature review and clinical guidelines for transgender speech therapy and
voice surgeries.

Deutsch, Madeline B. "Making It Count: Improving Estimates of the Size of
Transgender and Gender Nonconforming Populations." *LGBT Health* 3, no. 3
(2016): 181–85.

Recommendations to accurately capture the size and diversity of transgender and nonbinary populations in order to provide better health care.

dickey, lore m., Kelly M. Ducheny, and Randall D. Ehrbar. "Family Creation Options for Transgender and Gender Nonconforming People." *Psychology of Sexual Orientation and Gender Diversity* 3, no. 2 (2016): 173–79.
   Comprehensive overview of reproductive options for transgender and gender-nonconforming people, including assistive reproductive technologies and chestfeeding.

Feinberg, Leslie. "Trans Health Crisis: For Us It's Life or Death." *American Journal of Public Health* 91, no. 6 (2001): 897–900.
   A personal narrative about medical discrimination against gender-variant people, with suggestions for medical professionals to provide appropriate care.

Kattari, Shanna K., N. Eugene Walls, Darren L. Whitfield, and Lisa Langenderfer-Magruder. "Racial and Ethnic Differences in Experiences of Discrimination in Accessing Health Services among Transgender People in the United States." *International Journal of Transgenderism* 16, no. 2 (2015): 68–79.
   Study examining medical discrimination of transgender and gender-nonconforming people of color, particularly in emergency rooms, ambulances, and hospitals.

Klein, Augustus, and Sarit A. Golub. "Family Rejection as a Predictor of Suicide Attempts and Substance Misuse among Transgender and Gender Nonconforming Adults." *LGBT Health* 3, no. 3 (2016): 193–99.
   Data analysis and discussion of the link between gender identity–related family rejection and suicidality and other health risks; implications for public health interventions.

Miller, Lisa R., and Eric Anthony Grollman. "The Social Costs of Gender Nonconformity for Transgender Adults: Implications for Discrimination and Health." *Sociological Forum* 30, no. 3 (2015): 809–31.
   Analysis of the correlation between gender nonconformity and discrimination, and subsequent health risk behaviors and poor health for gender-nonconforming transgender people.

Porch, Maria, Robyn Stukalin, and Heather Weisbrod. "Complex Cases in Community Mental Health: Stories from the Castro and the Tenderloin." *Journal of Gay & Lesbian Mental Health* 18, no. 4 (2014): 393–411.
   Case studies and recommendations for the Informed Consent Model for medical providers working with transgender and gender-nonconforming clients.

Reisner, Sari L., Emily A. Greytak, Jeffrey T. Parsons, and Michele L. Ybarra. "Gender Minority Social Stress in Adolescence: Disparities in Adolescent Bullying and Substance Use by Gender Identity." *Journal of Sex Research* 52, no. 3 (2015): 243–56.

    Study of substance use and other health risk behaviors in youth revealed that transgender and gender-nonconforming youth experienced more peer bullying and reported more alcohol and illicit drug use; implications for public health interventions.

Sennott, Shannon, and Tones Smith. "Translating the Sex and Gender Continuums in Mental Health: A Transfeminist Approach to Client and Clinician Fears." *Journal of Gay & Lesbian Mental Health* 15, no. 2 (2011): 218–34.

    An introduction to the Identity Continuums, the Transfeminist Qualitative Assessment Tool, and the Allyship Practice Model, to improve care by medical and mental health providers.

Smalley, K. Bryant, Jacob C. Warren, and K. Nikki Barefoot. "Differences in Health Risk Behaviors across Understudied LGBT Subgroups." *Health Psychology* 35, no. 2 (2016): 103–14.

    A large-scale comparison of health risk behaviors between sexual and gender minority groups; major differences noted between binary transgender participants and nonbinary participants.

Whitehead, J., John Shaver, Rob Stephenson, and Peter A. Newman. "Outness, Stigma, and Primary Health Care Utilization among Rural LGBT Populations." *PLOS ONE* 11, no. 1 (2016).

    A study of barriers to primary health care and health risk factors among rural LGBT people; nonbinary people are well represented.

Wylie, Kevan, et al. "Good Practice Guidelines for the Assessment and Treatment of Adults with Gender Dysphoria." *Sexual and Relationship Therapy* 29, no. 2 (2014): 154–214.

    Clinical guidelines for appropriate care for transgender and gender-nonconforming adults, including primary care, gynecological and urological care, hormonal and surgical treatment, and mental health.

Wylie, Sarah A., Heather L. Corliss, Vanessa Boulanger, Lisa A. Prokop, and S. Bryn Austin. "Socially Assigned Gender Nonconformity: A Brief Measure for Use in Surveillance and Investigation of Health Disparities." *Sex Roles: A Journal of Research* 63, no. 3–4 (2010): 264–76.

    Data and discussion of negative health outcomes experienced by gender-nonconforming people, and recommendations for public health studies and tools.

SOCIAL SCIENCES

Ailles, Jennifer. "Pomosexual Play: Going beyond the Binaristic Limits of Gender?" *Journal of Bisexuality* 3, no. 3–4 (2004): 71–85.
   A discussion and analysis of pomosexual play as a method to destabilize binary gender.

Ansara, Y. Gavriel, and Peter Hegarty. "Methodologies of Misgendering: Recommendations for Reducing Cisgenderism in Psychological Research." *Feminism and Psychology* 24, no. 2 (2014): 259–70.
   A critique of cisgender bias in psychological publications and recommendations for reducing it.

Austin, Ashley. "'There I Am': A Grounded Theory Study of Young Adults Navigating a Transgender or Gender Nonconforming Identity within a Context of Oppression and Invisibility." *Sex Roles* 75, no. 5–6 (2016): 215–30.
   Research and analysis of the identity formation of transgender and gender-nonconforming young adults, with clinical implications.

Badruddoja, Roksana. "Queer Spaces, Places, and Gender: The Tropologies of Rupa and Ronica." *NWSA Journal* 20, no. 2 (2008): 156–88.
   An ethnographic examination of South Asian American genderqueer identities.

Bakshi, Sandeep. "A Comparative Analysis of Hijras and Drag Queens: The Subversive Possibilities and Limits of Parading Effeminacy and Negotiating Masculinity." *Journal of Homosexuality* 46, no. 3–4 (2004): 211–23.
   A comparison and discussion of the ways in which hijras and drag queens embody and perform gender.

Barr, Sebastian M., Stephanie L. Budge, and Jill L. Adelson. "Transgender Community Belongingness as a Mediator between Strength of Transgender Identity and Well-Being." *Journal of Counseling Psychology* 63, no. 1 (2016): 87–97.
   A large-scale study of transgender women, transgender men, and nonbinary people focused on community, identity, and mental health.

Beemyn, Genny. "Coloring outside the Lines of Gender and Sexuality: The Struggle of Nonbinary Students to Be Recognized." *Educational Forum* 79, no. 4 (2015): 359–61.
   A discussion of the needs of nonbinary college students and ways in which campuses can support them.

———. "The Experiences and Needs of Transgender Community College Students." *Community College Journal of Research and Practice* 36, no. 7 (2012): 504–10.

A discussion of the barriers faced by trans-spectrum community college students and suggestions to make campuses more inclusive and supportive.

Begun, Stephanie, and Shanna K. Kattari. "Conforming for Survival: Associations between Transgender Visual Conformity/Passing and Homelessness Experiences." *Journal of Gay & Lesbian Social Services* 28, no. 1 (2016): 54–66.
National survey on homeless experiences of transgender and gender-nonconforming individuals reveals that the inability to pass as a binary cisgender person correlates to negative experiences in homeless shelters; implications for social services are discussed.

Billies, Michelle. "Low Income LGBTGNC (Gender Nonconforming) Struggles over Shelters as Public Space." *ACME* 14, no. 4 (2015): 989–1007.
A participatory action research project exploring the intersections of LGBTGNC identities, race and ethnicity, and poverty in New York City.

Blackwood, Evelyn. "Gender Transgression in Colonial and Postcolonial Indonesia." *Journal of Asian Studies* 64, no. 4 (2005): 849–79.
An examination of tomboi and waria identities in historic and contemporary Indonesia.

———. "Tombois in West Sumatra: Constructing Masculinity and Erotic Desire." *Cultural Anthropology* 13, no. 4 (1998): 491–521.
An analysis of Minangkabau tomboi gender and sexual identity.

Blair, Karen L., and Rhea Ashley Hoskin. "Contemporary Understandings of Femme Identities and Related Experiences of Discrimination." *Psychology & Sexuality* 7, no. 2 (2015): 101–15.
Study examining the gender diversity of femme-identified individuals, as well as in-group femme-negativity.

———. "Experiences of Femme Identity: Coming Out, Invisibility and Femmephobia." *Psychology & Sexuality* 6, no. 3 (2015): 229–44.
Qualitative analysis of a survey on femme identity, gender identity and expression, and femmephobia in queer communities.

Boskey, Elizabeth R. "Understanding Transgender Identity Development in Childhood and Adolescence." *American Journal of Sexuality Education* 9, no. 4 (2014): 445–63.
An overview of the biological and social factors of transgender identity development, with implications for inclusive sexuality education.

Budge, Stephanie L., H. Kinton Rossman, and Kimberly A. S. Howard. "Coping and Psychological Distress among Genderqueer Individuals: The Moderating Effect of Social Support." *Journal of LGBT Issues in Counseling* 8, no. 1 (2014): 95–117.
    Study showing a direct relationship between social support and depression and anxiety symptoms among genderqueer individuals; implications for therapists working with genderqueer clients.

Callender, Charles, and Lee M. Kochems. "Men and Not-Men: Male Gender-Mixing Statuses and Homosexuality." *Journal of Homosexuality* 11, no. 3–4 (1985): 165–78.
    Discussion of gender variance among Native Americans; dated terminology is used, but still interesting and useful historically.

Case, Kim A., and S. Colton Meier. "Developing Allies to Transgender and Gender-Nonconforming Youth: Training for Counselors and Educators." *Journal of LGBT Youth* 11, no. 1 (2014): 62–82.
    An exploration of pedagogical approaches for K–12 educators and counselors supporting transgender and gender-nonconforming youth.

Chang, Sand C., and Anneliese A. Singh. "Affirming Psychological Practice with Transgender and Gender Nonconforming People of Color." *Psychology of Sexual Orientation and Gender Diversity* 3, no. 2 (2016): 140–47.
    Case study and guidelines for psychologists to support transgender and gender-nonconforming people of color.

Clare, Eli. "Stolen Bodies, Reclaimed Bodies: Disability and Queerness." *Public Culture* 13, no. 3 (2001): 359–65.
    Discussion of intersections of gender, queerness, and disability.

Corwin, Anna I. "Language and Gender Variance: Constructing Gender beyond the Male/Female Binary." *Electronic Journal of Human Sexuality* 12 (2009).
    Ethnographic analysis of nonbinary gender performance.

Davidson, Megan. "Seeking Refuge under the Umbrella: Inclusion, Exclusion, and Organizing within the Category Transgender." *Sexuality Research and Social Policy* 4, no. 4 (2007): 60–80.
    Exploration of the myriad definitions of "transgender" and ways in which activists organize for social change.

Dentice, Dianne, and Michelle Dietert. "Liminal Spaces and the Transgender Experience." *Theory in Action* 8, no. 2 (2015): 69–96.

Discussion of gender transition as a liminal state; interviews with binary and nonbinary transgender people.

Donatone, Brooke, and Katherine Rachlin. "An Intake Template for Transgender, Transsexual, Genderqueer, Gender Nonconforming, and Gender Variant College Students Seeking Mental Health Services." *Journal of College Student Psychotherapy* 27, no. 3 (2013): 200–11.

Concrete suggestions for college counselors to support transgender and genderqueer students during the initial assessment.

Driskill, Qwo-Li. "Doubleweaving Two-Spirit Critiques: Building Alliances between Native and Queer Studies." *GLQ: A Journal of Lesbian and Gay Studies* 16, no. 1–2 (2010): 69–92.

Argues that Two-Spirit critiques are crucial to produce fully intersectional theory and practice in queer studies.

———. "Stolen from Our Bodies: First Nations Two-Spirits/Queers and the Journey to a Sovereign Erotic." *Studies in American Indian Literatures* 16, no. 2 (2004): 50–64.

Discussion of historical trauma, decolonization, and Two-Spirit identities.

Edelman, Elijah Adiv. "'This Is Where You Fall Off My Map': Trans-Spectrum Spatialities in Washington, DC, Safety, and the Refusal to Submit to Somatic Erasure." *Journal of Homosexuality* 63, no. 3 (2016): 394–404.

Analysis of trans community–produced maps of Washington, DC, and the ways in which they construct trans narratives and provide data that are rare to locate elsewhere.

Ehrensaft, Diane. "Boys Will Be Girls, Girls Will Be Boys: Children Affect Parents as Parents Affect Children in Gender Nonconformity." *Psychoanalytic Psychology* 28, no. 4 (2011): 528–48.

Argues that gender nonconformity is healthy, not pathological; provides a framework for analyzing family dynamics around children's gender development.

———. "From Gender Identity Disorder to Gender Identity Creativity: True Gender Self Child Therapy." *Journal of Homosexuality* 59, no. 3 (2012): 337–56.

Case study and discussion of true gender self child therapy.

Factor, Rhonda, and Esther Rothblum. "Exploring Gender Identity and Community among Three Groups of Transgender Individuals in the United States: MTFs, FTMs, and Genderqueers." *Health Sociology Review* 17, no. 3 (2008): 235–53.

Survey and analysis of transgender and genderqueer people in terms of identity development and relationship to LGBT communities, with implications for health care professionals.

Fontanella, Lara, Mara Maretti, and Annalina Sarra. "Gender Fluidity across the
World: A Multilevel Item Response Theory Approach." *Quality & Quantity:
International Journal of Methodology* 48, no. 5 (2014): 2553–68.
Analysis of a large-scale study revealed nine gender profiles and concluded
that boundaries between the traditional classifications of male and female are
extremely fuzzy.

Giammattei, Shawn V. "Beyond the Binary: Trans-Negotiations in Couple and
Family Therapy." *Family Process* 54, no. 3 (2015): 418–34.
Case studies and current theory and research on gender minority stress and
affirming therapy approaches.

Gilbert, Miqqi Alicia. "Defeating Bigenderism: Changing Gender Assumptions in
the Twenty-First Century." *Hypatia* 24, no. 3 (2009): 93–112.
A discussion of the limitations of the gender binary and models for
challenging it.

Gilden, Andrew. "Preserving the Seeds of Gender Fluidity: Tribal Courts and
the Berdache Tradition." *Michigan Journal of Gender & Law* 13, no. 2 (2007):
237–72.
Comprehensive overview of indigenous gender variance, the effects of
colonialism and anthropology, and the Navajo tribal court's recognition of
traditional gender systems; some dated terminology.

Gonzalez, Maru, and Jesse McNulty. "Achieving Competency with Transgender
Youth: School Counselors as Collaborative Advocates." *Journal of LGBT Issues in
Counseling* 4, no. 3–4 (2010): 176–86.
Collaboration-specific strategies for school counselors to advocate for K–12
transgender and gender-nonconforming students.

Graham, Sharyn. "Negotiating Gender: Calalai' in Bugis Society." *Intersections:
Gender, History and Culture in the Asian Context*, no. 6 (2001).
Ethnographic analysis of Bugis gender roles and the lived experiences of five
calalai' individuals.

Hale, C. Jacob. "Leatherdyke Boys and Their Daddies: How to Have Sex without
Women or Men." *Social Text* no. 52–53 (1997): 223–36.
Autoethnographic discussion of gender play in BDSM communities.

Haritaworn, Jin. "Shifting Positionalities: Empirical Reflections on a Queer/Trans of
Colour Methodology." *Sociological Research Online* 13, no. 1 (2008).
Autoethnographic exploration of queer methodologies produced by queer and
trans (including genderqueer) people in diaspora.

Harper, Amney, and Anneliese Singh. "Supporting Ally Development with Families of Trans and Gender Nonconforming (TGNC) Youth." *Journal of LGBT Issues in Counseling* 8, no. 4 (2014): 376–88.

 A discussion of interventions and strategies for counselors working with the families of TGNC youth.

Harrison, Jack, Jaime Grant, and Jody L. Herman. "A Gender Not Listed Here: Genderqueers, Gender Rebels, and OtherWise in the National Transgender Discrimination Survey." *LGBTQ Policy Journal at the Harvard Kennedy School* 2 (2011–2012): 13–24.

 Large-scale study investigating violence and discrimination experienced by nonbinary transgender people; discusses the nuances of nonbinary gender categories and the importance of accurately capturing this data.

Hendricks, Michael L., and Rylan J. Testa. "A Conceptual Framework for Clinical Work with Transgender and Gender Nonconforming Clients: An Adaptation of the Minority Stress Model." *Professional Psychology: Research and Practice* 43, no. 5 (2012): 460–67.

 Overview of mental health issues experienced by transgender and gender-nonconforming people, with recommendations for psychologists to develop transgender competence.

Hidalgo, Marco A., Diane Ehrensaft, Amy C. Tishelman, Leslie F. Clark, Robert Garofalo, Stephen M. Rosenthal, Norman P. Spack, and Johanna Olson. "The Gender Affirmative Model: What We Know and What We Aim to Learn." *Human Development* 56, no. 5 (2013): 285–90.

 An outline of a gender affirmative model for working with gender-variant children.

Hobson, Amanda. "Designing and Implementing a Successful Gender-Neutral Housing Community." *Journal of College and Character* 15, no. 1 (2014): 33–38.

 Discusses strategies for gender-neutral housing on college campuses.

Hossain, Adnan. "Beyond Emasculation: Being Muslim and Becoming Hijra in South Asia." *Asian Studies Review* 36, no. 4 (2012): 495–513.

 Ethnographic analysis of hijra identities.

Johnston, Lynda. "Gender and Sexuality: Genderqueer Geographies?" *Progress in Human Geography* 40, no. 5 (2016): 668–78.

 Exploration of gender diversity in LGBTQI spaces and across geographical places.

Kristensen, Zoë E., and Matthew R. Broome. "Autistic Traits in an Internet Sample of Gender Variant UK Adults." *International Journal of Transgenderism* 16, no. 4 (2015): 234–45.

Analysis of AQ-10 scores of transgender adults, a large number of which identify as nonbinary; implications for treatment and further research.

Krum, Tiana E., Kyle S. Davis, and Paz M. Galupo. "Gender-Inclusive Housing Preferences: A Survey of College-Aged Transgender Students." *Journal of LGBT Youth* 10, no. 1–2 (2013): 64–82.

A survey of college-aged transgender and gender-nonconforming students regarding housing preferences, with recommended policies for campuses.

Kuper, Laura E., Robin Nussbaum, and Brian Mustanski. "Exploring the Diversity of Gender and Sexual Orientation Identities in an Online Sample of Transgender Individuals." *Journal of Sex Research* 49, no. 2–3 (2012): 244–54.

Analysis of transgender and genderqueer participants' sexual orientations and hormonal and surgical transition status and desire.

Lang, Sabine. "Native American Men-Women, Lesbians, Two-Spirits: Contemporary and Historical Perspectives." *Journal of Lesbian Studies* 20, no. 3–4 (2016): 299–323.

Overview of anthropological, decolonial, and historical approaches to indigenous gender systems, and discussion of contemporary Two-Spirit identities and concerns.

Langer, S. J. "Gender (Dis)Agreement: A Dialogue on the Clinical Implications of Gendered Language." *Journal of Gay & Lesbian Mental Health* 15, no. 3 (2011): 300–307.

A discussion on how the lack of nonbinary-specific language harms nonbinary psychotherapy patients, and suggestions for therapists to expand patient vocabulary and facilitate meaning making.

Leibowitz, Scott F., and Norman P. Spack. "The Development of a Gender Identity Psychosocial Clinic: Treatment Issues, Logistical Considerations, Interdisciplinary Cooperation, and Future Initiatives." *Child and Adolescent Psychiatric Clinics of North America* 20, no. 4 (2011): 701–24.

Discussion of the mental health risks and complex clinical needs of transgender and gender-nonconforming youth, with recommendations for specialized interdisciplinary treatment programs.

MacNeela, Pádraig, and Aisling Murphy. "Freedom, Invisibility, and Community: A Qualitative Study of Self-Identification with Asexuality." *Archives of Sexual Behavior* 44, no. 3 (2015): 799–812.

A study of asexual identity and community; a significant portion of participants also identified as a nonbinary gender.

Malpas, Jean. "Between Pink and Blue: A Multi-Dimensional Family Approach to Gender Nonconforming Children and Their Families." *Family Process* 50, no. 4 (2011): 453–70.
    Case studies and recommendations for multidimensional family approach therapy for gender-nonconforming children and their families.

Markman, Erin R. "Gender Identity Disorder, the Gender Binary, and Transgender Oppression: Implications for Ethical Social Work." *Smith College Studies in Social Work* 81, no. 4 (2011): 314–27.
    A critique of the binary gender oppression in diagnoses of gender identity disorder and a call for social workers to advocate for gender-nonconforming people and communities.

Matzner, Andrew. "'Transgender, Queens, *Mahu*, Whatever': An Oral History from Hawai'i." *Intersections: Gender, History and Culture in the Asian Context*, no. 6 (2001).
    The life narrative of Paige Peahi, who does not identify as a man and says she is different from women.

Middleton, Amy, publisher. *Archer Magazine*. http://archermagazine.com.au.
    Periodical focusing on sexuality, gender, and identity.

Moody, Chérie, and Nathan Grant Smith. "Suicide Protective Factors among Trans Adults." *Archives of Sexual Behavior* 42, no. 5 (2013): 739–52.
    Discussion of suicide prevention for transgender and nonbinary adults using data from a Canadian survey.

Morris, Jessica F., and Judy L. Van Raalte. "Transgender and Gender Nonconforming Athletes: Creating Safe Spaces for All." *Journal of Sport Psychology in Action* 7, no. 2 (2016): 121–32.
    Recommendations for sports psychologists and coaches for making transgender and gender-nonconforming athletes feel comfortable, understood, and included.

Nadal, Kevin L., Chassitty N. Whitman, Lindsey S. Davis, Tanya Erazo, and Kristin C. Davidoff. "Microaggressions toward Lesbian, Gay, Bisexual, Transgender, Queer, and Genderqueer People: A Review of the Literature." *Journal of Sex Research* 53, no. 4–5 (2015): 488–508.
    Literature review and analysis of microaggressions toward LGBTQ people.

Phillips, Layli, and Marla R. Stewart. "'I Am Just So Glad You Are Alive': New Perspectives on Non-Traditional, Non-Conforming, and Transgressive Expressions of Gender, Sexuality, and Race among African Americans." *Journal of African American Studies* 12, no. 4 (2008): 378–400.
  A model for understanding nonconforming gender, sexuality, and race in Black queers.

Rands, Kat. "Supporting Transgender and Gender-Nonconforming Youth through Teaching Mathematics for Social Justice." *Journal of LGBT Youth* 10, no. 1–2 (2013): 106–26.
  Discussion of approaches to gender-complex education and mathematics for social justice, with a proposal for a middle school assignment.

Reisner, Sari L., Sabra L. Katz-Wise, Allegra R. Gordon, Heather L. Corliss, and S. Bryn Austin. "Social Epidemiology of Depression and Anxiety by Gender Identity." *Journal of Adolescent Health* 59, no. 2 (2016): 203–8.
  Large-scale study on gender identity and mental health; discussion of transgender and gender-nonconforming identities as social determinants of depression and anxiety.

Roen, Katrina. "The Body as a Site of Gender-Related Distress: Ethical Considerations for Gender Variant Youth in Clinical Settings." *Journal of Homosexuality* 63, no. 3 (2016): 306–22.
  Discussion of self-harm among gender-variant youth and suggestions for clinical interventions, through a queer bioethics lens.

Roscoe, Will. "Bibliography of Berdache and Alternative Gender Roles among North American Indians." *Journal of Homosexuality* 14, no. 3–4 (1987): 81–171.
  An immense compendium of Native American terminology for gender-variant identities, organized by language family, and a comprehensive (for the time) list of anthropological references; some dated terminology.

———. "We'wha and Klah: The American Indian Berdache as Artist and Priest." *American Indian Quarterly* 12, no. 2 (1988): 127–50.
  Biographical information about two gender-variant Native Americans; some dated terminology, but rare rich description of these important people.

Ryan, Caitlin L., Jasmine M. Patraw, and Maree Bednar. "Discussing Princess Boys and Pregnant Men: Teaching about Gender Diversity and Transgender Experiences within an Elementary School Curriculum." *Journal of LGBT Youth* 10, no. 1–2 (2013): 83–105.
  Case study of a gender-inclusive elementary school curriculum.

Seelman, Kristie L. "Unequal Treatment of Transgender Individuals in Domestic
   Violence and Rape Crisis Programs." *Journal of Social Service Research* 41, no. 3
   (2015): 307–25.
      An investigation of the barriers faced by transgender and gender-
   nonconforming people attempting to access domestic violence and rape crisis
   services; includes implications for social services providers.

Shepherd, Laura J, and Laura Sjoberg. "Trans- Bodies in/of War(s):
   Cisprivilege and Contemporary Security Strategy." *Feminist Review* 101,
   no. 1 (2012): 5–23.
      Discussion about the erasure of genderqueer bodies in accounts of war and,
   conversely, the oppression of genderqueer bodies in security strategies.

Shotwell, Alexis, and Trevor Sangrey. "Resisting Definition: Gendering through
   Interaction and Relational Selfhood." *Hypatia* 24, no. 3 (2009): 56–76.
      Argues that transgender and genderqueer people play a role in the development
   of cisgender identities.

Spade, Dean. "Some Very Basic Tips for Making Higher Education More Accessible
   to Trans Students and Rethinking How We Talk about Gendered Bodies." *Radical
   Teacher*, no. 92 (2012): 57–62.
      Concrete suggestions for college instructors to make classrooms inclusive and
   supportive for transgender and gender-nonconforming students.

Stachowiak, Dana M. "Queering It Up, Strutting Our Threads, and Baring Our
   Souls: Genderqueer Individuals Negotiating Social and Felt Sense of Gender."
   Journal of Gender Studies, no. 2 (2016): 1–12.
      Ethnographic analysis of the ways in which genderqueer participants
   experience their genders.

Stephen, Lynn. "Sexualities and Genders in Zapotec Oaxaca." *Latin American
   Perspectives* 29, no. 2, iss. 123 (2002): 41–59.
      Ethnographic snapshots of gender and sexuality in Juchitán and Teotitlán del
   Valle, with historical context for Zapotec gender systems.

Tebbe, Elliot A., and Bonnie Moradi. "Suicide Risk in Trans Populations: An
   Application of Minority Stress Theory." *Journal of Counseling Psychology* 63,
   no. 5 (2016): 520–33.
      Study examining the relationships between minority stressors, social support,
   and substance use with depression and suicide risk in transgender and nonbinary
   populations; implications for therapeutic interventions.

ten Brummelhuis, Han. "Transformations of Transgender: The Case of the Thai
Kathoey." *Journal of Gay & Lesbian Social Services* 9, no. 2–3 (1999): 121–40.
Based on in-depth ethnographic fieldwork, this article discusses kathoey
identity and suggests appropriate social services.

Testa, Rylan J., Janice Habarth, Jayme Peta, Kimberly Balsam, and Walter Bockting.
"Development of the Gender Minority Stress and Resilience Measure." *Psychology
of Sexual Orientation and Gender Diversity* 2, no. 1 (2015): 65–77.
Development and evaluation of a new tool for assessing minority stress and
resilience in transgender and gender-nonconforming people, with suggestions
for use.

Wesley, Saylesh. "Twin-Spirited Woman/Sts'iyóye smestíyexw slhá:li." *TSQ:
Transgender Studies Quarterly* 1, no. 3 (2014): 338–51.
A call to Stó:lō grandmothers to support the reclamation of indigenous gender
and sexual identities.

West, Isaac. "PISSAR's Critically Queer and Disabled Politics." *Communication and
Critical/Cultural Studies* 7, no. 2 (2010): 156–75.
An analysis of the queer and disability politics of PISSAR (People In Search of
Safe and Accessible Restrooms).

Williams, H. Sharif. "Bodeme in Harlem: An African Diasporic Autoethnography."
Journal of Bisexuality 10, no. 1–2 (2010): 64–78.
An autoethnographic exploration of the Dagara concept bodeme and
genderqueer, bisexual, and polyamorous identities.

Williams, Walter L. "Persistence and Change in the Berdache Tradition among
Contemporary Lakota Indians." *Journal of Homosexuality* 11, no. 3–4 (1985):
191–200.
Ethnographic exploration of gender variance in contemporary Lakota
reservations; some dated terminology, but valuable data.

———. "Women, Men, and Others: Beyond Ethnocentrism in Gender Theory."
American Behavioral Scientist 31, no. 1 (1987): 135–41.
A discussion of indigenous gender systems and an argument for Western
gender scholars to avoid binary assumptions.

Worth, Heather. "Bad-Assed Honeys with a Difference: South Auckland Fa'afafine
Talk about Identity." *Intersections: Gender, History and Culture in the Asian
Context*, no. 6 (2001).

Ethnographic analysis of the fluid gender identities and presentations of eight fa'afafine individuals in South Auckland.

Wyss, Shannon E. "'This Was My Hell': The Violence Experienced by Gender Non-Conforming Youth in US High Schools." *International Journal of Qualitative Studies in Education* 17, no. 5 (2004): 709–30.
    An exploration of the physical and sexual harassment and violence experienced by seven gender-nonconforming high school students, and the impacts on mental health, academic achievement, and risk behaviors.

9

Theses and Dissertations

Graduate scholarship focusing on nonbinary gender identities has been produced in many disciplines. This chapter includes highly relevant graduate theses and dissertations, selected for strong focus on nonbinary gender-related terminology and topics in abstracts. Resources are organized according to disciplinary domain. The "Humanities" section includes history, linguistics and languages, literature, media studies, and performing and visual arts. The "Science" section includes biological psychology and medicine. The "Social Sciences" section includes cultural anthropology, education, political science, social psychology, sociology, and women and gender studies.

HUMANITIES

Bradley, Reeanna. "ARTivism: Gender and Artistic Expression at AWAC." MA thesis, University of Northern British Columbia, 2013.
>   Case study of art practice and gender expression at a homeless shelter.

Campbell, Michelle. "My Life as Mick Mounter: Performing Genders with the Chicago Kings." PhD diss., Northwestern University, 2005.
>   An autoethnographic examination of the performance of race, genders, and personas in theatre troupe Chicago Kings.

Cuevas, Teresa Jackqueline. "To(o) Queer the Chican@s: Disrupting Genders in the Post-Borderlands." PhD diss., University of Texas at Austin, 2010.

An exploration of nonnormative genders and sexualities in Mexican American literature.

Ebelherr, Abigail Lynn. "Fluid Bodies." MFA thesis, Iowa State University, 2012.
A short-story collection exploring transgender, genderqueer, and gay identities through folklore.

Halle, Craig Steven, Jr. "Iffy the Crumbsnatcher." PhD diss., Illinois State University, 2013.
A collection of poems and creative writing that explores a genderqueer character named Iffy; includes a theoretical discussion of poetics and identity.

Keller, Marie Margaret. "Salmacis' Alchemical Pool: Gender Diversity and the Transformation of Culture." PhD diss., Pacifica Graduate Institute, 2014.
An analysis of gender diversity in four myths from Ovid's *Metamorphoses*.

Krell, Elias Dylan. "Singing Strange: Transvocality in North American Music Performance." PhD diss., Northwestern University, 2014.
A performance ethnography of three transgender and genderqueer musicians: Lucas Silveira, Kelly Moe, and Joe Stevens.

MacLeod, Catriona. "Fictions of Androgyny in the German Bildungsroman." PhD diss., Harvard University, 1992.
A discussion of the androgynous "third sex" in German bildungsroman.

McArdle, Aych. "Transitional Spaces: Investigating the Role of Collaborative Art Practice in Generating Self-Representational Genderqueer Narratives." MAD thesis, Auckland University of Technology, 2014.
An action research project exploring collaborative arts practice and genderqueer self-representation.

Moon, Cameron. "The 'Hybrid Hero' in Western Dime Novels: An Analysis of Women's Gender Performance, Dress, and Identity in the Deadwood Dick Series." MS thesis, Colorado State University, 2012.
Discusses how Calamity Jane's androgynous dress challenges the gender binary.

Murphy, Annalyssa Gypsy. "Dissent along the Borders of the Fourth World: Native American Writings as Social Protest." PhD diss., Clark University, 2008.
An analysis of indigenous literature, including discussion of nonbinary trickster figures and their role in cultural resistance.

Robertson, Nyk. "Architect of Asylums: Spoken Word Creating Language for the Genderqueer Community." MA thesis, Simmons College, 2015.
An examination of ways in which slam poetry generates new language for genderqueer people to talk about their experiences and identities.

Rusell, Judith Kay. "Queers, Freaks, Hunchbacks, and Hermaphrodites: Psychosocial and Sexual Behavior in the Novels of Carson McCullers." PhD diss., Middle Tennessee State University, 1999.
An analysis of sex and gender expression in five Carson McCullers novels.

Schewe, Elizabeth. "Gender Migrants: Geographies of Transgenderism in Contemporary U.S. Life Writing, Fiction, and Film." PhD diss., University of Wisconsin, Madison, 2011.
Exploration of trans identities in media.

Schilling, LaChelle Elisabeth. "Queering (A)sexuality: Boundaries of Desire, Intimacy, and the Sacred." PhD diss., Claremont Graduate University, 2014.
A study of asexuality, queerness, and the sacred.

Shull, Dee (Daniel). "Communicative Acts of Identity: Non-Binary Individuals, Identity, and the Internet." MA thesis, California State University, East Bay, 2015.
Explores how nonbinary people express their identities online.

Snyder, Rachel. "The Androgyne Patriarchy in Japan: Contemporary Issues in Japanese Gender." MA thesis, University of Texas at Arlington, 2010.
Historical and media analysis of androgyny in Japan.

Tikkun, Kaitlyn Muriel. "Embodiment beyond the Binary: Sean Dorsey and the Trans Genderqueer Presence in Contemporary Concert Dance." MFA thesis, University of California, Irvine, 2010.
Ethnographic study of transgender choreographer and dancer Sean Dorsey and his trans and queer art programming and community.

Vayzman, Liena. "The Self-Portraits of Claude Cahun: Transgression, Self-Representation, and Avant-Garde Photography, 1917–1947." PhD diss., Yale University, 2002.
An analysis of the self-portraits of famed androgynous artist Claude Cahun.

Vreeland, Rebecca A. "LTTR: The Artists' Publication as a Medium for Radical Genderqueer Politics." MA thesis, San Francisco State University, 2010.

Discussion of a New York genderqueer artists' collective and their alternative media practices.

SCIENCE

Finnbogason, Signe. "Nonsuicidal Self-Injury in Queer Youth." MA thesis, University of British Columbia, 2010.

Large survey of LGBTQ and cisgender heterosexual adults in Canada reveals that the highest rate of nonsuicidal self-injury occurs in transgender and genderqueer populations; implications for clinicians are discussed.

Hooks, Barbara Mariko. "Mental Health Treatment Experiences of Transgender and Gender Nonconforming Adults." PsyD diss., Wright Institute, 2016.

Study revealing a positive correlation between mental health care satisfaction and trans-competent best practices; recommendations for all mental health providers to develop knowledge of binary and nonbinary transgender identities and treatment protocols.

Lewis, Jennifer. "Resilience among Transgender Adults Who Identify as Genderqueer: Implications for Health and Mental Health Treatment." PhD diss., New York University, 2008.

Two-year qualitative study on resilience among genderqueer individuals, with discussion of protective and risk factors and implications for medical and mental health interventions.

Martin, Chicora. "The Influence of Negative Educational Experiences on Health Behaviors among Gender Nonconforming American Indian/Alaska Native People." PhD diss., Colorado State University, 2013.

Quantitative analysis of the impact of harassment and policy barriers in higher education on transgender and gender-nonconforming First Nations people, focusing on substance use and suicidality.

Mogul-Adlin, Hannah. "Unanticipated: Healthcare Experiences of Gender Nonbinary Patients and Suggestions for Inclusive Care." MPH thesis, Yale University, 2015.

Study of nonbinary individuals' gender identities, health care experiences, and access to transition-related care; suggestions to medical providers for improved care.

Sadjadi, Sahar. "Diagnosing the Self: An Ethnography of Clinical Management of Gender in Children." PhD diss., Columbia University, 2014.

Study of clinical practices and diagnostic categories with regard to gender-nonconforming children in the United States.

Schulz, Sarah L. "Gender Identity: Pending? Identity Development and Health Care Experiences of Transmasculine/Genderqueer Identified Individuals." PhD diss., University of California, Berkeley, 2012.

Exploration of gender identities and health care experiences of transmasculine and genderqueer individuals; implications for health providers and health care organizations.

SOCIAL SCIENCES

Alie, Laura M. "Parental Acceptance of Transgender and Gender Non-conforming Children." PsyD diss., John F. Kennedy University, 2012.

An investigation of factors effecting parental acceptance or nonacceptance of transgender and gender-nonconforming children.

Bilodeau, Brent Laurence. "Genderism: Transgender Students, Binary Systems and Higher Education." PhD diss., Michigan State University, 2007.

An examination of ways in which the rigid gender binary results in systemic oppression on college campuses.

Bishop, Katelynn C. "Moments of Transformation: Gender, Sexuality, and Desire among Partners of Trans Men." MA thesis, University of California, Santa Barbara, 2012.

An exploration of the effects of gender transition on the gender and sexual identities of romantic and sexual partners.

Constantinides, Damon M. "Intersections of Gender and Intimacy in the Lives of Transgender People with Non-Binary Gender Identities." EdD diss., Widener University, 2011.

Using in-depth interviews with sixteen nonbinary people, the author conceptualizes a new model for friendship and sexual intimacy in the lives of nonbinary people; implications for educators, researchers, and clinicians.

Davidson, Skylar. "Gender Inequality: Nonbinary Transgender People in the Workplace." MA thesis, University of Massachusetts, Amherst, 2016.

A study of the hiring and employment outcomes of out nonbinary individuals.

di Bartolo, Adriana N. "Is There a Difference? The Impact of Campus Climate on Sexual Minority and Gender Minority Students' Levels of Outness." PhD diss., Claremont Graduate University, 2013.

A comparative analysis of sexual minority and gender minority students' outness, focusing on campus climate and intersectional identities.

Downing, Jordan Brooke. "Trans Identity Construction: Reconstituting the Body, Gender, and Sex." PhD diss., Clark University, 2013.
A qualitative exploration of the ways in which gender transition affects identity construction among transgender, genderqueer, and androgynous individuals.

Edelman, Elijah Adiv. "Articulating Bodies in Tapestries of Space: Mapping Ethnographies of Trans Social and Political Coalitions in Washington, DC." PhD diss., American University, 2012.
Community mapping project that reveals intersectional trans-spectrum experiences in Washington, DC.

Evans, Jennifer L. "Genderqueer Identity and Self-Perception." PsyD diss., California School of Professional Psychology, 2010.
An interview study exploring the experiences of AFAB genderqueer individuals.

Factor, Rhonda J. "Exploring Gender Diversity: A Comparison of Transgender Adults and Their Non-Transgender Siblings." PhD diss., University of Vermont, 2006.
A comparison of the experiences of trans women, trans men, and genderqueer individuals with their siblings; focusing on bodily experiences, gender presentation, social support, and discrimination.

Fogarty, Alison C. K. "Gender Ambiguity in the Workplace: Trans and Genderqueer Discrimination." PhD diss., Stanford University, 2015.
Qualitative analysis of workplace discrimination experienced by twenty-five transgender and genderqueer individuals in San Francisco.

Herman, Jody L. "Gender Regulation in the Built Environment: Gender-Segregated Public Facilities and the Movement for Change in Washington, DC, a Case Study Approach." PhD diss., George Washington University, 2010.
Participant action project examining gender segregation in public restrooms, locker rooms, and shelters, with discussion of public policy goals to protect transgender and gender-nonconforming people.

Hunt, Sarah E. "Trans/Formative Identities: Narrations of Decolonization in Mixed-Race and Transgender Lives." MA thesis, University of Victoria, 2007.
An autoethnographic exploration of indigenous and mixed-race gender identities.

Johnson, Daniel Ervin. "The Impact of Microaggressions in Therapy on
Transgender and Gender-Nonconforming Clients: A Concurrent Nested Design
Study." PsyD diss., University of the Rockies, 2014.
An investigation of 255 binary and nonbinary transgender clients' experiences
with microaggressions in therapy.

Klugman, Sam Shulman. "An Exploratory Study of the Experiences of Transgender
and Gender Nonconforming Students at Rutgers University." PsyD diss., Rutgers
University, 2014.
Qualitative needs assessment of transgender and gender-nonconforming
students at Rutgers University, in consultation with the LGBTQ Center at
Rutgers.

Lepak, Jamie Lynn. "Gender Identity: An Examination of Fears concerning
Reporting." MS thesis, Northeastern University, 2011.
A qualitative analysis of transgender and gender-nonconforming college
students and their experiences with victimization and seeking help.

Laing, Kelsie. "Towards Minoritarian Genderqueer Politics: Potentials of
Deleuzoguattarian Molecular Genderqueer Subjectivities and Bodies." MA thesis,
University of Victoria, 2010.
An ontological reading of genderqueer bodies and experiences.

Mahan, Ciara. "Teachers' Decision-Making Processes Related to Intervening in Peer
Aggression towards Gender Nonconforming and Perceived LGBTQ Students."
PhD diss., Pacific Graduate School of Psychology, 2007.
Qualitative study of eight high school teachers' understandings of
trans-antagonistic bullying and their decision-making processes around
intervention.

Mai, Thảo Yên. "Constructing the Vietnamese Queer Identities: A Hierarchy of
Class, Gender, and Sexuality." MA thesis, University of Helsinki, 2016.
A qualitative research project examining queer Vietnamese identities; author
interviewed seventeen individuals, including one genderqueer-identified person.

Manning, Elizabeth Joy. "Who Are the Men in 'Men Who Have Sex with Men'?"
MSW thesis, University of Victoria, 2010.
A study highlighting how the language used in HIV prevention excludes
transgender, genderqueer, and intersex individuals; implications for researchers
and policy makers.

Mar, Kobi. "Female-to-Male Transgender Spectrum People of Asian and Pacific Islander Descent." PsyD diss., Alliant International University, 2010.
    Discussion of the experiences of twelve API AFAB trans-spectrum individuals, with clinical implications.

Michael, Heather. "Queer Partner Abuse: An Exploration of Gender, Power, and Service Delivery." MSW thesis, University of Victoria, 2006.
    Qualitative analysis of the experiences of eight queer relationship abuse survivors; major themes include gender identity, gendered social services, and the impact of cisnormative understandings of relationship abuse.

Mountz, Sarah E. "Overrepresented, Underserved: The Experiences of LGBTQ Youth in Girls Detention Facilities in New York State." PhD diss., University of Washington, 2013.
    An ethnographic examination of the experiences of queer, transgender, and gender-nonconforming youth in the juvenile justice system.

Mushegain, Lorig M. "Genderfree: Liberating Psyche and Perception from the Constructs of Gender." MA thesis, Pacifica Graduate Institute, 2011.
    A deep examination of the author's transformation from living a gendered life to being gender-free, with discussion of how gender has been constructed in Western medicine and culture.

Ophelian, Annalise. "Diagnosing Difference: An Examination of the Psycho-social Impact of the Gender Identity Disorder Diagnosis on Transgender Lives." PsyD diss., Wright Institute, 2009.
    Analysis of thirteen transgender and gender-variant individuals' experiences with and thoughts about the GID diagnosis.

Peters, Melissa Minor. "Kuchus in the Balance: Queer Lives under Uganda's Anti-homosexuality Bill." PhD diss., Northwestern University, 2014.
    Ethnographic study of the identities and experiences of transgender and gender-nonconforming Ugandans.

Plis, Laura C. "Negotiating Lesbian and Queer Identities in Midwestern Young Adults." MS thesis, Purdue University, 2010.
    Examines identity construction of lesbian, genderqueer, and transgender emerging adults.

Saltzburg, Nicole L. "Developing a Model of Transmasculine Identity." PhD diss., University of Miami, 2010.

An exploration of transmasculine gender identities and therapeutic implications.

Seelman, Kristie L. "A Mixed Methods Examination of Structural Bigenderism and the Consequences for Transgender and Gender Variant People." PhD diss., University of Denver, 2013.

A discussion of the ways in which structural gender binarism impacts transgender and gender-variant people in social services settings and higher education.

Sell, Ingrid M. "Third Gender: A Qualitative Study of the Experience of Individuals Who Identify as Being Neither Man nor Woman." PhD diss., Institute of Transpersonal Psychology, 2001.

Qualitative analysis of in-depth interviews with thirty "third gender" individuals in the United States.

Seth, Bindu. "GenderQueer Identity: Examining Liminality through Narrative." PsyD diss., Chicago School of Professional Psychology, 2009.

Qualitative study of the "in-between" status of genderqueer individuals.

Shelton, Jama. "There's No Place Like Home? The Experiences of Unstably Housed Transgender and Gender Non-conforming Young People." PhD diss., City University of New York, 2013.

Analysis of housing instability among transgender and gender-nonconforming youth, with implications for social services.

Stachowiak, Dana Marie. "Queer(ing) Gender: A Critical Analysis of Thinking, Embodying, and Living Genderqueer." PhD diss., University of North Carolina at Greensboro, 2013.

A participatory action research project exploring the genderqueer body and the liminal spaces of identity.

Swanson, Hunter Greenwood. "Standards of Care: Transgender/Genderqueer Clients' Experiences with Mental Health Workers." MSW thesis, Smith College School for Social Work, 2009.

A qualitative study investigating twelve transgender and genderqueer individuals' experiences in therapy; focuses include quality of care and gatekeeping.

Wilson, Alexandria M. "N'Tacimowin Inna Nah': Coming in to Two-Spirit Identities." EdD diss., Harvard University, 2007.

Case study of Aboriginal Canadian Two-Spirit identities.

Wood, Caitlin. "Translating Gender: Exploring the Effect of Communicative
Barriers on Trans Identity." MA thesis, Southern Illinois University, Carbondale,
2015.
    An analysis of the experiences of five transgender and genderqueer individuals
with communicating their gender identities to others.

10

Fiction Books

This chapter provides an annotated bibliography of fiction books with nonbinary characters. Books are organized according to the following genres: erotica, fantasy, historical fiction, horror, literary fiction, mystery, picture books, romance, science fiction, urban fiction, and western. Books that span multiple genres are located under the primary genre, determined by Library of Congress subject headings and classification. Both adult and juvenile fiction are represented.

EROTICA

Bornstein, Kate, and Caitlin Sullivan. *Nearly Roadkill: An Infobahn Erotic Adventure*. New York: Serpent's Tail, 1996.
   Two genderless cybersex operators protest government intervention on the Internet.

Hill-Meyer, Tobi, ed. *Nerve Endings: The New Trans Erotic*. New York: Instar Books, 2017.
   An anthology of erotic short fiction by thirty contributors. Several writers and characters are nonbinary.

Rosenthal, Sam. *Rye*. Brooklyn, NY: Projekt, 2012.
   This erotic novel follows the kinky adventures of three genderqueer characters as they navigate gender, polyamory, and love together.

Taormino, Tristan, ed. *Take Me There: Trans and Genderqueer Erotica*. Berkeley, CA: Cleis, 2011.
  This twenty-nine-story erotica collection focuses on transgender and genderqueer desire, with notable writers including Kiki DeLovely, S. Bear Bergman, and Ivan Coyote.

FANTASY

Bradley, Marion Zimmer. *Lythande*. New York: Daw Books, 1986.
  In this series of novelettes, Lythande is a wandering mercenary magician sworn to fight against Chaos. While this character is biologically female and performs a masculine gender expression, their gender is ambiguous; both male and female pronouns are used at different times. The first story portrays Lythande neutrally until the final two paragraphs.

Flewelling, Lynn. *Tamir Triad, 1: The Bone Doll's Twin*. Sydney: HarperCollins, 2001.

———. *Tamir Triad, 2: Hidden Warrior*. New York: Bantam, 2001.

———. *Tamir Triad, 3: The Oracle's Queen*. New York: Bantam, 2006.
  This fantasy series is a coming-of-age story of a girl hidden in a boy's body. The gender narrative is interesting in this trilogy; Tobin begins as a boy and ends as a girl, but has a fluid and mixed gender identity for a portion in the middle.

Fox, Rose, and Daniel José Older, eds. *Long Hidden: Speculative Fiction from the Margins of History*. Framingham, MA: Crossed Genres, 2014.
  Speculative fiction short-story collection focusing on marginalized identities; includes several stories by nonbinary writers and/or featuring nonbinary characters.

Gaiman, Neil. *Neverwhere*. New York: Avon Books, 1997.
  Businessman Richard Mayhew helps a weak and bloody young woman on the street and enters a magical and dangerous underground world called London Below. One of the interesting characters they meet is the angel Islington, who is genderless and sexless and referred to with the pronoun "it," although sometimes other characters use "he" to refer to it. This novel is a companion to a television serial of the same title.

Hobb, Robin. *Realm of the Elderlings Series: Farseer Trilogy, Prequel: The Willful Princess and the Piebald Prince*. London: Harper, 2013.

———. *Realm of the Elderlings Series: Farseer Trilogy, 1: Assassin's Apprentice.* London: Harper, 1995.

———. *Realm of the Elderlings Series: Farseer Trilogy, 2: Royal Assassin.* London: Harper, 1996.

———. *Realm of the Elderlings Series: Farseer Trilogy, 3: Assassin's Quest.* London: Harper, 1997.

———. *Realm of the Elderlings Series: Liveship Traders Trilogy, 1: Ship of Magic.* London: Harper, 1998.

———. *Realm of the Elderlings Series: Liveship Traders Trilogy, 2: The Mad Ship.* London: Harper, 1999.

———. *Realm of the Elderlings Series: Liveship Traders Trilogy, 3: Ship of Destiny.* London: Harper, 2000.

———. *Realm of the Elderlings Series: Tawny Man Trilogy, 1: Fool's Errand.* London: Harper, 2001.

———. *Realm of the Elderlings Series: Tawny Man Trilogy, 2: The Golden Fool.* London: Harper, 2002.

———. *Realm of the Elderlings Series: Tawny Man Trilogy, 3: Fool's Fate.* London: Harper, 2003.

———. *Realm of the Elderlings Series: Rain Wild Chronicles, 1: Dragon Keeper.* London: Harper, 2009.

———. *Realm of the Elderlings Series: Rain Wild Chronicles, 2: Dragon Haven.* London: Harper, 2010.

———. *Realm of the Elderlings Series: Rain Wild Chronicles, 3: City of Dragons.* London: Harper, 2012.

———. *Realm of the Elderlings Series: Rain Wild Chronicles, 4: Blood of Dragons.* London: Harper, 2013.

———. *Realm of the Elderlings Series: Fitz and the Fool Trilogy, 1: Fool's Assassin.* London: Harper, 2014.

———. *Realm of the Elderlings Series: Fitz and the Fool Trilogy, 2: Fool's Quest.* London: Harper, 2015.

———. *Realm of the Elderlings Series: Fitz and the Fool Trilogy, 3: Assassin's Fate.* New York: Del Ray, 2017.
This fantasy series follows the adventures of royal bastard Fitz. Worldbuilding and character development are complex and interesting. One major character, the Fool, has ambiguous gender that has never been revealed.

Lam, Laura. *Micah Grey Trilogy, 1: Pantomime.* Nottingham, UK: Strange Chemistry, 2013.

———. *Micah Grey Trilogy, 2: Shadowplay.* Nottingham, UK: Strange Chemistry, 2014.

———. *Micah Grey Trilogy, 3: Masquerade.* London: Tor Books, 2017.
Intersex nonbinary teen Micah runs away from home to avoid genital surgery, joins the circus, and discovers that he has magical abilities.

Pratchett, Terry. *Discworld Series, 1: The Colour of Magic.* London: Corgi, 1983.

———. *Discworld Series, 2: The Light Fantastic.* London: Corgi, 1986.

———. *Discworld Series, 3: Equal Rites.* London: Corgi, 1987.

———. *Discworld Series, 4: Mort.* London: Corgi, 1987.

———. *Discworld Series, 5: Sourcery.* London: Gollancz, 1988.

———. *Discworld Series, 6: Wyrd Sisters.* London: Gollancz, 1988.

———. *Discworld Series, 7: Pyramids.* London: Gollancz, 1989.

———. *Discworld Series, 8: Guards! Guards!* London: Gollancz, 1989.

———. *Discworld Series, 9: Eric.* London: Gollancz, 1990.

———. *Discworld Series, 10: Moving Pictures.* London: Gollancz, 1990.

———. *Discworld Series, 11: Reaper Man.* London: Gollancz, 1991.

———. *Discworld Series, 12: Witches Abroad.* London: Gollancz, 1991.

———. *Discworld Series, 13: Small Gods.* London: Corgi, 1992.

———. *Discworld Series, 14: Lords and Ladies.* London: Gollancz, 1992.

———. *Discworld Series, 15: Men at Arms.* London: Corgi, 1993.

———. *Discworld Series, 16: Soul Music.* London: Corgi, 1994.

———. *Discworld Series, 17: Interesting Times.* London: Corgi, 1994.

———. *Discworld Series, 18: Maskerade.* London: Corgi, 1995.

———. *Discworld Series, 19: Feet of Clay.* London: Corgi, 1996.

———. *Discworld Series, 20: Hogfather.* London: Gollancz, 1996.

———. *Discworld Series, 21: Jingo.* London: Gollancz, 1997.

———. *Discworld Series, 22: The Last Continent.* London: Doubleday, 1998.

———. *Discworld Series, 23: Carpe Jugulum.* London: Doubleday, 1998.

———. *Discworld Series, 24: The Fifth Elephant.* London: Doubleday, 1999.

———. *Discworld Series, 25: The Truth.* London: Doubleday, 2000.

———. *Discworld Series, 26: Thief of Time.* London: Doubleday, 2001.

———. *Discworld Series, 27: The Last Hero.* London: Gollancz, 2001.

———. *Discworld Series, 28: The Amazing Maurice and His Educated Rodents.* London: Doubleday, 2001.

———. *Discworld Series, 29: Night Watch.* London: Doubleday, 2002.

———. *Discworld Series, 30: The Wee Free Men.* London: Doubleday, 2003.

———. *Discworld Series, 31: Monstrous Regiment.* London: Doubleday, 2003.

———. *Discworld Series, 32: A Hat Full of Sky.* London: Doubleday, 2004.

———. *Discworld Series, 33: Going Postal.* London: Doubleday, 2004.

———. *Discworld Series, 34: Thud!* London: Doubleday, 2005.

———. *Discworld Series, 35: Wintersmith.* London: Doubleday, 2006.

———. *Discworld Series, 36: Making Money.* London: Doubleday, 2007.

———. *Discworld Series, 37: Unseen Academicals.* London: Doubleday, 2009.

———. *Discworld Series, 38: I Shall Wear Midnight.* London: Doubleday, 2010.

———. *Discworld Series, 39: Snuff.* London: Doubleday, 2011.

———. *Discworld Series, 40: Raising Steam.* London: Doubleday, 2013.

———. *Discworld Series, 41: The Shepherd's Crown.* London: Doubleday, 2015.

Discworld is a long-running comedic series set in a fantasy world populated by humans as well as dwarfs, elves, witches, and other strange and magical characters. Several characters are genderfluid, multigendered, or have ambiguous gender: Altogether Andrews is several souls of both genders in one body; golems are not really male or female as they are artificial; and dwarves can be biologically male or female but both have beards and they use only one personal pronoun (he).

Riordan, Rick. *The Hammer of Thor*. Los Angeles: Disney Hyperion, 2016.
 The second in a fantasy trilogy based on Norse mythology; this book includes a genderfluid character.

Tepper, Sheri S. *The Revenants*. New York: Ace Fantasy Books, 1984.
 In this magical quest narrative, five characters strike out into the world, seek out magical items, learn important lessons, and work together to save the world. One protagonist, Jaer, is "the greatest riddle of all," a person who is sometimes physically male and sometimes physically female.

HISTORICAL FICTION

Arnold, June. *The Cook and the Carpenter*. Plainfield, VT: Daughters, 1973.
 A novel based on a large-scale lesbian feminist action that took place in 1970 in New York, written by one of the participants. Third-gender pronouns are used for everybody.

Woolf, Virginia. *Orlando: A Biography*. London: Hogarth, 1928.
 This important novel follows the exceptionally long life of a fascinating person named Orlando, who was born a biological male during Queen Elizabeth I's reign. In early adulthood, Orlando wakes up one day to discover that their body has mysteriously transformed into that of a biological female. For the rest of Orlando's more than three hundred years, they remain biologically female but gender fluid. Their adventures include politics, diplomacy, romance, and poetry, and they eventually marry another gender-nonconforming person.

HORROR

Somtow, SP. *Timmy Valentine Trilogy, 1: Vampire Junction*. Norfolk, VA: Donning, 1984.

———. *Timmy Valentine Trilogy, 2: Valentine*. New York: T. Doherty Associates, 1992.

———. *Timmy Valentine Trilogy, 3: Vanitas*. London: Gollancz, 1995.

A horror trilogy about a two-thousand-year-old vampire with the body of a twelve-year-old boy. Timmy is sexless and androgynous, but appears to identify as male. Supporting character PJ Gallagher is temporarily nonbinary in the second book.

LITERARY FICTION

Clark, Kristin Elizabeth. *Freakboy*. New York: Farrar Straus and Giroux, 2013.
   A young person struggles with coming to the realization that they are genderqueer. *Freakboy* is entirely in verse.

Strubel, Antje Rávic. *Snowed Under: An Episodic Novel*. Translated by Zaia Alexander. Los Angeles: Red Hen, 2008.
   In thirteen connected short stories, a couple visits a small Eastern European ski resort. Strubel plays with gender identity and other binaries.

Viramontes, Helena María. *Their Dogs Came with Them*. New York: Atria, 2007.
   A barrio in 1960s Los Angeles is threatened by freeway expansion, gang violence, poverty, and police surveillance. Character Turtle is androgynous.

White, Patrick. *The Twyborn Affair*. London: Jonathan Cape, 1979.
   A three-part novel about the life of a genderfluid person moving between identities, locations, and time periods.

MYSTERY

Nair, Anita. *A Cut-Like Wound*. London: Bitter Lemon, 2014.
   In this suspenseful thriller, Inspector Borei Gowda investigates a string of serial murders in Bangalore, India. The killer is a hijra, and sadly, the author seems to be somewhat confused about the nuances of cross-dressing versus gender identity. That said, there is some interesting exploration of sexual marginalization and gender diversity in India.

PICTURE BOOKS

Bergman, S. Bear, and Rachel Dougherty. *Is That for a Boy or a Girl?* Toronto: Flamingo Rampant, 2015.
   Some kids get frustrated with being told that their toys, interests, and activities are for "boys" or "girls" and decide to choose what fits them best.

Gonzalez, Maya Christina. *Call Me Tree / Llámame Arbol*. New York: Children's Book Press, 2014.

A bilingual Spanish/English rhyming book about being your authentic self and following your dreams. Protagonist Tree is gender neutral so that all children can identify with the story.

Kilodavis, Cheryl, and Suzanne DeSimone. *My Princess Boy: A Mom's Story about a Young Boy Who Loves to Dress Up*. New York: Aladdin, 2011.
A loving mother introduces her Princess Boy, a gender-creative child who loves wearing dresses and dancing. The Princess Boy could identify as male, female, both, or neither, which opens up those possibilities for young readers.

RANDom, WoMANtís. *Gummiband-Familien / Rubberband Families*. Berlin: w_ orten & meer, 2016.
A bilingual German/English picture book about family diversity, with inclusive language to allow children to see themselves and their family reflected.

Rothblatt, Phyllis. *All I Want to Be Is Me*. Lexington, KY: Self-published, 2011.
A beautifully illustrated children's book that encourages children to be themselves. Many genderfluid and gender-nonconforming children are represented, with a variety of ethnicities and levels of ability.

Savage, Sarah, and Fox Fisher. *Are You a Boy or Are You a Girl?* N.p.: TQUAL Books, 2015.
Children's book about a gender-neutral child.

ROMANCE

Dooland, A. E. *Under My Skin, 1: Under My Skin*. N.p.: Self-published, 2014.

———. *Under My Skin, 2: Flesh & Blood*. N.p.: Self-published, 2015.
Min Lee is living the perfect life—great job, loving boyfriend, and a wonderful family. But she is deeply unhappy and has body image issues. When she meets a beautiful young woman, she starts to rethink her sexuality and gender identity, and realizes that "she" isn't the right pronoun after all.

Garréta, Anne. *Sphinx*. Translated by Emma Ramadan. Dallas, TX: Deep Vellum, 2015.
A genderless love story, originally published in 1986 in French.

Garvin, Jeff. *Symptoms of Being Human*. New York: Balzer + Bray, 2016.
Genderfluid teen Riley explores their identity through blogging and navigates coming out and bullying.

Levithan, David. *Every Day*. New York: Knopf, 2012.

A wakes up in a different body every day, living a different life with different relationships. Because A is literally transitioning biologically on a daily basis, this entails gender fluidity as well. One day, A meets Rhiannon and falls in love.

Winterson, Jeanette. *The PowerBook*. New York: Knopf, 2000.

Language costumier Ali/Alix creates interactive stories for people, weaving magnificent transformations across time, space, and identity. On the Internet, you can be whoever you want to be, but you can't direct the outcome of your story. Ali/Alix, too, enters the stories and changes gender at will.

———. *Written on the Body*. New York: Knopf, 1992.

In this meandering romantic fiction, the narrator—only identified as "I"— muses about loves great and small, sex and intimacy, joy and loss. They have had both male and female lovers; one of whom stated that "you were the most beautiful creature male or female I had ever seen." For the entire book, our narrator is ungendered, and their gender (or lack thereof) is not questioned or commented upon.

SCIENCE FICTION

Asimov, Isaac. *The Gods Themselves*. London: Gollancz, 1972.

An Earth scientist works with an alien and a lunar-born human to save the universe. The alien society portrayed in this Hugo- and Nebula-winning novel has three genders.

Banks, Iain. *Culture Series, 1: Consider Phlebas*. London: Orbit, 1987.

———. *Culture Series, 2: The Player of Games*. London: Orbit, 1988.

———. *Culture Series, 3: Use of Weapons*. London: Orbit, 1990.

———. *Culture Series, 4: The State of the Art*. London: Orbit, 1991.

———. *Culture Series, 5: Excession*. London: Orbit, 1996.

———. *Culture Series, 6: Inversions*. London: Orbit, 1998.

———. *Culture Series, 7: Look to Windward*. London: Orbit, 2000.

———. *Culture Series, 8: Matter*. London: Orbit, 2008.

———. *Culture Series, 9: Surface Detail*. London: Orbit, 2010.

182

CHAPTER 10

——. *Culture Series, 10: The Hydrogen Sonata*. London: Orbit, 2012.

In a postscarcity society, enhanced genetics have allowed humanoid citizens to alter their bodies to change sex, a process that takes some time. Some citizens change back and forth numerous times. The Culture is an egalitarian society where not only is gender fluidity considered normal, it's actually expected.

Barker, Clive. *Imajica*. London: HarperCollins, 1991.

This massive fantasy tome recounts the reunion of Earth, known as the Fifth Dominion, with four other Dominions; while also describing the complex relationships and movements of three extraordinary people as they travel amid the Dominions. *Imajica* explores love, spirituality, and gender: main character Pie 'oh' pah is a shapeshifting alien who is a third sex with the pronoun "it."

Bashe, Kayla. *To Stand in the Light*. N.p.: Self-published, 2015.

Nonbinary half-demon superhero Shadow meets a street kid named Bean, mentors her, and falls in love.

Bujold, Lois McMaster. *Vorkosigan Saga, 1: Falling Free*. New York: Baen Books, 1988.

——. *Vorkosigan Saga, 2: Shards of Honor*. New York: Baen Books, 1986.

——. *Vorkosigan Saga, 3: Barrayar*. New York: Baen Books, 1991.

——. *Vorkosigan Saga, 4: The Warrior's Apprentice*. New York: Baen Books, 1986.

——. *Vorkosigan Saga, 5: The Vor Game*. New York: Baen Books, 1990.

——. *Vorkosigan Saga, 6: Cetaganda*. New York: Baen Books, 1995.

——. *Vorkosigan Saga, 7: Ethan of Athos*. New York: Baen Books, 1986.

——. *Vorkosigan Saga, 8: Borders of Infinity*. New York: Baen Books, 1987.

——. *Vorkosigan Saga, 9: Brothers in Arms*. New York: Baen Books, 1988.

——. *Vorkosigan Saga, 10: Mirror Dance*. New York: Baen Books, 1994.

——. *Vorkosigan Saga, 11: Memory*. New York: Baen Books, 1996.

——. *Vorkosigan Saga, 12: Komarr*. New York: Baen Books, 1998.

——. *Vorkosigan Saga, 13: A Civil Campaign*. New York: Baen Books, 1999.

——. *Vorkosigan Saga, 14: Diplomatic Immunity*. New York: Baen Books, 2002.

———. *Vorkosigan Saga, 15: Captain Vorpatril's Alliance.* New York: Baen Books, 2012.

———. *Vorkosigan Saga, 16: CryoBurn.* New York: Baen Books, 2010.
This sweeping science fiction series follows protagonist Miles Vorkosigan throughout his entire life (and a bit before). Miles's mother is from Beta Colony, which has a third sex/gender and is an egalitarian and nonviolent culture. Bel Thorne is a major character in the series and refers to itself as a "herm" and with the personal pronoun "it," which is not perceived as disrespectful.

Bull, Emma. *Bone Dance: A Fantasy for Technophiles.* New York: Ace Books, 1991.
This urban fantasy follows gender-neutral protagonist Sparrow as they barter scavenged electronics and repair work in a postnuclear America. As a bioengineered posthuman, Sparrow is biologically sexless as well as being androgynous in expression and neutral in gender.

Butler, Octavia E. *Xenogenesis Series, 1: Dawn.* New York: Warner Books, 1987.

———. *Xenogenesis Series, 2: Adulthood Rites.* New York: Warner Books, 1988.

———. *Xenogenesis Series, 3: Imago.* New York: Warner Books, 1989.
This science fiction trilogy, later published in an omnibus edition as *Lilith's Brood*, follows Lilith and her children after they are saved by an alien race called the Oankali after nuclear war destroys Earth. The Oankali have three sexes/genders: male, female, and ooloi. The ooloi have the capability to manipulate genetic material, and work to create a hybrid human-Oankali species.

Constantine, Storm. *Wraeththu Chronicles, 1: The Enchantments of Flesh and Spirit.* London: Macdonald Futura, 1987.

———. *Wraeththu Chronicles, 2: The Bewitchments of Love and Hate.* London: Macdonald Futura, 1988.

———. *Wraeththu Chronicles, 3: The Fulfillments of Fate and Desire.* London: Macdonald Futura, 1989.

———. *Wraeththu Histories, 1: The Wraiths of Will and Pleasure.* New York: Tor Books, 2003.

———. *Wraeththu Histories, 2: The Shades of Time and Memory.* New York: Tor Books, 2004.

———. *Wraeththu Histories, 3: The Ghosts of Blood and Innocence.* Stafford, UK: Immanion, 2005.

———. *Wraeththu Novellas, 1: The Hienama: A Story of the Sulh*. Stafford, UK: Immanion, 2005.

———. *Wraeththu Novellas, 2: Student of Kyme: A Story of the Sulh*. Stafford, UK: Immanion, 2008.

———. *Wraeththu Series: The Moonshawl*. Stafford, UK: Immanion, 2014.
    The Wraeththu are a posthuman species that evolved to be functionally intersex and androgynously gendered. They live in tribal communities on a postapocalyptic Earth, where they challenge humans for world control. This series of novels and short stories has complex worldbuilding that explores spirituality, gender, and technology.

Delany, Samuel R. *Stars in My Pocket Like Grains of Sand*. Toronto: Bantam, 1984.
    In the future, thousands of planets are colonized by humans and aliens, some of whom have three sexes.

———. *Trouble on Triton: An Ambiguous Heterotopia*. London: Wesleyan University Press, 1976.
    On Neptune's moon Triton, gender and sexual diversity have exploded, sexual attitudes are highly permissive, and each individual is free to express themselves as they like. Delany has created a world of fluidity and a novel about exploring knowledge and ideas of utopia.

Dickinson, Seth. "Sekhmet Hunts the Dying Gnosis: A Computation." *Beneath Ceaseless Skies* 143 (March 20, 2014). http://www.beneath-ceaseless-skies.com/stories/sekhmet-hunts-the-dying-gnosis-a-computation.
    In this short science fiction story, a character named Coeus is a transhuman with unknown biological sex who uses the pronoun "ze."

Egan, Greg. *Distress*. New York: HarperPaperbacks, 1995.
    On an artificial island named Stateless, a physics conference is being held in order to decide on a new Theory of Everything. In this future world, there are five new genders, and Egan uses epicene pronouns. One of the main characters, Akili Kuwale, is asexual and gender neutral and uses the pronouns "ve," "ver," and "vis."

Gardner, James Alan. *Commitment Hour*. New York: Avon Books, 1998.
    In the small village of Tober Cove, children change their sex every year until the age of twenty-one, when they must commit to being male, female, or "Neut" (both).

Gentle, Mary. *Orthe Series, 1: Golden Witchbreed*. London: Gollancz, 1983.

———. *Orthe Series, 2: Ancient Light*. London: Gollancz, 1987.

British envoy Lynne de Lisle Christie visits the planet Orthe to establish diplomatic relations. Ortheans are humanoid but not human; one of the differences between humans and Ortheans is that Orthean children have no biological sex and are gender neutral until puberty.

Gilman, Carolyn Ives. *Halfway Human*. New York: Avon, 1998.
   Tedla is a beautiful young alien who has tried to commit suicide; Val is an expert in alien cultures who is called to assist in recuperation. Tedla soon reveals that it is a "bland," a gender-neutral asexual person from the closed planet Gammadis. Val fights to protect Tedla from the government while Tedla tells a sordid story of eugenics, sex crimes, and slavery in a world where men and women are considered people and neuters are not.

Krasnostein, Alisa, and Julia Rios, eds. *Kaleidoscope: Diverse YA Science Fiction and Fantasy Stories*. Yokine, Perth, Australia: Twelfth Planet, 2014.
   This science fiction/fantasy anthology is a terrific collection of short stories centering on characters who are marginalized in terms of ethnicity, dis/ability, gender identity, sexuality, religion, and more. Dirk Flinthart's "Vanilla" has nonbinary characters.

Leckie, Ann. *Imperial Radch Trilogy, 1: Ancillary Justice*. New York: Orbit, 2013.

———. *Imperial Radch Trilogy, 2: Ancillary Sword*. New York: Orbit, 2014.

———. *Imperial Radch Trilogy, 3: Ancillary Mercy*. New York: Orbit, 2015.
   Breq was once the Justice of Toren, an intelligent starship. Now, though, Breq has a human body with the artificial intelligence of the ship, and is on a quest to attain vengeance for the Justice of Toren's destruction. This science fiction opera is set in the Radch Empire, where people are not distinguished by gender and everybody is referred to with she/her pronouns.

Le Guin, Ursula K. *The Left Hand of Darkness*. London: Macdonald, 1969.
   On the bleak world Winter, the inhabitants have no sex characteristics except during their fertile period or kemmer, in which their body transforms to match the reproductive capability of their closest partner also in kemmer. This neutrality punctuated by ambisexuality shapes their society, as there are no genders and thus no gender roles.

Leigh, Stephen. *Dark Water's Embrace*. New York: Avon, 1998.
   A group of interstellar explorers were stranded on the planet Mictlan generations ago. The descendants culturally evolved into a small society that highly values reproduction, as infertility rates are staggering due to the ecology of their new planet. Doctor Anaïs, struggling with infertility herself, discovers a

preserved alien body from the extinct previous occupants and learns the solution to her culture's reproduction failures: a third sex, known as the Sa or "midmale," which counteracted biological mutations.

MacFarlane, Alex Dally, ed. *Aliens: Recent Encounters*. Gaithersburg, MD: Prime Books, 2013.
 This science fiction anthology is edited by a nonbinary person, and Nancy Kress's "My Mother, Dancing" uses the pronoun "hir/s" exclusively.

Mandelo, Brit, ed. *Beyond Binary: Genderqueer and Sexually Fluid Speculative Fiction*. Maple Shade, NJ: Lethe, 2012.
 This speculative fiction anthology explores genderqueer and sexually fluid identities in seventeen short stories taking place across space and time. Characters are gay, lesbian, bisexual, queer, and asexual; women, men, and nonbinary; people, aliens, and androids.

McDonald, Ian. *India in 2047, 1: River of Gods*. London: Simon & Schuster, 2004.

———. *India in 2047, 2: Cyberabad Days*. London: Gollancz, 2009.
 In 2047, India is set to celebrate one hundred years of independence. The country has separated into competing states rife with political and caste tension and struggling with severe droughts. Technology has advanced so extraordinarily that people can choose to surgically transition to a neutral gender and artificial intelligences are passing as human.

McIntyre, Vonda N. *Dreamsnake*. Boston: Houghton Mifflin, 1978.
 Snake is a traveling snake-healer in a postapocalyptic world of advanced biotechnology, nuclear wastelands, tribalism, and gender equality. Sexuality and sexual relations are fluid and self-determined. One character's gender is unspecified; they have both a husband and a wife, and McIntyre manages to avoid using a pronoun for them.

Piercy, Marge. *Woman on the Edge of Time*. New York: Knopf, 1976.
 After a Latina woman is forcibly committed to a mental institution, she is contacted by an androgynous person from a utopian future who tells her that her life is important and will impact the future.

Reynolds, Alastair. *On the Steel Breeze*. London: Gollancz, 2013.
 The second in a trilogy about interstellar travel and colonization, this book has a supporting character who uses ve/vis/vir pronouns.

Robinson, Kim Stanley. *2312*. London: Orbit, 2012.
In the year 2312, Mercury, Mars, and Venus, as well as several moons, are inhabited by humans. Many people have quantum computers with artificial intelligence implanted in their bodies. And physical sex and gender are not rigid or static, with many people identifying outside the gender binary and/or with "gynandromorphous" bodies.

Schmatz, Pat. *Lizard Radio*. Somerville, MA: Candlewick, 2015.
In this dystopian novel, a teenage "bender" (nonbinary person) is sent to an indoctrination camp to conform to societal norms.

Scott, Melissa. *Shadow Man*. New York: Tor Books, 1995.
In this science fiction novel, two societies collide, forcing social change. Concord culture recognizes five sexes: fems, herms, mems, men, and women. Each sex has a corresponding gender and unique set of pronouns. Hara has a two-gender system and must relax rigid expectations in order to fit into interstellar civilization.

Sriduangkaew, Benjanun. "Silent Bridge, Pale Cascade." *Clarkesworld Magazine* 87 (December 2013). http://clarkesworldmagazine.com/sriduangkaew_12_13.
In this short story, Lunha is a military general who changes gender frequently and has been rebuilt after dying in service of the Hegemony. A secondary character, Operative Isren, is neutrois and uses the pronoun "they."

Stross, Charles. *Glasshouse*. New York: Ace Books, 2006.
In a future world, people can live in any kind of body they want. Robin and Kay decide to join an experiment where they are given new identities and bodies and sent to a model of a late twentieth-century Euro-American society.

Sturgeon, Theodore. *Venus Plus X*. New York: Pyramid Books, 1960.
In a future utopia, gender no longer exists.

Wells, Ankaret. *Requite Series, 1: The Maker's Mask*. London: Self-published, 2010.

——. *Requite Series, 2: The Hawkwood War*. London: Self-published, 2010.

——. *Requite Series, 3: Heavy Ice*. London: Self-published, 2013.
This science fiction romance trilogy includes genderqueer/intersex characters called epicons. In the first two books, epicons are referred to as "it"; this is changed to "they" for the third book. Epicon Innes is a bodyguard and major character, with a complex and witty personality.

Westerfeld, Scott. *Leviathan Trilogy, 1: Leviathan*. New York: Simon Pulse, 2009.

———. *Leviathan Trilogy, 2: Behemoth*. New York: Simon Pulse, 2010.

———. *Leviathan Trilogy, 3: Goliath*. New York: Simon Pulse, 2011.
   In this alternate-history steampunk adventure, a prince and a commoner are thrown together during World War I. Protagonist Deryn/Dylan's gender identity is fluid and difficult to categorize.

Witt, LA. *Static*. Hillsborough, NJ: Riptide, 2014.
   In this paranormal romance story, Alex is a shifter, someone who can change sex. After receiving an implant that blocks this ability, Alex is unwillingly outed to their boyfriend.

URBAN FICTION

Breedlove, Lynn. *Godspeed*. New York: St. Martin's, 2002.
   A gender-indeterminate bike messenger has to choose between addiction and love.

Brezenoff, Steven. *Brooklyn, Burning*. Minneapolis: Carolrhoda Lab, 2011.
   Kid and Scout are street kids who ran away from home because of family intolerance. They bond over music and fall in love while dealing with food and housing insecurity, an ongoing arson investigation, and parental neglect. Neither protagonist is gendered throughout the entire book; it is clear that both are gender nonconforming, but neither their biological sex nor their gender identities are ever explicitly named.

Feinberg, Leslie. *Drag King Dreams*. New York: Carroll & Graf, 2006.
   Max Rabinowitz is a bouncer in a Manhattan drag club and a tired former rabble-rouser until one of his friends is killed in a gender-motivated murder. He begins to come out of his loner shell and build community with other gender rebels in the clubs and in an online virtual reality game.

———. *Stone Butch Blues*. Ithaca, NY: Firebrand Books, 1993.
   Jess runs away from a homophobic family and finds a new home in the butch/femme community. S/he experiments with testosterone and feels between genders.

Lowrey, Sassafras. *Lost Boi*. Vancouver, BC: Arsenal Pulp, 2015.
   A genderqueer street punk retelling of Peter Pan.

———. *Roving Pack*. Brooklyn, NY: PoMo Freakshow, 2012.
A group of straightedge punks explore gender fluidity in Portland, Oregon.

Reynolds, Sheri. *The Sweet In-Between: A Novel*. New York: Shaye Areheart Books, 2008.
Kendra, a.k.a. Kenny, is living with her father's girlfriend while he is in jail, worried that she might get kicked out when she turns eighteen, and obsessed with the murder of a young woman by her neighbor. Throughout the book, Kenny's gender is ambiguous.

Woods, Chavisa. *The Albino Album*. New York: Seven Stories, 2013.
A girl with an unpronounceable name mistakenly causes her mother's death, grows up in a series of queer/punk homes, and becomes an ecoterrorist. One of the secondary characters is an intersex person who identifies as both male and female; pronouns "they" and "he" are used interchangeably.

WESTERN

Lawrence, Caroline. *Western Mysteries, 1: The Case of the Deadly Desperados*. New York: Putnam, 2012.

———. *Western Mysteries, 2: The Case of the Good-Looking Corpse*. London: Orion Children's, 2012.

———. *Western Mysteries, 3: P. K. Pinkerton and the Pistol-Packing Widows*. New York: Putnam, 2014.
This series of Wild West fiction is set in 1860s Nevada Territory and features protagonist P. K. "Pinky" Pinkerton, orphaned kid detective. Pinky is ambiguously gendered, sometimes dresses in "girl drag" and sometimes "boy drag" depending on what a situation calls for, and doesn't reveal their gender until the end of the third book.

11

Organizations and Associations

This chapter provides an annotated list of organizations and associations that produce scholarship on, support, and advocate for nonbinary people. Resources are organized according to geographic location (United States or international); beginning with professional associations, followed by advocacy organizations, and ending with support organizations. Many of the listed resources have a wider focus on transgender people or LGBTQ people as a whole. Selection was determined by a resource specifically including nonbinary people within the umbrella.

A professional association is defined as "a body of persons engaged in the same profession, formed usually to control entry into the profession, maintain standards, and represent the profession in discussions with other bodies."[1] Professional associations are generally nonprofit and are often connected with the academic discipline that corresponds to the profession. They often disseminate scholarship and set standards and best practices through journals and white papers. The professional associations highlighted in this chapter have been included either because they have service groups focusing on nonbinary issues, or they have produced standards and best practices that positively impact nonbinary people.

Advocacy organizations are nonprofit organizations that serve the community through legal and educational advocacy. Support organizations provide social support through online and in-person meetings, events, and forums. Resources for this section are focused on organizations that have a regional rather than local impact and specifically include nonbinary identities. Most major cities in the United States have trans support groups, although not all are formal organizations. The best way to find your local group is to do an Internet search for "[your city] transgender support" or inquire with a relevant regional organization.

PROFESSIONAL ASSOCIATIONS

United States

American Academy of Child & Adolescent Psychiatry, Sexual Orientation and Gender Identity Issues Committee. http://www.aacap.org.
  This committee serves in an educational, research, and advisory capacity concerning LGBT issues in child and adolescent psychiatry.

American Academy of Pediatrics, Section on Lesbian, Gay, Bisexual and Transgender Health and Wellness. https://www.aap.org/en-us/about-the-aap/Committees-Councils-Sections/solgbt/Pages/home.aspx.
  This group of pediatricians and other health providers focuses on LGBT children, parents, and health providers.

American Academy of Physician Assistants, LBGT PA Caucus. http://www.lbgpa.org.
  This group provides education and advocacy for LGBT health care equality.

American Academy of Religion, Status of Lesbian, Gay, Bisexual, Transgender, Intersex, & Queer Persons in the Profession Committee. https://www.aarweb.org/node/116.
  This committee advocates for the academic freedom and status of LGBTIQ religious studies professionals.

American Alliance of Museums, LGBTQ Alliance. http://www.aam-us.org/resources/professional-networks/lgbtq.
  This committee advocates for inclusion and visibility of LGBTQ museum professionals, patrons, programming, and collections.

American Anthropological Association, Association for Queer Anthropology Section. http://queeranthro.org.
  This association promotes anthropological research and education on sexual and gender diversity, and advocates for diversity within the profession.

American Association of Law Libraries, Lesbian & Gay Issues Standing Committee. http://www.aallnet.org/sections/sr/lgissues.

This committee advocates for nondiscrimination policies and diversity in law librarianship, and produces scholarship on sexual orientation and gender identity and the law.

American Association of Sexuality Educators, Counselors and Therapists. "Position on Reparative Therapy." https://www.aasect.org/position-reparative -therapy.

An official position that sexual and gender diversity is not pathological and that "reparative therapy" is harmful.

American Association of University Professors, Committee on Sexual Diversity and Gender Identity. https://www.aaup.org/about/committees/standing -committees#sdgicomm.

This committee provides education about sexual and gender diversity and promotes campus inclusion.

American Bar Association, Sexual Orientation and Gender Identity Committee of the Section of Civil Rights and Social Justice. http://apps.americanbar.org/dch/ committee.cfm?com=IR516000.

This committee educates the legal profession, develops policies, and files amicus briefs to support equal justice for LGBT people.

American Folklore Society, Lesbian Gay Bisexual Transgender Queer and Allies (LGBTQA) Section. http://www.afsnet.org/?page=LGBTQA.

This group encourages folklore research into LGBTQ culture and supports LGBTQ folklore researchers.

American Geriatrics Society, Needs of Older Gay and Lesbian, Bisexual and Transgendered Persons Special Interest Group. http://www.americangeriatrics. org/about_us/who_we_are/sections__special_interest_groups.

This group focuses on health research and advocacy for older GLBT people.

American Historical Association, Committee on LGBT History. http://clgbthistory .org.

This committee promotes the study and visibility of queer history.

American Humanist Association, LGBTQ Humanist Alliance. http://lgbthumanists .org.

This group works toward social progress for LGBTQ people.

American Library Association, Gay, Lesbian, Bisexual, and Transgender Round
Table. http://www.ala.org/glbtrt.
   This group supports the information and access needs of GLBT library
professionals and patrons.

American Musicological Society, LGBTQ Study Group. http://ams-lgbtq.org.
   This group promotes awareness and research in LGBTQ music studies, and
seeks to create a positive environment to come out in academia.

American Philosophical Association, LGBT People in the Profession Committee.
http://www.apaonline.org/members/group.aspx?id=110434.
   This committee monitors the status of LGBT philosophers and promotes equal
opportunity.

American Political Science Association, Committee on the Status of Lesbians, Gays,
Bisexuals, and Transgender Individuals in the Profession. http://www.apsanet
.org/statuscommitteelgbt.
   This committee advances research on LGBT issues, supports LGBT political
scientists, and develops curriculum materials.

American Political Science Association, Lesbian, Gay, Bisexual, Transgender
Caucus. http://www.apsanet.org/RESOURCES/For-the-Public/Political-Science
-Organizations/Caucuses-in-Political-Science/Lesbian-Gay-Bisexual-Transgender
-Caucus.
   This group is the primary association for LGBT members of the APSA, and
promotes research on sexuality, gender, and political theory and behavior.

American Psychoanalytic Association, Committee on Gender & Sexuality. http://
www.apsa.org/content/social-issues.
   This committee produces scholarship and best practices regarding gender and
sexuality in psychoanalysis. They have disseminated several position statements
focusing on sexual and gender diversity, including bullying, conversion therapy,
and civil rights.

American Psychological Association, Office on Sexual Orientation and Gender
Diversity. http://www.apa.org/pi/lgbt/index.aspx.
   This office advances psychological knowledge on sexual and gender diversity,
including best practice guidelines, state and federal advocacy, and policy
statements.

American Psychological Association, Society for the Psychological Study of Lesbian,
Gay, Bisexual and Transgender Issues. http://www.apa.org/about/division/div44
.aspx.

This division supports research, provides education, and creates best practices on sexual and gender diversity and psychology. They produced a fact sheet on nonbinary identities in 2015: http://www.apadivisions.org/division-44/resources/advocacy/non-binary-facts.pdf

American Society for Public Administration, LGBT Advocacy Alliance. https://lgbtaspa.wordpress.com.
This group focuses on LGBT public policy, research and education, and cultural competency for public administration professionals.

Association of American Law Schools, Section on Sexual Orientation and Gender Identity Issues. http://www.aals.org/services/sections/#directory.
This group advocates for legal improvement for sexual and gender diversity issues.

Association of American Medical Colleges (AAMC), AAMC Advisory Committee on Sexual Orientation, Gender Identity, and Sex Development (Axis). https://www.aamc.org/initiatives/diversity/431398/standingcommittee.html.
This committee supports diversity and inclusion in the medical profession, and promotes the health of people who are LGBT, gender nonconforming, and/or born with differences of sex development.

Association for Contextual Behavioral Science, LGBTQA Special Interest Group. https://contextualscience.org/lgbtqa_special_interest_group.
This group promotes research with sexual and gender minority communities, develops cultural competency trainings for providers, and provides a safe space for LGBTQA members.

Association for Lesbian, Gay, Bisexual & Transgender Issues in Counseling. http://www.algbtic.org.
This association promotes awareness for counselors and advocacy for clients.

Association for Theatre in Higher Education, LGBTQ Focus Group. http://www.athe.org/members/group.aspx?id=130353.
This group promotes LGBTQ perspectives in theatre, creates guidelines and ethical standards, and encourages research and artistic expression.

Children's Literature Association, Diversity Committee. http://www.childlitassn.org/diversity-committee.
This committee supports diversity in children's literature.

College Art Association, Queer Caucus for Art. http://www.queercaucusforart.org.
This group represents the interests of queer arts professionals and sponsors an annual queer art exhibition.

GLMA: Health Professionals Advancing LGBT Equality. http://www.glma.org.
    This association promotes health care equality for LGBT patients and health
    care professionals.

Medical Library Association, LGBT Health Science Librarians Special Interest
    Group. http://lgbt.mlanet.org.
    This group identifies, collects, and disseminates LGBT health care information.

National Art Education Association, LGBTQ+ Issues Group. https://www
    .arteducators.org/community/articles/69-lgbtq-issues-group.
    This group works against misrepresentation and bias to create safer spaces on
    campus and in society.

National Communication Association, Caucus on Lesbian, Gay, Bisexual,
    Transgender and Queer Concerns and the GLBTQ Communication Studies
    Division (NCA GLBTQ). https://glbtqcaucus.wordpress.com.
    These groups promote LGBTQ scholarship and ensures equity for LGBTQ
    members.

National Latina/o Psychological Association, Orgullo Latina/o: Sexual Orientation
    and Gender Identity Interest Group. http://www.nlpa.ws/special-interest-groups.
    This group promotes affirmative and intersectional LGBTQI Latina/o practices.

National Organization of Gay and Lesbian Scientists and Technical Professionals.
    http://www.noglstp.org.
    This association empowers LGBTQ STEM professionals and educates the
    public about LGBTQ STEM issues.

Organization of American Historians, Committee on the Status of Lesbian, Gay,
    Bisexual, Transgender, and Queer (LGBTQ) Historians and Histories. http://
    www.oah.org/about/governance/committees/service-committees/#lgbtq.
    This committee supports LGBTQ historians and promotes LGBTQ histories.

Pacific Sociological Association, Committee on the Status of LGBTQ Persons in
    Sociology. http://pacificsoc.org/committees/committee-on-the-status-of-lgbtq
    -persons-in-sociology.
    This committee monitors the participation of LGBTQ sociologists and
    members.

Society for Cinema & Media Studies, Queer Caucus. http://www.cmstudies.org/?
    page=caucus_queer.
    This group promotes the study of LGBTQ screen and media cultures.

Society of American Archivists, Lesbian and Gay Archivists' Roundtable. http://
www2.archivists.org/groups/lesbian-and-gay-archives-roundtable-lagar.
    This group promotes the preservation and research use of LGBTQ archives and
historical materials.

International

Association of Internet Researchers. "Diversity and Inclusivity." Adopted
unanimously by the Executive Committee August 8, 2014. https://aoir.org/
diversity-and-inclusivity.
    This association promotes ethical Internet research. AoIR includes gender
identity and expression in their inclusion statement.

Association of Moving Image Archivists, LGBT Interest Group. http://www.amia
net.org/community/committees.
    This group works to preserve LGBT moving images and promotes diversity
within the association.

British Psychological Society, Psychology of Sexualities Section. http://www.bps.org
.uk/networks-and-communities/member-microsite/psychology-sexualities-
section.
    This group develops sexuality and gender-inclusive research, theory, and
practice.

Canadian Psychological Association, Section on Sexual Orientation & Gender
Identity. http://www.sogii.ca.
    This group disseminates research and practice-based information on sexual
orientation and gender identity issues in psychology, taking a nonpathologizing
stance.

European Professional Association for Transgender Health. http://epath.eu.
    This association promotes knowledge and scholarship relating to transgender
health.

GLADD: The Association of LGBT Doctors & Dentists. https://gladd.co.uk.
    This association represents LGBT doctors and dentists in the UK.

International Communication Association, Lesbian, Gay, Bisexual, Transgender &
Queer Studies Interest Group. http://www.icahdq.org/group/glbtstudies.
    This group encourages research on LGBTQ representations and discourses,
and supports LGBTQ scholars in the field.

International Federation of Library Associations, LGBTQ Users Special Interest
   Group. http://www.ifla.org/about-lgbtq.
      This group supports the full range of LGBTQ information needs and library
   services.

International Lesbian, Gay, Bi, Trans, and Intersex Law Association. http://www
   .ilglaw.org.
      This association is dedicated to legal equality for LGBTI people.

International Society for Traumatic Stress Studies, LGBT Special Interest Group.
   http://www.istss.org/about-istss/special-interest-groups/lesbian,-gay,-bisexual
   -and-transgender-(lgbt)-sig.aspx.
      This group encourages research on and quality health care for LGBT trauma
   survivors.

NACADA: The Global Community for Academic Advising, Commission for
   LGBTQA Advising and Advocacy. http://www.nacada.ksu.edu/Community/
   Commission-Interest-Groups/Advising-Specific-Populations-III/Commission
   -for-LGBTQA-Advising-and-Advocacy.aspx.
      This group focuses on promoting success for LGBTQA students.

Special Libraries Association, GLBT Issues Caucus. http://lgbt.sla.org.
      This group shares resources and supports GLBTQ members of the association.

World Medical Association. "WMA Statement on Transgender People." Adopted by
   the 66th WMA General Assembly, Moscow, Russia, October 2015. http://www
   .wma.net/en/30publications/10policies/t13.
      The World Medical Association advocates for human rights, medical ethics,
   and public health. This official statement describes the transgender spectrum and
   provides health recommendations for medical providers.

World Professional Association for Transgender Health. http://www.wpath.org.
      This association promotes academic and clinical research for transgender
   health, and also produces the Standards of Care and Ethical Guidelines used by
   health professionals.

ADVOCACY ORGANIZATIONS

United States

American Civil Liberties Union (ACLU). Transgender Rights. https://www.aclu.org/
   issues/lgbt-rights/transgender-rights.

The ACLU provides legal and community advocacy to protect civil liberties for all people. This page describes their work on transgender issues.

Campus Pride. Trans Policy Clearinghouse. https://www.campuspride.org/tpc.
Campus Pride works for safer and more inclusive campuses for LGBTQ students. This page provides transgender-related resources.

Family Equality Council. http://www.familyequality.org.
Family Equality Council supports LGBTQ families and works to change policies.

Gay, Lesbian and Straight Education Network. https://www.glsen.org.
GLSEN works to create safe schools for queer and gender-diverse youth.

Gender Diversity. http://www.genderdiversity.org.
Gender Diversity promotes inclusive learning environments via policy, training, and direct assistance to youth and families.

Genders & Sexualities Alliance Network. https://gsanetwork.org.
GSA Network empowers and trains LGBTQ youth to work toward racial and gender justice in schools and communities.

GLBTQ Legal Advocates & Defenders (GLAD). https://www.glad.org.
GLAD fights for equality for LGBTQ people and people with HIV.

Human Rights Campaign. http://www.hrc.org.
HRC advocates for LGBTQ rights and educates the public.

Intersex and Genderqueer Recognition Project. http://www.intersexrecognition.org.
This organization works toward the legal recognition of intersex and genderqueer people.

Lambda Legal. http://www.lambdalegal.org.
Lambda Legal works for LGBTQ civil rights through litigation, education, and public policy.

National Center for Lesbian Rights. http://www.nclrights.org.
NCLR advocates for LGBTQ equality. They have released many statements and participated in litigation on trans rights.

National Center for Transgender Equality. http://www.transequality.org.
NCTE works to improve public policy and legal and social status for transgender people.

National LGBTQ Task Force. http://www.thetaskforce.org.
  The Task Force trains activists and advocates for LGBTQ equality.

PFLAG. https://www.pflag.org.
  PFLAG is a family and ally organization that educates and supports families
  and advocates for LGBTQ equality.

Sylvia Rivera Law Project. https://srlp.org.
  SRLP works to improve access to social, health, and legal services for
  transgender and gender-variant people.

Transgender Law Center. https://transgenderlawcenter.org.
  Transgender Law Center advocates for transgender people through legal and
  policy change.

Trans Student Educational Resources. http://www.transstudent.org.
  TSER empowers transgender and gender-nonconforming students to improve
  their campus environments.

Trans Youth Equality Foundation. http://www.transyouthequality.org.
  Trans Youth Equality Foundation advocates for gender-variant youth and their
  families.

International

Gay & Lesbian Alliance Against Defamation (GLAAD). http://www.glaad.org.
  GLAAD works to improve LGBTQ representation in entertainment, news, and
  digital media.

Gender DynamiX. https://genderdynamix.org.za.
  Gender DynamiX is a human rights organization for trans and gender-
  nonconforming people in Africa.

Gender Identity Research and Education Society. http://www.gires.org.uk.
  GIRES provides education and training about trans issues and advocates for
  trans people in the UK.

Global Action for Trans Equality. https://transactivists.org.
  GATE facilitates local, national, and international trans activism.

International Lesbian, Gay, Bisexual, Trans and Intersex Association (ILGA)
  Europe. Trans Advocacy. http://www.ilga-europe.org/what-we-do/our-advocacy
  -work/trans-and-intersex/trans.

ILGA Europe advocates for LGBTI equality through litigation, public policy, and education. This page describes their trans-specific work.

Press for Change. http://www.pfc.org.uk.
   Press for Change is a UK legal organization focusing on transgender rights.

Scottish Transgender Alliance. http://www.scottishtrans.org.
   This Scotland-based organization works to improve social and legal equality for transgender people.

Transgender Europe. http://tgeu.org.
   Transgender Europe advocates for transgender human rights, promotes and disseminates research, and raises awareness and visibility.

Transgender Victoria. http://www.transgendervictoria.com.
   This Australian organization works to improve legal standing, public policy, and health and social services for trans and gender-diverse people.

SUPPORT ORGANIZATIONS

United States

Bay Area American Indians Two-Spirits (BAAITS). http://www.baaits.org.
   BAAITS is a community social and support organization for Two-Spirit people; they hold an annual powwow that attracts participants nationwide and beyond.

Gender Spectrum. https://www.genderspectrum.org.
   Gender Spectrum provides education and training for more inclusive schools, and also hosts social and support groups both in person and online.

Renaissance Education Association. http://www.ren.org.
   Renaissance Education Association is a network of local chapters that host support groups for transgender people.

International

The Beaumont Society. http://www.beaumontsociety.org.uk.
   The Beaumont Society provides social support through online discussion forums, a magazine, and educational resources.

The Gender Trust. http://gendertrust.org.uk.
   The Gender Trust is a membership-based mutual support organization that also provides workplace trainings and public education.

Gendered Intelligence. http://genderedintelligence.co.uk.
   Gendered Intelligence is a UK-based organization that hosts trans youth
support groups, one-on-one mentoring for trans students, and training and
education to families and schools.

Genderqueer Australia. http://www.genderqueer.org.au.
   Genderqueer Australia is a peer support group for genderqueer and trans
Australians; the website also includes educational resources and a gender-neutral
restroom locator.

Laura's Playground: Forums. http://www.lauras-playground.com/forums.
   Laura's Playground is a transgender resources website. The discussion forums
are organized by identities and issues; one is devoted to nonbinary identities, and
several others have nonbinary-relevant threads.

Mermaids UK. http://www.mermaidsuk.org.uk.
   Mermaids UK supports gender-diverse children and their families through a
helpline, e-mail support, online discussion forums, in-person support groups,
and weekend retreats.

Minus18. https://minus18.org.au.
   An Australian organization providing social support and peer mentoring for
LGBTI youth.

Tiwhanawhana. http://www.tiwhanawhana.com.
   Tiwhanawhana is a Wellington, New Zealand, social and support group for
takatāpui people (Māori people with diverse sexual and gender identities).

Trans Lifeline. http://www.translifeline.org.
   Trans Lifeline is a crisis line for transgender people, staffed by transgender
volunteers.

T-Vox. http://t-vox.org.
   An online resources hub and chatroom for transgender, nonbinary, and
intersex people.

Zoe Belle Gender Collective. http://www.zbgc.com.au.
   Zoe Belle Gender Collective is an Australian organization that provides
resources and support, including online support forums for trans and gender-
diverse youth.

NOTE

1. *Collins English Dictionary: Complete and Unabridged 2012 Digital Edition*, s.v.
"professional association" (New York: HarperCollins, 2012).

12

Online Resources

This chapter provides an annotated list of online resources relevant to non-binary gender identities. Resources are organized under the following types: apps, articles, blogs, commercial and informational websites, and forums and social media. Apps are mobile-friendly websites or iOS or Android applications that perform a specific function for the user, such as locating restrooms, doctors, or dates. Articles include both journalistic news articles and personal essays. Blogs are online personal journals that focus on politics, health, images, news, and personal life. Commercial and informational websites include merchandise and resource and education sites. Forums and social media are community-oriented platforms for people to connect and share. Twitter profiles are not included due to the enormous number of nonbinary people on Twitter; they are also very easy to locate by searching on Twitter or a browser. In addition, multimedia-focused online resources are not included because multimedia is the subject of chapter 13.

Resources were selected according to the following criteria: popularity, authority, accuracy, and currency. Popularity was measured in traffic, shares, and comments. Authority was judged by the identity of the author(s) or creator(s); either they are nonbinary themselves or have a record of being nonbinary allies. For informational resources, historical and cultural accuracy was important; if, for example, an article made a blanket statement about First Nations gender identities, that would be inaccurate and thus not included. In terms of currency, only resources that were updated recently were included; criteria was one week for social media, one month for blogs, and six months for static websites.

Online resources, particularly participatory social media, have a short life span. Web pages often don't survive one hundred days before they are taken down, rerouted, or archived.[1] Websites have an average life of two to five years.[2] Many social media pages have a brief burst of activity and then lapse when moderators become bored or busy with other things. Therefore, by the time the reader attempts to access any of the following resources, the link may be dead. To locate a resource with a broken link, try a browser search for "[article or site name] [author or creator name]."

APPS

GENDR. Developed by Mightybell in 2016. http://www.gendr.co.
  An iOS and Android dating app for the gender-variant and queer community.

My Trans Health. Founded by Kade Clark. http://mytranshealth.com.
  A mobile-friendly website to locate medical, mental health, legal, and crisis providers that are trans-competent.

Pronouns. Developed by Manu Gill for Minus 18. https://minus18.org.au/pronouns -app.
  An interactive pronoun practice app.

Quist. Founded by Sarah Prager in 2013. http://www.quistapp.com.
  An iOS and Android queer history app.

RAD Remedy. Founded by Eliot Colin, Rachel Hennessy, and Riley Johnson in 2014. http://radremedy.org.
  A mobile-friendly website for trans, gender-nonconforming, intersex, and queer folks to locate competent and respectful health providers.

REFUGE Restrooms. Created by Teagan Widmer in 2014. http://www .refugerestrooms.org.
  An iOS app that helps users locate gender-neutral and ADA-accessible restrooms.

ARTICLES

Allen, Joshua, and Alok Vaid-Menon. "SOFT: A Gender Non-Conforming Photo Series by Zara Julius." *Unlabelled*, April 18, 2017. http://www.unlabelledmagazine

.com/single-post/2017/04/18/SOFT-A-Gender-Non-conforming-Photo-Series-by-Zara-Julius.
  Photojournalism exploring gender nonconformity.

Anderson, West. "Transitioning While Nonbinary." *The Body Is Not an Apology*, October 17, 2016. https://thebodyisnotanapology.com/magazine/transitioning-while-non-binary.
  Personal essay about nonbinary transition.

âpihtawikosisân. "Language, Culture, and Two-Spirit Identity." âpihtawikosisân (blog), March 29, 2012. http://apihtawikosisan.com/2012/03/language-culture-and-two-spirit-identity.
  An in-depth discussion of indigenous gender roles and language used to discuss and define gender.

Ballou, Adrian. "10 Myths about Non-Binary People It's Time to Unlearn." Everyday Feminism. December 6, 2014. http://everydayfeminism.com/2014/12/myths-non-binary-people.
  An informational essay to educate cisgender people about nonbinary gender.

Beeby, Dean. "Federal Government Offers First Gender-Neutral Travel Document." CBC News. November 7, 2016. http://www.cbc.ca/news/politics/gender-neutral-trudeau-passport-travel-identification-male-female-1.3835344.
  Report on Canada's decision to accept gender-neutral documents from visitors.

Berendzen, Gerri. "AP Style for First Time Allows Use of They as Singular Pronoun." American Copy Editors Society. March 24, 2017. http://www.copydesk.org/blog/2017/03/24/ap-style-for-first-time-allows-use-of-they-as-singular-pronoun.
  Report on new entries in the Associated Press stylebook, including singular "they" as a gender-neutral pronoun.

Binkley, Collin. "He? She? Ze? Colleges Add Gender-Free Pronouns, Alter Policy." *Seattle Times*, September 18, 2015. http://www.seattletimes.com/nation-world/nation/he-she-ze-colleges-add-gender-free-pronouns-to-forms.
  Report on colleges and universities that offer gender-neutral pronouns during the registration process.

Blake, Heidi. "Briton Is Recognised as World's First Officially Genderless Person." *Telegraph*, March 15, 2010. http://www.telegraph.co.uk/news/newstopics/howaboutthat/7446850/Briton-is-recognised-as-worlds-first-officially-genderless-person.html.

Report on Norrie May-Welby, who was the first person to have a birth certificate list no specific gender.

Brooks, Jon. "A New Generation Overthrows Gender." NPR. May 2, 2017. http://www.npr.org/sections/health-shots/2017/05/02/526067768/a-new-generation-overthrows-gender.
Article about a nonbinary thirteen-year-old.

Burin, Margaret. "Kunghah: Sistergirls and Brotherboys Unite to Strengthen Spirits." ABC News. November 20, 2016. http://www.abc.net.au/news/2016-11-21/sistergirls-and-brotherboys-unite-to-strengthen-spirits/8040928.
Discusses gender-diverse Aboriginal identities in Australia.

Foden-Vencil, Kristian. "Neither Male nor Female: Oregon Resident Legally Recognized as Third Gender." NPR. June 17, 2016. http://www.npr.org/2016/06/17/482480188/neither-male-nor-female-oregon-resident-legally-recognized-as-third-gender.
Report on Jamie Shupe, the first person in the United States to obtain a legal gender change to nonbinary.

Godfrey, John. "Kiwis First to Officially Recognize Third Gender." *Nonprofit Quarterly*, July 20, 2015. https://nonprofitquarterly.org/2015/07/20/kiwis-first-to-officially-recognize-third-gender.
Report on New Zealand's third gender category in government data collection.

Graden, Kyle. "I Knew I Had a Non-Binary Gender Identity in Kindergarten." *Huffington Post*, March 15, 2017. http://www.huffingtonpost.com/entry/i-knew-i-had-a-non-binary-gender-identity-in-kindergarten_us_58c965a1e4b02c06957328f4.
A personal essay about nonbinary identity and the difficulties with restrooms and locker rooms in school.

Hamish. "The Disappearance of the Two-Spirit Traditions in Canada." *The Drummer's Revenge* (blog), August 11, 2009. https://thedrummersrevenge.wordpress.com/2009/08/11/the-disappearance-of-the-two-spirit-traditions-in-canada.
Historical essay about the impact of colonialism on Two-Spirit traditions in Canada.

Harris, Kathleen. "Canadian Passport Will Have New Marker for Transgender Travellers, Justice Minister Says." CBC News. May 4, 2017. http://www.cbc.ca/beta/news/politics/passport-transgender-c16-1.4099066.

Article discussing Canada's plan to implement a third gender option on passports.

Independent Lens. "A Map of Gender-Diverse Cultures." PBS. August 11, 2015. http://www.pbs.org/independentlens/content/two-spirits_map-html. Discussion of culturally specific gender identities; includes map.

Kennedy, Merrit. "Tinder Now Lets Users Identify as Genders Other Than Male or Female." NPR. November 15, 2016. http://www.npr.org/sections/thetwo-way/2016/11/15/502197048/tinder-now-lets-users-identify-as-genders-other-than-male-or-female. Report on dating app Tinder's expanded gender options.

Khaleeli, Homa. "Hijra: India's Third Gender Claims Its Place in Law." *Guardian*, April 16, 2014. https://www.theguardian.com/society/2014/apr/16/india-third-gender-claims-place-in-law. Report on India's government recognition of hijra as a third gender.

Lopez, German. "Gender Is Not Just Male or Female: 12 People across the Gender Spectrum Explain Why." Vox. September 28, 2016. http://www.vox.com/identities/2016/9/28/12660752/gender-binary-spectrum-queer. Interviews with twelve nonbinary people about their gender identities.

Masters, Jeffrey. "Asia Kate Dillon Talks Discovering the Word Non-Binary: 'I Cried.'" *Huffington Post*, April 13, 2017. http://www.huffingtonpost.com/entry/asia-kate-dillon-talks-discovering-the-word-non-binary_us_58ef1685e4b0156697224c7a. Discusses actor Asia Kate Dillon's gender identity as well as their being the first nonbinary person to play a nonbinary person on television.

Masters, Ryan. "Santa Cruz County Resident Is First Legally Nonbinary Person in California." *Santa Cruz Sentinel*, October 4, 2016. http://www.santacruzsentinel.com/article/NE/20161004/NEWS/161009844. Report on Sara Kelly Keenan's legal gender change to nonbinary.

Miller, Lisa. "The Trans-Everything CEO." *New York*, September 7, 2014. http://nymag.com/news/features/martine-rothblatt-transgender-ceo. Describes the life and work of Martine Rothblatt, a trans woman CEO who sees gender as a spectrum rather than a binary.

Minosh, Kai. "Why Non-Natives Appropriating 'Two-Spirit' Hurts." *Black Girl Dangerous* (blog), July 21, 2016. http://www.blackgirldangerous.org/2016/07/appropriating-two-spirit.

Personal essay about Two-Spirit identity and why non-Native appropriation is wrong.

Ngubane, Sandiso. "Gender Free: Sandiso Ngubane on Fashion as a Form of Fearless Self-Expression." *The Way of Us* (blog), December 1, 2016. https://superbalist. com/thewayofus/2016/01/12/gender-free/482.
    Discusses genderqueer self-representation through fashion choices.

O'Hara, Mary Emily. "Californian Becomes Second US Citizen Granted 'Non-Binary' Gender Status." NBC News. September 26, 2016. http://www.nbcnews. com/feature/nbc-out/californian-becomes-second-us-citizen-granted-non-binary-gender-status-n654611.
    Report on Sara Kelly Keenan, the first person in California to be legally recognized as nonbinary.

———. "Court Rulings Raise Number of Legally Non-Binary Californians to Seven." NBC News. February 16, 2017. http://www.nbcnews.com/feature/nbc -out/court-ruling-raises-number-legally-nonbinary-californians-seven-n721676.
    Report on the increase in nonbinary legal gender changes in California.

———. "Judge Grants Oregon Resident the Right to be Genderless." NBC News. March 23, 2017. http://www.nbcnews.com/feature/nbc-out/judge-grants-oregon-resident-right-be-genderless-n736971.
    Report on Patch, the first legally agender person in the United States.

———. "Movement for Third Gender Option 'Exploding' in U.S." NBC News. December 15, 2016. http://www.nbcnews.com/feature/nbc-out/movement-third-gender-option-exploding-u-s-n696446.
    Discusses the first legally designated nonbinary Americans' cases and experiences.

Okrent, Arika. "The *Washington Post* Style Guide Now Accepts Singular 'They.'" Mental Floss. December 10, 2015. http://mentalfloss.com/article/72262/ washington-post-style-guide-now-accepts-singular-they.
    Report on the updated gender-neutral pronoun guidelines in the *Washington Post* style guide.

Pietrasik, Tom. "India's Third Gender—In Pictures." *Guardian*, April 16, 2014. https://www.theguardian.com/society/gallery/2014/apr/16/india-third-gender-in -pictures.
    Photojournalism exploring hijra identity.

Pullin, Zachary. "Two Spirit: The Story of a Movement Unfolds." *Native Peoples Magazine*, May–June 2014. http://www.nativepeoples.com/Native-Peoples/May -June-2014/Two-Spirit-The-Story-of-a-Movement-Unfolds.
   A historical essay about Two-Spirit history and traditions, with personal anecdotes.

Rivas, Jorge. "Native Americans Talk Gender Identity at a 'Two-Spirit' Powwow." Fusion. February 9, 2015. http://fusion.net/story/46014/native-americans-talk-gender-identity-at-a-two-spirit-powwow.
   Report on the Bay Area American Indian Two-Spirit (BAAITS) powwow.

Scolari, Rosalie. "Genderqueer Feminist Porn Star: Jiz Lee." The Scavenger. August 14, 2010. http://www.thescavenger.net/sex-gender-sexuality-diversity-archived/65-queer/393-genderqueer-feminist-porn-star-jiz-lee-74398.html.
   An interview with genderqueer adult actor Jiz Lee.

Segal, Corinne. "In California, Non-Binary Activists Pushing for ID Options Reach New Frontier." PBS NewsHour. October 23, 2016. http://www.pbs.org/newshour/updates/nonbinary-intersex-california.
   Report on nonbinary and intersex legal gender changes in California.

Shackelford, Ashleigh. "Why I'm Nonbinary but Don't Use 'They/Them.'" *Wear Your Voice: Intersectional Feminist Media*, July 7, 2016. http://wearyourvoicemag.com/identities/why-im-nonbinary-but-dont-use-theythem.
   Personal essay by a Black fat DFAB nonbinary person about gender identity and pronouns.

Shupe, Jamie. "I Am the First Official Genderless Person in the United States." *Guardian*, June 16, 2016. https://www.theguardian.com/commentisfree/2016/jun/16/i-am-first-official-genderless-person-united-states.
   Personal essay by Jamie Shupe about their legal gender change.

Slovic, Beth. "Portland State University Moves beyond Male and Female: Students Can Now Identify as Agender, Genderqueer or Nonbinary." *Willamette Week*, November 8, 2016. http://www.wweek.com/news/2016/10/15/portland-state -university-moves-beyond-male-and-female.
   Report on expanded gender options for PSU students.

Sterritt, Angela. "Indigenous Languages Recognize Gender States Not Even Named in English." *Globe and Mail*, March 10, 2016. https://beta.theglobeandmail.com/life/health-and-fitness/health/indigenous-languages-recognize-gender-states-not -even-named-in-english/article29130778.

Explores traditional indigenous gender identities and language used to discuss gender.

Talusan, Meredith. "Telling Trans Stories beyond 'Born in the Wrong Body.'" BuzzFeed. May 14, 2016. https://www.buzzfeed.com/meredithtalusan/telling-trans-stories-beyond-born-in-the-wrong-body.
    A collaborative group interview about gender identity, dysphoria, and the "wrong body" model.

Thomas, Jacob J. "What It's Like to Come Out as Gay, Then Come Out as Nonbinary." BuzzFeed. December 9, 2016. https://www.buzzfeed.com/jacobjthomas/coming-out-as-nonbinary.
    A personal essay about the joys and hardships of coming out.

Tobia, Jacob. "First Legal Non-Binary Person in the US: 'I Didn't Just Reset the Parameters, I Got Rid of Them.'" Out, June 20, 2016. http://www.out.com/out-exclusives/2016/6/20/first-legal-non-binary-person-us-i-didnt-just-reset-parameters-i-got-rid.
    An interview with nonbinary trailblazer Jamie Shupe.

Tramontana, Mary Katharine. "Gender Fuck." The New Inquiry. October 30, 2015. http://thenewinquiry.com/features/gender-fuck.
    An interview with genderqueer adult actor Jiz Lee.

Tsjeng, Zing. "Teens These Days Are Queer AF, New Study Says." Broadly, March 10, 2016. https://broadly.vice.com/en_us/article/teens-these-days-are-queer-af-new-study-says.
    Report on a survey of generation Z youth and their attitudes toward gender.

Urquhart, Evan. "What the Heck Is Genderqueer?" Slate, March 24, 2015. http://www.slate.com/blogs/outward/2015/03/24/genderqueer_what_does_it_mean_and_where_does_it_come_from.html.
    An informational essay about genderqueer identities.

Wilchins, Riki. "Op-Ed: Transgender Dinosaurs and the Rise of the Genderqueers." Advocate, December 6, 2012. http://www.advocate.com/commentary/riki-wilchins/2012/12/06/transgender-dinosaurs-and-rise-genderqueers.
    Personal essay about changing ideas about transgender identities and experiences.

Williams, Walter L. "The 'Two-Spirit' People of Indigenous North Americans." Guardian, October 11, 2010. https://www.theguardian.com/music/2010/oct/11/two-spirit-people-north-america.

Historical essay about indigenous sexual and gender diversity.

Williamson, Lucy. "In Pictures: Indonesia's Waria." BBC News. 2008. http://news.bbc.
co.uk/2/shared/spl/hi/picture_gallery/08/asia_pac_indonesia0s_waria/html/1.stm.
Photojournalism exploring waria identity.

Wilson, Alexandria. "Two-Spirit People, Body Sovereignty and Gender
Self-Determination." *Red Rising Magazine*, September 21, 2015. http://
redrisingmagazine.ca/two-spirit-people-body-sovereignty-and-gender-self
-determination.
Historical essay about Two-Spirit identities and ways in which homophobia,
transphobia, and misogyny have entered indigenous communities and impacted
Two-Spirit traditions.

Ziyad, Hari. "What I Learned from Being Non-Binary While Still Being Perceived
as a Man." *Everyday Feminism*, February 5, 2016. http://everydayfeminism.
com/2016/02/genderqueer-amab-experience.
A personal essay about being genderqueer and assigned male at birth.

BLOGS

Bornstein, Kate. *Kate Bornstein Is a Queer and Pleasant Danger—This Is Her Blog*.
http://katebornstein.typepad.com
Personal blog of famous writer and activist Kate Bornstein; includes tour dates.

Brown, Lydia X. Z. *Autistic Hoya*. http://www.autistichoya.com.
Political blog by an autistic nonbinary person of color.

Cory. *Fuck Yeah Monster Enbies*. http://fuckyeahmonsterenbies.tumblr.com.
Images of canon and noncanon nonbinary paranormal creatures.

Devin. *Transparent Gender*. http://www.transparentgender.com.
Transition blog of an androgynous person of color.

Dopp, Sarah (Founder). *Genderfork: Beauty in Ambiguity*. http://genderfork.com.
A moderated blog showcasing nonbinary images, videos, and news.

Fairy JerBear. *Fairy JerBear's Queer/Trans Musings from the City Different—Santa
Fe, NM*. https://jerbearinsantafe.wordpress.com.
Personal and news blog by an agender trans femme person.

Faucette, Avory. *Radically Queer: Learn, Question, Make Change*. https://
radicallyqueer.wordpress.com.
Personal blog of a queer legal activist.

Gethen, Pax Ahimsa. *The Funcrunch Files.* http://funcrunch.org/blog.
    Personal blog of a Black queer agender trans male.

Leonard, Selissa. *Holding Patterns and High Tea.* https://holdingpatternsandhightea.
    wordpress.com.
    Personal blog by a disabled nonbinary person.

Lodge, Cassian. *The Genderqueer Activist.* http://mxactivist.tumblr.com.
    An activism and news blog focusing on genderqueer issues.

McCann, Hannah. *BINARYTHIS.* https://binarythis.com.
    A gender studies blog that explores popular culture.

Micah. *Neutrois Nonsense: An Intimate Exploration of Identity and Life Wisdom
    beyond the Gender Binary.* https://neutrois.me.
    Combination transition blog and community guest post blog.

Nkozi, max, no, and Danny (Moderators). *Ask a Nonbinary.* http://askanonbinary
    .tumblr.com.
    A blog for people to submit questions about nonbinary identity.

Piepzna-Samarasinha, Leah Lakshmi. *Brown Star Girl.* http://www.brownstargirl.org.
    Personal blog and website of a nonbinary disabled poet and performance artist
    of color.

River, Arleigh, Avery, and Kass (Admins). *2 Cute 2 Be Cis.* http://nonbinarycuties
    .tumblr.com.
    A nonbinary selfie-sharing blog.

Shackelford, Ashleigh. *Black Fat Femme.* http://blackfatfemme.com.
    Personal blog of a Black hood feminist.

Smashing the Binary. http://smashingthebinary.tumblr.com.
    A photo and image blog celebrating nonbinary identities.

smith, s. e. *This Ain't Livin'.* http://meloukhia.net.
    Personal website of a disabled nonbinary writer and activist.

What the Heck Gender Am I? http://what-the-heck-gender-am-i.tumblr.com.
    A blog for people to query the identity term that best matches their gender.
    Includes lists of gender terms.

COMMERCIAL AND INFORMATIONAL WEBSITES

Abernathey, Marti. International Transgender Day of Remembrance. https://tdor
    .info.

An annual list memorializing victims who died due to anti-transgender violence; updated in November for the Trans Day of Remembrance.

Bond, Justin Vivian. Justin Vivian Bond. http://www.justinvivianbond.com.
Personal and commercial website of transgenre artist Mx Justin Vivian Bond.

Dowling, Aydian (Creator). Point 5cc: International Transgender Clothing Company. Established in 2011. http://point5cc.com.
Clothing created for the trans and gender-nonconforming community; a percentage of proceeds goes to binders and breast forms for trans people in need.

failedslacker. Pronoun Dressing Room. http://www.pronouns.failedslacker.com.
An interactive pronoun practice website.

Ford, Tyler. My Friend Tyler. http://myfriendtyler.com.
Personal and commercial website of agender social media star Tyler Ford.

Forward Together. Trans Day of Resilience. Established in 2015. http://tdor.co.
Celebrates trans and gender-diverse communities of color through art.

Geeks OUT. Established in 2010. http://geeksout.org.
News, popular culture analysis, and events for the LGBTQ geek community.

Mic Network. Unerased: Counting Transgender Lives. https://mic.com/unerased.
Database counting transgender murders since 2010.

Native OUT. http://nativeout.com.
Two-Spirit news, multimedia, and resources.

Oram, Sonny (Founder). Qwear. http://www.qwearfashion.com.
Fashion website focusing on the LGBTQ community, with special attention to people of color, fat people, femmes, and others often erased in the community.

Patriquin, Lane (Creator). Life outside the Binary: Nonbinary Transgender Information Centre. http://lifeoutsidethebinary.com.
A wide variety of nonbinary resources, including news, a glossary, and information about pronouns, coming out, and transition.

Practice with Pronouns. http://www.practicewithpronouns.com.
An interactive pronoun practice website.

Roxie, Marilyn. Genderqueer and Non-Binary Identities. http://genderqueerid .com.
Nonbinary resource site focusing on history, media, news, health, and more. Blog no longer updated.

Shaw, Adrienne. LGBTQ Video Game Archive. https://lgbtqgamearchive.com.
A curated collection of video games with LGBTQ content.

Stringer, JAC. Midwest GenderQueer. http://midwestgenderqueer.com.
Personal and commercial website for genderqueer activist and educator JAC
Stringer.

Tobia, Jacob. Jacob Tobia: Speaker—Writer—Advocate. http://www.jacobtobia.com.
Personal and commercial website for nonbinary performer and internet
personality Jacob Tobia.

Toi. Afro-Genderqueer. http://www.afrogenderqueer.com.
Personal and commercial website for genderqueer philosophactivist Toi.

Trans Cafe. http://www.trans.cafe.
A nonbinary-inclusive trans news and resources website; focuses on health,
identity, lifestyle, relationships, career, and crisis.

Trans Respect versus Transphobia Worldwide. http://transrespect.org.
Monitors homicides of transgender and gender-diverse people worldwide,
maps legal and social status changes of trans people worldwide, and surveys trans
social experiences.

Vita, Anita Dolce (Owner, Creative Director, and Editor-in-Chief). DapperQ:
Transgressing Men's Fashion. Established 2009. http://www.dapperq.com.
Menswear and style website for transmasculine people and butch women.

Zagria. A Gender Variance Who's Who. http://zagria.blogspot.com.
A trans history and biography website.

FORUMS AND SOCIAL MEDIA

Adorable Agender Angels. https://www.facebook.com/groups/1141689869254977.
A Facebook group focused on support for agender people.

Alex (glenyan) and Sam (samfeasor) (Moderators). The Genderqueer Community.
http://genderqueer.livejournal.com.
A forum for genderqueer people and their friends, families, and significant
others.

Androgynes: Living beyond Gender. Yahoo! Groups. https://groups.yahoo.com/neo/
groups/androgynes/info.
An e-mail forum for androgynes.

Asexual Visibility & Education Network (AVEN). Gender Discussion. http://www
.asexuality.org/en/forum/57-gender-discussion.
   A forum for discussing trans, nonbinary, and gender-nonconforming topics.

BronyHoney (Moderator). NonBinary. https://www.reddit.com/r/NonBinary.
   A forum for discussing nonbinary identities and experiences.

FTM and AFAB Nonbinary. https://www.facebook.com/groups/5684495199
14806.
   Support group for trans men and AFAB nonbinary people.

FTM MTF NB Help & Support. https://www.facebook.com/
groups/187360438336510.
   A Facebook group for the entire trans spectrum, focused on social support and
   selling and donating transition-related items.

Genderfluid Rocks. https://www.facebook.com/Genderfluidrocks.
   A Facebook page that shares memes and articles relating to trans and
   nonbinary identities.

Genderqueer Gengar. https://www.facebook.com/genderqueergengar.
   A Facebook meme page focusing on transgender and genderqueer humor.

Genderqueer Mercury. https://www.facebook.com/genderqueermercurythesjw.
   A Facebook meme page focusing on transgender and genderqueer humor.

NB Physical Transition Discussion Group. https://www.facebook.com/
groups/1051917641515383.
   A Facebook group for discussion and support around nonbinary transition.

The Non-Binary Collective. https://www.facebook.com/thenonbinarycollective.
   A Facebook page focusing on news, information, resources, and support for
   nonbinary people.

Non-Binary Gender Pride. https://www.facebook.com/groups/160116852020
9978.
   A Facebook group focused on social support for nonbinary people.

Non-Binary Non-Monogamy. https://www.facebook.com/
groups/1725178407808885.
   Support group for nonmonogamous nonbinary people.

Nonbinary POC Only! https://www.facebook.com/groups/nonbinarypoconly.
   Support group for nonbinary people of color.

Non-Binary Pregnancy and Parenting Support. https://www.facebook.com/
groups/1117781851639369.
   Support group for nonbinary parents.

Non-Binary Support. https://www.facebook.com/groups/405942152906314.
   A Facebook group focused on social support for nonbinary people.

#relatable #trans #n #enby #probZ. https://www.facebook.com/
groups/1114381241915174.
   A Facebook group for trans and nonbinary people to share memes and support
one another.

SaturnMoth (Moderator). Androgyny. https://www.reddit.com/r/androgyny.
   A forum for discussing androgynous identities and experiences.

A Supportive Cafe the Non-Binary Way. https://www.facebook.com/
groups/316809975345505.
   A Facebook group for nonbinary people focused on social support and trading
clothing and transition-related items.

tapioca_fetish, trimalchio-worktime, and CedarWolf (Moderators). Genderfluid.
https://www.reddit.com/r/genderfluid.
   A forum for discussing genderfluid identities and experiences.

TransGender-GenderQueer. https://www.facebook.com/groups/213396725394276.
   Support group for transgender and genderqueer people.

ZorbaTHut (Moderator). Agender. https://www.reddit.com/r/agender.
   A forum for discussing agender identities and experiences.

NOTES

1. Mike Ashenfelder, "The Average Lifespan of a Webpage," *The Signal* (blog),
November 8, 2011, https://blogs.loc.gov/thesignal/2011/11/the-average-lifespan-of
-a-webpage.

2. Andy Crestodina, "Website Lifespan and You," *Orbit Media* (blog), March 2010,
https://www.orbitmedia.com/blog/website-lifespan-and-you.

13

Multimedia

This chapter provides an annotated bibliography of multimedia made by nonbinary people and/or with nonbinary content, separated into "Visual Media," "Performing Media," and "Multidisciplinary Media." Visual media includes chapbooks and zines; comics, including online and print; and painting, drawing, and photography. Performing media includes music, radio, and theatre. Multidisciplinary media includes film and television, both traditional and online; games for all platforms, including online; multigenre art; and performance art. Many of these resources emerged during the queercore movement, a postpunk subgenre of music and associated DIY cultural production; chapbooks and zines in particular. Chapbooks and zines are small self-published paperback booklets; chapbooks generally contain poetry or fiction, and zines can contain creative nonfiction, poetry, art, comics, and other writing and image genres. Perzines are a subtype of zine that focus on autobiographical material.

VISUAL MEDIA

Chapbooks and Zines

Cannibal, Clementine. *Licking Stars off Ceilings*. 2005–2012.
    A twenty-four-issue perzine exploring riot grrrl, sexuality, gender, and mental illness.

Davis, Vaginal. *Crude*. 1976–1980. http://vaginaldavis.com/zine.shtml.
    One of the zines that started the queercore movement.

——. *Dowager*. 1972–1975. http://vaginaldavis.com/zine.shtml.
    One of the zines that started the queercore movement.

——. *Fertile La Toyah Jackson*. 1982–1991. http://vaginaldavis.com/zine.shtml.
    One of the zines that started the queercore movement.

——. *Shrimp*. 1993. http://vaginaldavis.com/zine.shtml.
    Queercore zine.

——. *Sucker*. 1995–1997. http://vaginaldavis.com/zine.shtml.
    Queercore zine.

——. *Yes, Ms. Davis*. 1994. http://vaginaldavis.com/zine.shtml.
    Queercore zine.

Jackson, Khari, and Malcolm Shanks. *Decolonizing Gender: A Curriculum*. 2017.
    https://issuu.com/jkharij/docs/decolonizing_gender_zine_v2.compres.
    A zine with instructions on how to facilitate a decolonizing gender workshop.

Morrigan, Clementine. *Seawitch*. ca. 2015.
    A zine series exploring sobriety, trauma, gender, and polyamory.

Piepzna-Samarasinha, Leah Lakshmi. *Femme Shark Communique*. ca .2008.
    A manifesto uplifting femmes.

Robo, Aung. *The Non-Binary Coloring Book*. New Santa Fe, IN: Self-published,
    2016. http://www.aungrobo.us/nbcb.
    Coloring book celebrating nonbinary bodies.

Soto, Christopher (a.k.a. Loma). *Sad Girl Poems*. http://siblingrivalrypress.bigcartel
    .com/product/sad-girl-poems-by-christopher-soto.
    Poetry chapbook by a queer Latin@ punk.

Vaid-Menon, Alok. *Femme in Public*. 2017. https://www.alokvmenon.com/store/
    fipchapbook.
    Poetry chapbook by performance artist and writer Alok Vaid-Menon.

Comics

AK. *Full-Spectrum Therapy*. http://fst.smackjeeves.com.
    A queer supernatural horror comic.

Akamatsu, Ken. *UQ Holder!* New York: Kodansha Comics USA, 2013–present.
Supernatural manga with a society of demihumans whose children are born
sexless and choose a gender at age sixteen.

Arakawa, Hiromu. *Fullmetal Alchemist*. Japan: Square Enix, 2001–2010.
A twenty-seven-volume science fiction manga series; character Envy is genderless.

C., Taylor. *Monsterkind*. 2012–present. http://monsterkind.enenkay.com.
A fantasy web comic about a human social worker helping monsters; character
Louise Spence is nonbinary.

Claremont, Chris, and Dwayne Turner. *Sovereign Seven*. New York: DC Comics,
1995–1998.
Superhero series that includes a character with ambiguous gender.

Costa, Mari. *Peritale*. 2015–present. http://www.peritale.com.
A fantasy web comic; one fairy character is nonbinary.

DiDomenick, Jocelyn Samara. *Rain LGBT*. 2010–present. http://rainlgbt.
smackjeeves.com.
Slice-of-life web comic about a trans girl; includes a genderfluid character.

Edwards, Dylan. *Valley of the Silk Sky*. 2015–present. http://valleyofthesilksky
.tumblr.com.
A queer YA science fiction web comic.

Fedoruk, Kadi. *Blindsprings*. http://www.blindsprings.com.
A web comic exploring coming-of-age with a magical theme; includes several
nonbinary characters.

Furedi, Chelsey. *Rock and Riot*. http://rockandriotcomic.com.
A web comic about two rival teen gangs set in the 1950s; includes several
nonbinary characters.

Gaiman, Neil. *The Sandman*. New York: DC Comics, 1989–present.
Long-running monthly comic about dreams, stories, and choices. Character
Desire is simultaneously genderless and all genders.

Gil, Joamette (Editor). *Power & Magic: The Queer Witch Comics Anthology*.
Portland, OR: Power & Magic, 2016.
A collection of comics focusing on queer witches of color.

Gisele. *Star Trip*. 2013–present. http://startripcomic.com.
A space adventure web comic with several nonbinary characters.

Hagio, Moto. *They Were Eleven*. Japan: Shogakukan, 1975.
    A science fiction manga with a character of indeterminate gender.

Halla, Valerie. *Goodbye to Halos*. 2015–present. http://www.goodbyetohalos.com.
    A queer fantasy web comic.

Heimpel, Noel Arthur. *Ignition Zero*. 2011–2016. http://ignitionzero.com.
    An urban fantasy web comic with queer characters.

Howard, Abby. *The Last Halloween*. http://www.last-halloween.com.
    A horror web comic about a post–monster uprising. Mona's parent is
    nonbinary, as are some monsters.

Labelle, Sophie. *The Assignment*. 2016. https://www.etsy.com/shop/assignedmale.
    Comics about trans and gender-nonconforming youth.

——. *Dating Tips for Trans and Queer Weirdos*. 2017. https://www.etsy.com/shop/
    assignedmale.
    Comics about trans and gender-nonconforming youth.

——. *Dear Cis People*. 2015. https://www.etsy.com/shop/assignedmale.
    Comics about trans and gender-nonconforming youth.

——. *Gender Euphoria*. 2015. https://www.etsy.com/shop/assignedmale.
    Comics about trans and gender-nonconforming youth.

——. *The Genderific Coloring Book*. ND. https://www.etsy.com/shop/assignedmale.
    Comics about trans and gender-nonconforming youth.

——. *Gender Liberation and Warm Fuzzies*. 2016. https://www.etsy.com/shop/
    assignedmale.
    Comics about trans and gender-nonconforming youth.

——. *Nail Polish*. 2016. https://www.etsy.com/shop/assignedmale.
    Comics about trans and gender-nonconforming youth.

——. *Ultra Chicken Fun-Time Super Special*. 2017. https://www.etsy.com/shop/
    assignedmale.
    Comics about trans and gender-nonconforming youth.

Lee, Adrien. *White Noise*. 2011–present. http://www.white-noise-comic.com.
    A supernatural web comic with a character that uses ne/nem/nir pronouns.

Lehkonen, Hanna-Pirita. *The Immortal Nerd*. 2015–present. http://www.webtoons
    .com/en/comedy/immortal-nerd/list?title_no=579.

Science fiction web comic with a nonbinary transfeminine main character.

Lim, Elisha. *100 Crushes*. Toronto: Koyama, 2014.
Compilation of five years of work by a genderqueer artist.

Merey, Ilike. *a + e 4ever*. Maple Shade, NJ: Lethe, 2011.
A tender graphic novel about a genderqueer friendship.

Monster, Sfé. *Eth's Skin*. 2014–present. http://www.eths-skin.com.
Fantasy series about a nonbinary fisherperson who accidentally takes a selkie skin.

——. *Kyle and Atticus*. 2011–2013. http://kyleandatticus.tumblr.com.
Genderqueer comic about a kid named Kyle and their best friend Atticus.

Morrison, Zack. *Paranatural*. 2011–present. http://www.paranatural.net.
Web comic about superpowered middle schoolers; character RJ is nonbinary.

Nagai, Go. *Mazinger Z*. Tokyo: Shueisha, 1972–1973; Kodansha, 1973–1974.
A mecha manga series that includes a half-man, half-woman character.

Nations, Erin. http://erin-nations.tumblr.com.
Nonbinary trans man comic artist.

Parker, Ethan. *Ethan Draws Stuff*. http://ethandrawsstuff.tumblr.com.
An online comic by a Black nonbinary illustrator.

Ptah, Erin. *But I'm a Cat Person*. 2011–present. http://erinptah.com/catperson.
Fantasy web comic that includes a bigender character.

R., Carro. *ChRIStIS*. 2011–present. http://christis-comic.tumblr.com.
Web comic about a teenage half angel; several characters are nonbinary.

Ritchie, Ronnie. *GQutie!* 2014–present. http://gqutiecomics.com.
Autobiographical web comic by a genderqueer person.

Robin, Taylor. *Never Satisfied*. 2015–present. http://www.neversatisfiedcomic.com.
Web comic about a magician's apprentice; includes several nonbinary characters.

Robot Hugs. 2009–present. http://www.robot-hugs.com.
Partly autobiographical web comic by a nonbinary person.

Rufin, Catalina. *The Fairy Warriors*. 2016–present. http://cargocollective.com/catalinarufin.

Web and print comic about fairies; includes several nonbinary characters.

Sol. *Psychonaut*. 2016. https://tapastic.com/series/Psychonaut.
A web comic about a genderqueer alien.

Stevenson, Noelle, Grace Ellis, Shannon Watters, and Brooke A. Allen. *Lumberjanes*. Los Angeles: Boom! Studios, 2014–present.
A comic book series about a group of friends at a supernatural camp; includes trans and genderqueer characters.

Stiffler, A., and K. Copeland. *Chaoslife*. 2011–present. http://chaoslife.findchaos.com.
Semiautobiographical web comic about an agender person and their girlfriend.

Takahashi, Rumiko (Writer). *Ranma ½*. Japan: Shogakukan, 1987–1996.
A thirty-eight-volume manga series about a boy who transforms into a girl every time he is splashed with cold water.

Thompson, Craig. *Habibi*. New York: Pantheon, 2011.
Graphic novel about two former slaves growing up together; includes hijra periphery characters.

Togashi, Yoshihiro. *Hunter X Hunter*. Japan: Shueisha, 1998–present.
A manga series about a boy training to become a hunter; includes a genderless chimera character.

Vaughan, Brian K., and Adrian Alphona. *Runaways*. New York: Marvel Comics, 2003–2009.
Comic series about superpowered teenagers; includes a shapeshifter character who can gender shift.

Wolf, Tikva. *Kimchi Cuddles*. 2013–present. http://kimchicuddles.com.
Web comic exploring poly, queer, and genderqueer identities.

Yuki, Kaori. *Angel Sanctuary*. San Francisco: Viz Media, 2004–2007.
Fantasy manga series about an angel journeying to reunite with his dead sister; includes several characters that are ambiguously gendered or two souls sharing one body.

Painting, Drawing, and Photography

Baier, J. Jackie. http://fotografie.jackiebaier.de.
Photographer specializing in gender-nonconforming nightlife.

Bazant, Micah. Micah Bazant: Making Social Change Look Irresistible. https://www
.micahbazant.com.
  Illustrator focusing on trans and POC representation.

Deragon, Sarah. The Identity Project. http://www.identityprojectsf.com.
  Photo project exploring gender and sexuality.

Grosland, Em. http://www.emgrosland.com.
  Visual art by a pangender person.

Harper, Rhys. Transcending Gender Project. http://www.transcending
gender.org.
  Photo project exploring gender.

Harris, Amanda Arkansassy. Femme Space. http://www.femmespace.net.
  Photo project uplifting femme identities.

Lewis, Jamal T. http://www.jamaltlewis.com/photography.
  Jamal T. Lewis is a multidisciplinary artist exploring race, class, gender, and
  sexuality.

McDaniel, Shoog. Shoog McD (@shooglet). https://www.instagram.com/shooglet.
  Photography by a Southern queer nonbinary fat photographer and artist.

Muñoz, Sal. FEMME. http://www.salmunoz.com/femme.html.
  Photo project celebrating femmes of all identities.

Philomene, Laurence. http://www.laurencephilomene.com.
  Portraits of gender-variant people.

Roxie, Marilyn. http://marilynroxie.com.
  Marilyn Roxie is a photographer and digital artist focusing on androgyny and
  queer culture.

Sleepless, Eli. https://www.instagram.com/elisleepless.
  Photography by a genderqueer Latinx.

Soper, Basil Vaughn, and Johanna C. Case. Transilient. http://www.wearetransi
lient.com.
  A photography and interview project documenting trans and gender-
  nonconforming people.

Vita, Anita Dolce. Hi Femme! https://www.instagram.com/hifemme.
  A femme and POC visibility project.

Volcano, Del LaGrace. http://www.dellagracevolcano.com.
   Photographer exploring genderqueerness.

PERFORMING MEDIA
Music

Adorable, Sarah, and Cindy Wonderful. Scream Club. https://screamclub.band
   camp.com.
   Genderqueer hip-hop.

Anohni. http://anohni.com.
   Former lead singer of Antony and the Johnsons.

Bailey, Shamir. https://www.youtube.com/channel/
   UCRsYhNKO6Mp62WVDE0W1ZuQ.
   Genderqueer singer-songwriter.

Barton Stink, Heidi. https://bartonstink.bandcamp.com.
   Genderqueer homo-hop artist.

Blanco, Mykki. http://mykkiblancoworld.com.
   Genderqueer rapper.

Blazes, Johnny. *Johnny Blazes and the Pretty Boys.* http://johnnyblazes.com.
   Vaudeville covers with a genderqueer front person.

Bond, Justin Vivian. https://justinvivianbond.bandcamp.com.
   Nonbinary singer-songwriter.

Boucher, Claire Elise. Grimes. http://www.grimesmusic.com.
   A synth-pop artist who identifies as gender neutral.

Breedlove, Lynn. Tribe 8. 1991–2005.
   One of the first queercore bands. Lynn Breedlove, genderqueer drummer, was a
   founding member.

Bruce, Liv, and Ben Hopkins. PWR BTTM. https://pwrbttm.bandcamp.com.
   Queer garage punk.

Brynn, Tannrr, Camille, and Erik. Slouch. https://sloucholympia.bandcamp.com.
   Queer punk band.

Castricum, Simona. https://soundcloud.com/simonacastricum.
   Electronic music exploring gender nonconformity.

Cox, Rachel Maria. https://rachelmariacox.bandcamp.com.
 Indie music by a nonbinary singer-songwriter.

Cyrus, Miley Ray. https://www.mileycyrus.com.
 Pop singer who doesn't identify as male or female.

Davis, Melo, Em Boltz, and Ro Samarth. MALLRAT. https://mallrat.bandcamp.com.
 Emo punk music about gender, race, and trauma.

Davis, Vaginal. The Afro Sisters. http://www.vaginaldavis.com/disc.shtml.
 Art pop with a genderqueer front person.

———. Black Fag. http://www.vaginaldavis.com/disc.shtml.
 Art punk with a genderqueer front person.

———. !Cholita! The Female Menudo. http://www.vaginaldavis.com/disc.shtml.
 Art pop with a genderqueer front person.

———. Pedro, Muriel & Esther. http://www.vaginaldavis.com/disc.shtml.
 Art punk with a genderqueer front person.

Denitzio, Lauren. Worriers. https://worriers.bandcamp.com.
 Melodic punk with a nonbinary front person.

Ganito, Mars, and Joe McCann. Aye Nako. https://ayenako.org.
 Queer punk band.

Greer, Evan. http://evangreer.org.
 Genderqueer singer-songwriter.

Imaginary Hockey League. https://imaginaryhockeyleague.bandcamp.com.
 Nonbinary emo music.

José, Mabel, and Rory. Anybody but the Cops. https://anybodybutthecops.
 bandcamp.com.
 Queer punk band.

Lester, CN. http://www.cnlester.com.
 Nonbinary singer-songwriter.

Lomes. Pigeon Pit. https://pigeonpit.bandcamp.com.
 Pop punk by an agender musician.

Lydia and Francis. *Different Devils*. https://soundcloud.com/differentdevils.
 Queercore band.

Mama Alto. http://www.mamaalto.com.
    Nonbinary femme person of color who sings jazz and cabaret.

M(x)Blouse. https://www.mxblouselive.com.
    Queer nonbinary rapper.

Ngcobo, Siya. UMLILO. https://soundcloud.com/umlilosa.
    Electronic music by the "future kwaai" diva Umlilo.

PizzaCupcake and FXBoi. GAYmous. https://gaymous.bandcamp.com.
    Queer synth-pop.

P-Orridge, Genesis Breyer. *Psychic TV*. https://myspace.com/ptv3.
    Industrial band with a nonbinary member.

———. *Throbbing Gristle*. http://www.throbbing-gristle.com.
    Industrial band with a nonbinary member.

Pureka, Chris. https://www.chrispureka.com.
    Genderqueer folk musician.

Register, Kym, Will Hackney, Brad Cook, Phil Cook, Matt McCaughan, and Jon
    Ashley. Loamlands. https://loamlands.bandcamp.com.
    Indie folk with a genderqueer front person.

Samson, JD. Le Tigre. https://www.facebook.com/LeTigreWorld.
    An electroclash band with a nonbinary member.

———. MEN. https://menmakemusic.bandcamp.com.
    Dance music with a nonbinary band member.

Shanholtzer-Dvorak, Danielle. The World Is a Beautiful Place and I Am No Longer
    Afraid to Die. http://theworldis.bandcamp.com.
    Emo band with a nonbinary front person.

Sol Patches. https://soundcloud.com/solpatches.
    Queer hip-hop.

Spoon, Rae. http://www.raespoon.com.
    Indie folk by a nonbinary person.

Sumner, Eliot. http://eliotsumnerofficialmusic.tumblr.com.
    A genderqueer singer-songwriter.

Sylvae, Viridian. Hagazussa. https://hagazussa.bandcamp.com.

Black metal by a nonbinary trans woman.

Unger-Weiss, Izabella. Izzy and the Chimera. https://izzyandthechimera.band
camp.com.
Folk-pop by a nonbinary trans woman.

Way, Gerard. My Chemical Romance. https://www.youtube.com/user/
mychemicalromance.
Rock band with a lead vocalist who identifies with both genders.

Radio

Arring, Caleb (Host). *Beyond Gender Podcast*. http://www.beyondgenderpod.com.
A weekly podcast exploring trans identities.

Breedlove, Lynn. *The Unka Lynnee & Aunty Cindy Show*. 2005–2007. http://
unkalynnee.blogspot.com.
Radio show hosted by genderqueer icon Lynn Breedlove.

Carpenter, Luzviminda Uzuri (Host). *#LuluNation + #SadBoisHypeClub*. 2014–
2015. https://www.mixcloud.com/discover/lulunation%2Bsadboishypeclub.
A podcast interviewing queer and trans people of color.

Du Bois, Jim (Host). "Transgender History Project at the U of M." *Access
Minnesota*, February 15, 2015. http://www.accessminnesotaonline.
com/2015/02/11/transgender-history-project-at-the-u-of-m.
A radio show talking about the history of the Tretter Collection and a new
grant to study transgender history in the upper Midwest.

Du Bois, Jim (Host). "Transgender Politics." *Access Minnesota*, April 24, 2016.
http://www.accessminnesotaonline.com/2016/04/20/transgender-politics.
A radio show focusing on transgender and gender-nonconforming rights in
relation to bathroom politics.

Fink, Joseph, and Jeffrey Cranor (Writers). *Welcome to Nightvale*. 2012–present.
http://www.welcometonightvale.com.
A supernatural podcast narrated by Cecil Baldwin; character Sheriff Sam uses
gender-neutral pronouns, and the show in general is inclusive with regard to
gender-neutral language.

Hallward, Anne (Creator), and Gabe Grabin (Producer). "Being Gender Neutral."
Safe Space Radio, February 10, 2014. http://safespaceradio.com/2014/02/being
-gender-neutral.

An interview with a gender-neutral high schooler.

Jesse and Sean (Hosts). *Gendercast: Our Transmasculine Genderqueery*. 2011–2013. http://gendercast.libsyn.com.
Podcast series about transmasculine genderqueer identities.

Kirk, Jennifer, and Zoë Kirk-Robinson (Hosts). *T-Vox*. 2008–2014. http://t-vox.org/resources/podcasts.
Podcast series about genderqueer, intersex, and transsexual identities.

Lugo, Emma (Host). *Transpositive PDX*. Portland, OR: KBOO, 2016–present. http://kboo.fm/program/transpositive-pdx-0.
Podcast focusing on transgender communities in Portland.

McCarthy, Julie (Host). "A Journey of Pain and Beauty: On Becoming Transgender in India" (Radio Interview). *NPR: All Things Considered*, April 18, 2014. http://www.npr.org/sections/parallels/2014/04/18/304548675/a-journey-of-pain-and-beauty-on-becoming-transgender-in-india.
A radio show about a hijra's transition experience.

Theatre

Bornstein, Kate. *Hidden: A Gender*. 1991.
A play exploring Bornstein's own experiences and those of historical intersex person Herculine Barbin.

Mac, Taylor (Playwright). *Hir: A Play*. Evanston, IL: Northwestern University Press, 2015.
A play about a genderqueer person and their family.

Pearle, Daniel (Playwright). *A Kid Like Jake*. Dramatists Play Service, 2015.
A play about a family struggling to handle their young child's gender identity.

MULTIDISCIPLINARY MEDIA
Film and Television

Anand, Vivek (Producer). *Project Bolo*. Mumbai: Solaris Pictures, 2011. http://www.projectbolo.com.
Documentary film series exploring LGBT identities in India.

Andrews, Julie (Creator). *Julie's Greenroom*. New York: Jim Henson Co., and Los Gatos, CA: Netflix, 2017.

Live-action puppet program for children, including a gender-neutral puppet named Riley.

Ansolabehere, Joe, and Paul Germain (Creators). "Neither Boy nor Girl." In *Lloyd in Space*. Burbank, CA: Walt Disney Television, 2002.
Animated series about a high school in space; this episode features an alien who has no gender identity or sex until the age of thirteen, when they choose for themselves.

Araki, Tetsurō. *Attack on Titan*. Flower Mound, TX: FUNimation, 2014.
Anime about superpowered Titans battling humans; includes a deliberately ungendered character.

Avanzino, Peter (Director). *Futurama: The Beast with a Billion Backs*. Los Angeles: 20th Century Fox Home Entertainment, 2008.
Animated science fiction comedy featuring a pangender alien courting everybody in the universe.

Benski, Thomas, Fred Grinstein, Elvira Lind, and Nikki Calabrese (Producers). *Twiz & Tuck*. London: Pulse Films, 2017.
Six-part documentary series following two best friends, a trans man and a genderfluid person, as they undertake a bachelor party road trip.

Bergsmark, Ester Martin (Director). *She Male Snails*. Denmark: Upfront Films, 2012.
Documentary about being nonbinary, directed by a nonbinary person.

———. *Something Must Break*. Sweden: Garagefilm, 2014.
Film about young love and being nonbinary, directed by a nonbinary person.

Bhatt, Mahesh (Director). *Tamanna*. India: Spark Films, 1997.
Film based on a true story of a hijra rescuing a baby girl and raising her.

Bornstein, Kate. *Adventures in the Gender Trade*. New York: Filmakers Library, 1994.
Kate Bornstein shares hir journey and introduces several other people who resist traditional gender identities and roles.

Browning, Tod. *Freaks*. Beverly Hills, CA: Metro-Goldwyn-Mayer, 1932.
Film about carnival sideshow performers; includes Josephine Joseph, billed as "Half Woman—Half Man."

Burton, LaVar (Director). "Cogenitor." In *Enterprise*. Los Angeles: Paramount Network Television, April 30, 2003.

The *Enterprise* encounters an alien race that has a third gender that is necessary for reproduction.

Cruz, Leigh, Bion, Lucien, Z, Jo, and Manon. Out of This Binary. https://www.youtube.com/user/OutOfThisBinary.
Seven nonbinary people sharing about their experiences.

Curland, Martin. *Zerophilia*. United States: Scrambled Eggs Productions, 2007.
Romantic comedy about a person who can change their sex and gender at will.

Davis, Vaginal (Writer, Director, Actor). *Fertile La Toyah Jackson Video Magazine*. 1992. http://vaginaldavis.com/film.shtml.
Short film by celebrated genderqueer celebrity Vaginal Davis.

———. *Fertile La Toyah Jackson Video Magazine Kinky Issue*. 1993. http://vaginaldavis.com/film.shtml.
Short film by celebrated genderqueer celebrity Vaginal Davis.

———. *Fertile's Last Dance*. 1987. http://vaginaldavis.com/film.shtml.
Short film by celebrated genderqueer celebrity Vaginal Davis.

———. *Fra unter Einfluss*. 2001. http://vaginaldavis.com/film.shtml.
Short film by celebrated genderqueer celebrity Vaginal Davis.

———. *Le Petite Tonkinoise*. 2001. http://vaginaldavis.com/film.shtml.
Short film by celebrated genderqueer celebrity Vaginal Davis.

———. *The Other Newest One*. 2001. http://vaginaldavis.com/film.shtml.
Short film by celebrated genderqueer celebrity Vaginal Davis.

———. *The White to Be Angry*. 1999. http://vaginaldavis.com/film.shtml.
Short film by celebrated genderqueer celebrity Vaginal Davis.

Dezaki, Satoshi, and Tsuneo Tominaga (Directors). *They Were Eleven*. Japan: Kitty Films, 1986.
A science fiction anime with a character of indeterminate gender.

Dodge, Harry, and Silas Howard. *By Hook or By Crook*. Los Angeles: Steakhaus Productions, 2001.
A queer buddy film.

Dunham, Lena, and Jenni Konner (Producers). *Suited*. New York: HBO, 2016.
Documentary film about gender-neutral clothing.

Ernst, Rhys (Director). *We've Been Around*. http://www.wevebeenaround.com.
     A collection of documentary short films about trans and gender-
     nonconforming pioneers.

Fernandez, Scout (Producer). *Roaming Gender*. https://www.youtube.com/channel/
     UCTsLF-pQo0UNIcNp4J8RHsA.
     Web documentary series exploring gender variance.

Flannigan, Tracy (Director). 2004. *Rise Above: The Tribe 8 Documentary*. Los
     Angeles: Red Hill Pictures.
     Documentary about Lynn Breedlove's band Tribe 8.

Fox, Amy (Producer). *The Switch*. Vancouver, BC: OutTV, 2016–present.
     A web comedy about a trans woman; includes a nonbinary character.

Gaiman, Neil (Creator). *Neverwhere*. UK: BBC Two, 1996.
     Television series adapted from Gaiman's fantasy novel of the same name;
     includes a nongendered angel.

Green, M. "Gender Rebel." In *Real Momentum*. United States: Friction Films, 2006.
     Four-part documentary exploring the identities of three gender-variant people.

Greenfield-Sanders, Timothy (Filmmaker). *The Trans List*. New York: HBO, 2016.
     Documentary about eleven transgender people, including nonbinary femme
     Alok Vaid-Menon.

Hall, Jordan (Creator), and Spencer Maybee (Director). *Carmilla*. Canada: KindaTV,
     2014–2016. https://www.youtube.com/user/VervegirlMagazine.
     Web series about a group of supernatural college students; includes a
     nonbinary character.

Hamer, Dean, and Joe Wilson (Directors). *Kumu Hina*. PBS Independent Lens, May
     4, 2015. http://kumuhina.com.
     Documentary film about a māhū mentor.

Harmon, Dan, and Justin Roiland (Creators). *Rick and Morty*. Burbank, CA: Adult
     Swim, 2013–present.
     An animated series about a mad scientist and his grandson; hivemind character
     Unity appears as both male and female.

Houston, Shine Louise (Founder/Director). *Crash Pad Series*. Pink and White
     Productions. https://crashpadseries.com.
     A queer adult film series.

Huang, Kathy (Director). *Tales of the Waria*. Global Voices series, Independent
Television Service (ITVS) International, June 3, 2012. http://itvs.org/films/tales
-of-the-waria.
     Documentary about waria identities.

Igarashi, Takuya. *Ouran High School Host Club*. Flower Mound, TX: FUNimation,
2006.
     Anime about a high school club; includes an androgynous character who states
that gender does not dominate their personality.

———. *Soul Eater*. Flower Mound, TX: FUNimation, 2012.
     Supernatural anime about warriors bonded with living weapons; includes an
androgynous character whose gender is never revealed.

Irie, Yasuhiro (Director). *Fullmetal Alchemist: Brotherhood*. Japan: Bones, 2009–2010.
     A science fiction anime series that includes a genderless character.

Iuchi, Shuji (Director). *Ranma ½: Big Trouble in Nekonron, China*. Japan: Kitty
Films, 1991.
     An anime film about a boy who transforms into a girl every time he is splashed
with cold water.

Johnson, Kenneth (Creator). *Alien Nation*. Beverly Hills, CA: 20th Century Fox,
1989–1990.
     Buddy cop series about a human-alien team; the aliens have a third sex.

Jordenö, Sara (Director). *Kiki*. United States and Sweden: 2016.
     A documentary exploring ball culture in New York.

Kōjina, Hiroshi (Director). *Hunter X Hunter*. Japan: Madhouse, 2011–2014.
     An anime series about a boy who is training to be a Hunter; includes a
genderless chimera character.

Koppelman, Brian, David Levien, and Andrew Ross Sorkin (Creators). *Billions*. New
York: Showtime, 2016–present.
     Television drama about a federal prosecutor; includes a nonbinary character.

Larrainzar, Jacque (Creator). *Omecihuatl*. 2015. https://queeringthemuseum.
org/2015/11/02/omecihuatl-reclaiming-gender-through-undocumented-stories.
     Digital storytelling about culturally specific genders.

Lee, Alexander L. (Director). *A Night in the Woods*. Self-produced, 2012.
     Short film about a zombie apocalypse, featuring a genderqueer person.

Lee, Jiz. Jiz Lee: Gender Queer Porn Star. http://jizlee.com/film.
Adult films by a genderqueer performer.

Lewis, Jamal (Director). *Diary of a Banji Cunt*. ND. http://www.jamaltlewis.com/
diaryofabanjicunt.
Web comedy exploring race, gender, and class.

———. *No Fats, No Femmes*. 2016. http://nofatsnofemmes.com.
Documentary exploring queer dating and love.

Losier, Marie (Director). *The Ballad of Genesis and Lady Jaye*. New Yorker Video, 2011.
Documentary about the pandrogyne project, a body modification project
between two lovers to look alike and become one being.

M., Celeste. https://www.youtube.com/channel/UCnLu3StU9CSJSAouZhh1khQ.
An asexual nonbinary person sharing their thoughts and experiences.

MacDonald, Kirsty. *Assume Nothing*. Auckland, NZ: Girl-On-A-Bike Films, 2009.
Biographical film exploring nonbinary artists' work.

Malkin, Anna (Creator). *Queer Story Archive*. http://onmyplanet.ca/mundo.
An autobiographical video project examining queer lives; includes genderqueer
stories.

McKinnon, Elijah (Creator). *Two Queens in a Kitchen*. OpenTV, 2016. http://www
.weareopen.tv/2qik.
A queer cooking show.

McMullan, Chelsea (Director). *My Prairie Home*. Montreal: National Film Board of
Canada, 2013.
Documentary about Rae Spoon, genderqueer singer-songwriter.

Michaels, Lorne (Creator). *Saturday Night Live*. New York: NBC Studios, 1990–1994.
Sketch comedy show that had a recurring character named Pat, who was
gender ambiguous.

Mitchell, Elizabeth, Ali Ekeroma Cowley, Maka Makatoa, and Ali Cowley
(Directors). *bro'Town*. New Zealand: Firehorse Films, 2004–2009.
An adult animated comedy series about a group of young men in a Pacific
Islander community; includes a fa'afafine character.

Mitchell, John Cameron. *Shortbus*. New York: Thinkfilm, 2007.
Film about a weekly salon called Shortbus, run by a nonbinary person played
by Justin Vivian Bond.

Mizushima, Seiji (Director). *Fullmetal Alchemist*. Japan: Bones, 2003–2004.
  A science fiction anime series that includes a genderless character.

Mochizuki, Tomomi, and Tsutomu Shibayama (Directors). *Ranma ½*. Japan: Kitty Films, 1989.
  An eighteen-episode anime series about a boy who transforms into a girl every time he is splashed with cold water.

Nakamura, Ryūtarō. *Kino's Journey*. Houston, TX: ADV Films, 2003.
  Animated series about a young androgynous person traveling from town to town and finding adventure.

Nibley, Lydia (Filmmaker). *Two Spirits*. Riding the Tiger Productions, 2010.
  A documentary film about Fred Martinez, a nádleehí Navajo youth who was murdered.

Nishimura, Junji (Director). *Ranma ½: Super Indiscriminate Decisive Battle! Team Ranma vs. the Legendary Phoenix*. Japan: Kitty Films, 1994.
  An anime film about a boy who transforms into a girl every time he is splashed with cold water.

Ōnuma, Shin. *Baka and Test*. Flower Mound, TX: FUNimation, 2010.
  Anime about a school where students battle for amenities; includes a character who is a third gender.

P., Lane. https://www.youtube.com/user/JohannDrivesMyBus.
  Transition vlog by a nonbinary person.

Peddle, Daniel (Director). *The Aggressives*. Chatsworth, CA: Image Entertainment, 2006.
  A documentary film about six aggressives, Black gender-nonconforming lesbians.

Peterson, Michael (Writer), and Ian Toynton (Director). "The Girl in the Mask." In *Bones*. United States: 20th Century Fox Television, 2009.
  A forensics team has a visiting scientist who is ambiguously gendered, with a visual kei aesthetic.

Richards, Jen (Creator). *We Happy Trans*: A Place for Sharing Positive Trans* Perspectives*. http://wehappytrans.com.
  Vlog series focusing on positive trans experiences.

Rivera, Ignacio. *They*. ND. http://www.ignaciogrivera.com/films.html.
  An experimental short exploring a genderfluid person's journey.

Roddenberry, Gene (Creator). "The Outcast." In *Star Trek, the Next Generation.* Hollywood, CA: Paramount Pictures, 1992.
The Enterprise encounters an alien race for whom gender is forbidden.

Rose, Alex. "Being Nonbinary: A Gender Discussion." YouTube video. October 31, 2016. https://youtu.be/s_szh0N9gA8.
A short video about nonbinary gender.

Sawai, Koji, and Junji Nishimura (Directors). *Ranma ½ Nettōhen.* Japan: Kitty Films, 1989–1992.
A 143-episode anime series about a boy who transforms into a girl every time he is splashed with cold water.

Shavelson, Lonny (Director). *Three to Infinity: Beyond Two Genders.* Berkeley, CA: Photowords Films, 2015.
A documentary about nonbinary gender.

Shiva, Alexandra, Sean MacDonald, and Michelle Gucovsky (Directors). *Bombay Eunuch.* New York: Gidalya Pictures, 2001.
Documentary about hijras.

Shizuno, Kōbun. *Knights of Sidonia.* Tokyo: Polygon Pictures, 2014.
Space adventure anime in which humans have evolved a third gender.

Skurnik, Jonathan (Director). *The Family Journey.* Skurnik Productions, 2010. http://youthandgendermediaproject.org.
Documentary focusing on parents and siblings of gender-questioning youth.

———. *I'm Just Anneke.* Skurnik Productions, 2010. http://youthandgendermediaproject.org.
Documentary about a twelve-year-old taking hormone blockers and exploring their gender.

Stewart, Milo. https://www.youtube.com/user/RoryDeganRepresent.
A nonbinary vlogger.

Sugar, Rebecca (Creator). *Steven Universe.* Atlanta: Cartoon Network, 2013–present.
Animated television series about alien humanoids called Gems and a young person's coming of age; several characters are nonbinary and otherwise queer.

Suzuki, Akira (Director). *Ranma ½: Nihao My Concubine.* Japan: Kitty Films, 1992.
An anime film about a boy who transforms into a girl every time he is splashed with cold water.

TEDx Talks. "Beyond the Gender Binary: Yee Won Chong at TEDxRainier."
    YouTube video. December 13, 2012. https://youtu.be/-Lm4vxZrAig.
    A TED Talk about nonbinary gender.

Tom, Jes. *Weird Queer Comedy Babe*. http://www.jestomdotcom.com.
    Queer stand-up comedy show.

Torrington, Sean, and Terry Torrington (Directors). *SlayTV*. Brooklyn, NY: Blunted
    Muse Productions, 2017. http://slaytv.com.
    An online media network for Black LGBTQ stories.

Treut, Monika. *Gendernauts: A Journey through Shifting Identities*. New York: First
    Run Features, 1999.
    Documentary about a group of gender-variant artists in San Francisco.

Tsukerman, Slava (Director). *Liquid Sky*. United States: WINTERtainment, 1982.
    Science fiction film with two androgynous characters.

Uekrongtham, Ekachai (Director). *Beautiful Boxer*. Los Angeles: Regent Releasing,
    2005.
    Biographical film about a kathoey boxer.

Vogt-Roberts, Jordan (Director). *The Kings of Summer*. Los Angeles: CBS Films,
    2013.
    A coming-of-age comedy film that includes a character who doesn't have a
    gender.

Ward, Pendleton (Creator). *Adventure Time*. Atlanta: Cartoon Network, 2010–
    present.
    Animated series following a boy and his dog as they adventure in a
    postapocalyptic world; sentient robot BMO seems to be bigender.

Wilchins, Riki. "The MANgina Monologues (A One Trans Show)." YouTube video.
    2009. https://www.youtube.com/watch?v=82UU5JE12ZM.
    Stand-up comedy by genderqueer activist and writer Riki Wilchins.

Wu, Adrian. *Wumingbong*. https://www.youtube.com/channel/UCStxBkM_Il-
    aMjjAJwYvy8Q.
    Transition vlog of a neutrois person.

Yun, Hye. *Hey Yun the Web Series*. http://www.heyheyyun.com.
    A web comedy about a genderqueer person.

Zeka, Alessandra (Director). *Harsh Beauty*. San Francisco: Frameline, 2005.
    Documentary following three hijras over three years.

Games

ACE Team (Developer). *Zeno Clash*. 2009. http://store.steampowered.com/app/22200.
A PC punk fantasy game; the primary antagonist is genderfluid.

Aqualuft Games (Developer). *Queen at Arms*. 2016. http://store.steampowered.com/app/362020.
PC visual novel with a player character who is assigned female at birth, cross-dresses as a boy to hide their identity, and then gets to choose whether to be male, female, or nonbinary.

Cole, Alayna (Developer). *Fairy Tale*. 2015. http://alaynamcole.com/fairy-tale.
A browser-based fairy-tale adventure with gender-neutral characters.

Crawford, Jeremy, James Wyatt, Robert J. Schwalb, and Bruce R. Cordell. *Dungeons & Dragons: Player's Handbook, 5th Edition*. Renton, WA: Wizards of the Coast.
Tabletop role-playing game with canon nonbinary characters.

Date Nighto (Developer). *Hustle Cat*. 2016. http://store.steampowered.com/app/453340.
PC visual novel that allows the player to use nonbinary pronouns.

Failbetter Games (Developer). *Fallen London*. 2009. http://fallenlondon.storynexus.com.
Browser-based game based in a Gothic underworld; game offers nonbinary player character option.

———. *Sunless Sea*. 2015. https://www.failbettergames.com/sunless.
Browser-based game in the Fallen London universe; game offers nonbinary player character option.

Fox, Toby (Designer). *Undertale*. 2015. http://undertale.com.
A PC and Mac role-playing game with several characters that use they/them pronouns.

Garfield, Richard (Designer). *Magic: The Gathering*. Wizards of the Coast, 1993.
A tabletop deck-building game with several canon nonbinary characters.

Grimes, Arielle (Developer). *BrokenFolx*. 2014. https://ariellegrimes.itch.io/brokenfolx.
Browser-based game exploring queer identities.

Jagex (Developer). *Runescape*. 2001. http://www.runescape.com/community.
A PC MMORPG with a genderfluid character.

MidBoss (Developer). *2064: Read Only Memories*. 2017. http://readonlymemori.es.
    PC, Mac, and PlayStation cyberpunk game; several characters use they/them
    pronouns.

Motion Twin (Developer). *Mush*. 2013. http://mush.twinoid.com.
    An online multiplayer game with sixteen playable characters, one of whom is
    nonbinary.

Peffer, Jessica, Dana Pull, and Darren Hill (Developers). *Flight Rising*. 2013. http://
    www1.flightrising.com.
    Web-based game featuring dragon breeding; Scribbles the dragon uses they/
    them pronouns.

Preloaded (Developer). *The End*. 2011. http://playtheend.com/game.
    A PC game designed for young adults to explore gender presentation and identity.

Sonic (Developer). *Nights into Dreams*. 1996. http://store.steampowered.com/
    app/219950.
    An action video game featuring an androgynous character.

Squinkifer, Dietrich (Developer). *Dominique Pamplemousse*. 2014. http://store
    .steampowered.com/app/270310.
    A stop-motion PC adventure game that explores gender.

Telltale Games (Developer). *Tales of Monkey Island*. 2009. http://store.steam
    powered.com/app/31170.
    A PC adventure game with a gender-ambiguous player character.

TinyCo (Developer). *Marvel Avengers Academy*. 2016. http://www.tinyco.com/
    tinyco-games/marvel-avengers-academy.
    A superhero mobile game; character Singularity from the A-Force Winter
    Event is nonbinary.

Voltage Entertainment (Developer). *Astoria: Fate's Kiss*. 2016. https://www.astoria
    fateskiss.com.
    A mobile dating sim game featuring a canon nonbinary character, Alex.

Multigenre Art

Adsit, Lexi (Managing Director), and Devi K (Executive Director). *Peacock
    Rebellion*. http://www.peacockrebellion.org.
    Collaborative art project by queer and trans POC.

Anthony, Adelina. http://www.adelinaanthony.com.
    A queer Xicanx artist working with film, poetry, and theatre.

Bryce, AJ (Director). *Trans-Genre: A Showcase of Transgender Artists, Musicians, Writers and Performers.* http://trans-genre.net.
    Multimedia art collaboration showcasing gender-variant artists' works.

Fluffy. *BusyBee.* http://beesbuzz.biz.
    Comics, music, and visual art by a nonbinary artist.

LeRoy, Océan. http://www.oceanleroy.com.
    Nonbinary artist who works with video, singing, and poetry slam.

Lewis, Jamal. *Queer HBCU.* http://www.queerhbcu.com.
    A digital multimedia project exploring race and gender.

New York Times. Transgender Today. http://www.nytimes.com/interactive/projects/storywall/transgender-today.
    A multimedia personal narrative collection looking at gender diversity.

Olive-or-Oliver. http://www.oliveoroliver.com.
    A nonbinary artist who works with music, theatre, video, and performance art.

Rivera, Ignacio. http://www.ignaciogrivera.com.
    Two-Spirit slam poet, filmmaker, and writer.

Takahashi, Ginger Brooks, K8 Hardy, Emily Roysdon, and Ulrike Müller. *LTTR.* http://www.lttr.org.
    A genderqueer art collective creating multigenre art.

Trouble, Courtney. http://courtneytrouble.com.
    Photography, two- and three-dimensional art, and adult film by a nonbinary artist.

Waxman, Tobaron. http://www.tobaron.com.
    Artist exploring gender and diaspora through two- and three-dimensional art, installations, and performance art.

Wild Gender. *Wild Gender: Fabulous, Flagrant Gender Variance.* http://wildgender.com.
    A collaborative art project exploring gender fluidity.

Performance Art

Breedlove, Lynn. *One Freak Show*. 2004–2005. http://www.lynnbreedlove.com/
   onefreakshow/index.html.
   Standup comedy series by legendary genderqueer rocker Lynn Breedlove.

Colins, Gavin Mikey (Director). *FemmeInPublic*. https://vimeo.com/211267675.
   A photography and live performance spectacle celebrating femme identities.

FAFSWAG Arts Collective. https://fafswag.com.
   An LGBT Pacific Islander arts collective that produces and facilitates
   performance art and vogue balls.

Gibson, Andrea. http://www.andreagibson.org.
   A genderqueer slam poet.

Grant, Taunee. *?Jump! Run! Androgynite!?* ca. 2002.
   Spoken word piece about the pains of androgynous transition.

Jina, Kieron. http://kieronjina.com.
   Innovative performance artist Kieron Jina uses collaborative dance and theatre
   to explore gender dynamics.

Lowrey, Kestryl Cael. *PoMo Freakshow*. http://pomofreakshow.com/kessmain.
   Performance artist exploring gender, sex, and sexuality.

Norman, Sarah-Jane. https://www.sarahjanenorman.com.
   A cross-disciplinary artist whose primary medium is the body.

P-Orridge, Genesis Breyer, and Lady Jaye Breyer. *The Pandrogeny Project*.
   1993–present.
   Body modification project by two lovers who wanted to become one person;
   although Lady Jaye passed away, Genesis continues to transition.

Stringer, JAC. *Midwest GenderQueer*. https://www.youtube.com/user/
   MidwestGenderQueer.
   Performance art, music, dance, and spoken word by a genderqueer person.

Appendix A
Glossary

AFAB (also DFAB): Assigned (or designated) female at birth.

affirmed gender: The gender one has transitioned to and identifies as.

agender: A person who is genderless.

aggressive: A (primarily African American) term for a person assigned female at birth who presents masculine; some identify as nonbinary.

ake:śkassi: A Blackfoot term meaning "acts like a woman" used for persons assigned male at birth who occupy an alternate gender role.

akhnuchik: A Yup'ik term meaning "man-woman" used for persons assigned male at birth who occupy an alternate gender role.

alha'ya'o: A Bella Coola term used for persons assigned male at birth who occupy an alternate gender role.

Alyha: A Mohave name for a mythical figure with an alternate gender role.

AMAB (also DMAB): Assigned (or designated) male at birth.

androgyne: A person who identifies as in-between or ambiguously gendered.

androgynous: Clothing, hair, and other style markers that are in between or ambiguously gendered.

angut"guaq: A Kuskokwim River Yup'ik term meaning "manlike" used for persons assigned female at birth who occupy an alternate gender role.

aranaruaq: A Kuskokwim River Yup'ik term meaning "womanlike" used for persons assigned male at birth who occupy an alternate gender role.

aranu'tiq: A Chugach term meaning "man-woman" used for persons assigned male at birth who occupy an alternate gender role.

asegi udanto: A term meaning "other heart" used by some Cherokee Two-Spirit people to describe a third gender option that is neither male nor female.
ashtime: Maale (Ethiopia) third gender.
a'yahkwêw: Plains Cree third gender.
ayekkwe: A Cree term meaning "split testicles" used for persons assigned male at birth who occupy an alternate gender role.
bakla (also bayot and bantut): A Philippines third gender role for people assigned male at birth.
ballroom community: A primarily African American and Latinx subculture in which sexual and gender-diverse people participate in dance competitions. People are often grouped into houses led by housemothers.
berdache: A derogatory colonial (and old anthropological) term describing indigenous gender and sexual variance.
biatti (also miati): A Hidatsa term meaning "woman-compelled" used for persons assigned male at birth who occupy an alternate gender role.
bigender: A person who identifies as two genders, either at the same time, or moving between.
binding: Flattening one's chest using binders, sports bras, or bandages.
bissu: Buginese intersex people who identify as a blend of all four genders; a metagender. They dress distinctively and have an important spiritual role in society.
biza'ah: Teotitlán del Valle (Oaxaca, Mexico) alternate gender for people assigned male at birth.
boi: A (primarily African American) person assigned female at birth who leans masculine or butch.
boté: A Crow term meaning "not man, not woman" used for persons assigned male at birth who occupy an alternate gender role.
bottom surgery: Genital surgery to create a vagina or penis; can also refer to hysterectomy.
brotherboy: An Aboriginal Australian term for a person assigned female at birth who occupies an alternate gender role.
burrnesha (also sworn virgin): An alternate gender role in Albania. Balkan sworn virgins are assigned female at birth, and take on a masculine role in the community. Dating from fifteenth-century tribal law, this role was originated when a family lost all its men from combat and needed a patriarch.

butch: Originally, a style and gender role performed by masculine lesbians. Now expanded to sometimes mean a nonbinary gender identity that typically involves masculine style markers.

calabai: Buginese people assigned male at birth who have traditional female behaviors and occupy a unique societal role as wedding planners.

calalai (also calalai'): Buginese people assigned female at birth who occupy a male role without the desire to be men.

cisgender: A person who identifies as the gender they were assigned at birth; nontransgender.

cisnormativity: The assumption that all people are cisgender.

cissexism: Biased toward cisgender people.

clocking: Reading or perceiving somebody's transgender status.

coming out: The process of disclosing one's sexual or gender identity.

cross-dresser: A person who wears clothing of another gender.

demiboy: A person who is partially boy.

demigirl: A person who is partially girl.

devadasi: An Indian term used for a person assigned female at birth who is dedicated to the goddess Yellamma and occupies an alternate gender role.

drag: Theatrical performance of masculinity (drag kings) or femininity (drag queens).

dysphoria: An intense feeling of discomfort with one's assigned gender. Can include body dysphoria, in which sexual characteristics feel wrong; or social dysphoria, caused by misgendering interactions.

enby: Diminutive of nonbinary.

epicene: An adjective indicating androgyny or lack of gender.

fa'afafine: Samoan AMAB feminine individuals who do not identify as men or women. Translates to "in the manner of a woman."

femme: Originally, a style and gender role performed by feminine lesbians. Now expanded to sometimes mean a nonbinary gender identity that typically involves feminine style markers.

femminiello: An Italian term meaning "little woman-man" used for persons assigned male at birth who occupy an alternate gender role.

gatxan: A Tlingit term meaning "halfman-halfwoman" used for persons assigned male at birth who occupy an alternate gender role.

gender bending: The act of playing with one's gender expression.

gender binary: The idea that there are only two genders, male and female.

gender confirmation surgery (also sexual reassignment surgery): Surgical interventions to bring a person's body more in line with their gender identity.
gender expression: The act of articulating one's gender through clothing, hairstyle, and other gender cues.
genderfluid: A person who moves fluidly between two or more genders.
genderfuck: A transgressive identity or style that purposely challenges binary ideas of gender.
gender identity: The way a person feels about their gender. This important part of an individual's identity is generally formulated quite young, as early as three years old.
gender marker: A legal gender designation on identity documents.
gender neutral: A neutral gender identity or expression. Some gender-neutral people identify as agender or neutrois. Also refers to spaces (like restrooms) and language (like pronouns) that are not gendered.
gender nonconforming: Individuals who do not conform to binary gender roles and expression.
gender outlaw: Term coined by Kate Bornstein to describe her gender identity, which is politicized and neither male nor female.
gender policing: The act of imposing gender norms on another person.
gender presentation: The ways in which an individual expresses their gender. Can include clothing, hairstyle, makeup, reducing or enlarging secondary sex characteristics, gait, vocal pitch and style, and nonverbal communication.
genderqueer: An umbrella term for a person who is not exclusively male or female; often has a political connotation.
gender spectrum: The idea that gender is not binary but rather a spectrum of possibilities.
gender variant: Gender identities that are nonstandard; can include binary trans people.
guevedoche: A nonbinary gender role in the Dominican Republic for individuals with a very prevalent intersex condition. Translates to "testicles at twelve."
hijra: Indian person assigned male at birth who has traditional female behaviors. They bless infants and dance at weddings as spiritual bargainers. As of 2014, hijras are legally recognized as a third gender in India.
hoobuk: A Muskogean term meaning "eunuch" used for persons assigned male at birth who occupy an alternate gender role.

hwami: A Mohave term for persons assigned female at birth who occupy an alternate gender role.

ickoue ne kioussa: An Illinois term meaning "hunting women" used for persons assigned female at birth who occupy an alternate gender role.

înahpîkasoht: Plains Cree term for a woman accepted as a man.

intersex: An individual whose sex is somewhere between typical male and female characteristics, in terms of chromosomes, hormones, genital appearance, reproductive organs, or secondary sex characteristics. Intersex individuals can identify as binary cisgender, binary transgender, or nonbinary gender.

iskwêhkân: Plains Cree for "fake woman," but without negative connotations.

iskwêw ka napêwayat: Plains Cree term for a woman dressed as a man.

í-wa-musp (also iwop-naiip): A Yuki term meaning "man-woman" used for persons assigned male at birth who occupy an alternate gender role.

kathoey: A third gender category in Thailand meaning "ladyboy." Kathoeys can be traced in Thai culture from a creation myth.

katsotse: A Zuni term meaning "girl-boy" used for persons assigned female at birth who occupy an alternate gender role.

keknatsa'nxwix^W: A Quinault term meaning "part woman" used for persons assigned male at birth who occupy an alternate gender role.

khanith: An Oman alternate gender role for people assigned male at birth.

khawaja sara: A third gender designation in Pakistan, used as an alternative to hijra.

kocek: Turkish people assigned male at birth who dress in feminine clothing and identify as a third gender. During the Ottoman Empire, the kocek were highly respected dance performers.

Kolhama(na): A Zuni name for a mythical figure who occupies an alternate gender role.

kupalhke:tek: A Kutenai term meaning "to imitate a woman" used for persons assigned male at birth who occupy an alternate gender role.

Kwasaitaka: A Hopi name meaning "Skirt Man" used for a mythical figure with an alternate gender role.

lhamana (also lha'ma): A Zuni term used for persons assigned male at birth who occupy an alternate gender role.

lila witkowin: A Lakota term meaning "crazy woman" used for persons assigned female at birth who occupy an alternate gender role.

māhū: A third gender in Hawaii. Māhū can be assigned male or female at birth and have an important cultural role as healers and teachers.

ma'kalí (also mé'mi): A Flathead term used for persons assigned male at birth who occupy an alternate gender role.

mangaiko: Mbo (Democratic Republic of the Congo) third gender.

masculine of center (also MOC): Lesbians, trans men, and nonbinary people who are more masculine than feminine.

mashoga: Kenyan coast third gender.

misgender: The act of improperly gendering somebody; for example, by using incorrect pronouns.

mixu'ga: An Osage term meaning "moon instructed" used for persons assigned male at birth who occupy an alternate gender role.

m'nuhtokwae: A Potawatomi term meaning "supernatural, extraordinary" plus the female suffix, used for persons assigned male at birth who occupy an alternate gender role.

musp-íwap naip: A Yuki term meaning "woman man-girl" used for persons assigned female at birth who occupy an alternate gender role.

muxe: A Zapotec third gender in Oaxaca, Mexico. Muxe are assigned male at birth and have a respected and important role in society, traditionally caring for their parents as they age. Vestidas wear long hair and dresses; pintadas wear men's clothing and makeup.

Mx: A gender-neutral title, used in place of Mrs., Ms., Miss, and Mr.

nádle (also nádleeh or nádleehí): A Navajo term meaning "being transformed" or "one who changes time and again" used for people occupying an alternate gender role.

napêhkân: Plains Cree for "fake man," but without negative connotations.

napêw iskwêwisêhot: Plains Cree term for a man who dresses as a woman.

Ńa-yénnas-ganné: An Apache name meaning "man-woman warrior" used for a mythical figure with an alternate gender role.

ńdé'sdzan: An Apache term meaning "man-woman" used for persons assigned male at birth who occupy an alternate gender role.

neutrois: A neutral or null gender.

ninauposkitzipxpe: A Blackfoot term meaning "manly hearted woman" used for persons assigned female at birth who occupy an alternate gender role.

nonbinary: An umbrella term for people who are not exclusively male or female.

okitcitakwe: An Ojibwa term meaning "warrior woman" used for persons assigned female at birth who occupy an alternate gender role.

packing: Wearing a phallus under one's clothing.

palao'ana: Micronesian third gender.

pangender: Somebody who identifies as multiple or all genders.

passing: Being perceived as one's true gender. Can also refer to others' perceptions of one's ethnicity, ability, or sexual orientation.

pronouns: Parts of speech used to refer to somebody instead of using their name. Includes he/him and she/her as well as a host of gender-neutral pronouns such as ze/hir.

quariwarmi: Prior to Spanish conquest, third gender Incan shamans.

queer: An umbrella term describing sexual and gender diversity. Can also be a distinct identity term and is often politicized.

Radical Faeries: A counterculture movement incorporating queer consciousness, ecofeminism, and neo-pagan spirituality. Although it began with gay men, the movement now includes a wide range of genders and sexualities, including nonbinary people.

sādhin: An Indian term used for a person assigned female at birth who occupies a male role and is viewed as being genderless.

sakwo'mapi akikwan: A Blackfoot term meaning "boy-girl" used for persons assigned female at birth who occupy an alternate gender role.

sexual reassignment surgery (also gender confirmation surgery): Surgical interventions to bring a person's body more in line with their gender identity.

shiángge: A Winnebago term meaning "eunuch" used for persons assigned male at birth who occupy an alternate gender role.

sipiniq: An Inuit term for an infant whose sex changes at birth.

sistagirl (also sistergirl): An Aboriginal Australian term for a person assigned male at birth who occupies an alternate gender role.

st'a'mia: A Sanpoil term used for persons assigned male at birth who occupy an alternate gender role.

stealth: The act of concealing one's transgender status.

stud: A (primarily African American or Latinx) term for an assigned female at birth person who is masculine; some identify as nonbinary.

sworn virgin (also burrnesha): An alternate gender role in Albania. Balkan sworn virgins are assigned female at birth, and take on a masculine role in the community. Dating from fifteenth-century tribal law, this role was originated when a family lost all its men from combat and needed a patriarch.

takatāpui: Māori people with diverse sexual and gender identities.

tangwuwaip (also tangowaip): A Western Shoshone term meaning "man-woman" used for persons who occupy an alternate gender role.

tawkxwa'nsix^W: A Quinault term meaning "man-acting" used for persons assigned female at birth who occupy an alternate gender role.

third gender: A primarily anthropological term referring to culturally specific genders that are not exclusively male or female.

títqattek: A Kutenai term meaning "pretending to be a man" used for persons assigned female at birth who occupy an alternate gender role.

top surgery: Surgery to sculpt the chest; includes mastectomy and breast implants.

transfeminine: An assigned male at birth person who has a feminine gender expression or identity.

transgender (or trans): An umbrella term for any individual who does not identify with the gender assigned to them at birth. Transgender people can be binary or nonbinary.

transition: The act of transitioning from the gender assigned at birth to an individual's true gender identity. Many nonbinary people do not transition, either because they do not want or need to, or because the financial, social, or other cost is too high. Transition can include medical, surgical, and/or social factors.

transmasculine: An assigned female at birth person who has a masculine gender expression or identity.

transmisogyny: Sexism toward trans women.

transphobia: Hatred or fear of transgender people.

transsexual (sometimes spelled transexual): An older umbrella term for people who do not identify with the gender they were assigned at birth; people with this identity often pursue medical and surgical transition.

transvestite: An older term for a person who cross-dresses, or wears clothing of a different gender; also historically used for transfeminine people.

travesti: A Latin American term that includes third gender people and transgender women.

tübasa: A Northern Shoshone term meaning "sterile" used for persons who occupy an alternate gender role.

tucking: The act of tucking the penis between the legs, using tape or a gaff, in order to make the pelvis area flat and smooth.

tüdayap [i] **(also tuyayap):** An Owens Valley Paiute term meaning "dress like other sex" used for persons assigned male at birth who occupy an alternate gender role.

tuva'sa (also tüvasa): A Northern Paiute term meaning "sterile" used for persons who occupy an alternate gender role.

Two-Spirit (also two-spirit): An English-language umbrella term for First Nations and Native American gender and sexual identities unique to these cultures.

Tyakutyi: A Yup'ik name meaning "what kind of people are those two" used for a mythical figure with an alternate gender role.

wakashu: Androgynous Japanese "beautiful youths" of the seventeenth, eighteenth, and nineteenth centuries.

waria: An Indonesian gender category that encompasses cross-dressers, binary transgender people, and third gender people. The word is a combination of wanita ("woman") and pria ("man").

w"citc: A Tlingit term meaning "boy whose sex changes at birth."

wi:k'ovat: A Pima-Papago term meaning "like a girl" used for persons assigned male at birth who occupy an alternate gender role.

winkta (also wingkta): A Dakota term meaning "would-be woman" used for persons assigned male at birth who occupy an alternate gender role.

winkte (also wingkte): A Lakota term meaning "would-be woman" used for persons assigned male at birth who occupy an alternate gender role.

winox:tca' akitcita: A Dakota term meaning "women police" used for persons assigned female at birth who occupy an alternate gender role.

witkowin: A Dakota term meaning "crazy woman" used for persons assigned female at birth who occupy an alternate gender role.

wós: A Wappo term meaning "hermaphrodite" used for persons assigned male at birth who occupy an alternate gender role.

x-gender: A Japanese transgender identity that is neither male nor female. In the Japanese transgender community, this gender is sometimes represented as FTX or MTX, indicating an alternate transition path.

yinyang ren: A Chinese gender role for people who encompass both feminine (yin) and masculine (yang) qualities. These people are generally bisexual and present androgynously.

yuk allakuyaaq: A St. Lawrence Island Yup'ik term meaning "different, distinct person" used for persons assigned male at birth who occupy an alternate gender role.

Appendix B
Pronoun Usage

Gender pronouns are parts of speech used to refer to a person without using their name. The most well-known gender pronouns are he/him/his and she/her/hers, but there are also several alternate pronouns. The most common gender neutral pronouns are they/them/theirs[1] and ze/hir/hirs.

It can be very difficult to start using a new pronoun. Most people have spent their entire life using "he" and "she" and these pronouns are automatic. It takes a lot of practice to make the new pronoun habitual. One way to train yourself is to talk about the person to your pet or to yourself (in the car or while washing dishes, for instance).[2] Web comic *Robot Hugs* created an excellent didactic comic describing respectful pronoun use; see the first three panels below:[3]

FIGURE A2.1

"Pronoun Dos and Don'ts" by *Robot Hugs*; originally appeared at http://www.robot-hugs.com/pronoun-etiquette/ on September 9, 2014. Reprinted with permission of *Robot Hugs*.

The following chart illustrates the most common gender pronouns:

Pronoun Chart

Subject Pronoun	Object Pronoun	Possessive Adjective	Possessive Pronoun	Reflexive Pronoun
He	Him	His	His	Himself
She	Her	Her	Hers	Herself
They	Them	Their	Theirs	Themself
Ze	Hir	Hir	Hirs	Hirself
E	Em	Eir	Eirs	Emself

FIGURE A2.2
Pronoun Chart created by Charlie McNabb.

NOTES

1. For more information on using "they" as a singular pronoun, see Davey Shlasko, "How Using 'They' as a Singular Pronoun Can Change the World," *Feministing*, February 3, 2015, http://feministing.com/2015/02/03/how-using-they-as-a-singular-pronoun-can-change-the-world.

2. You can also practice with the Pronoun Dressing Room (http://www.pronouns.failedslacker.com), Practice with Pronouns (http://www.practicewithpronouns.com), and the Pronouns App (https://minus18.org.au/pronouns-app).

3. For the full comic, see http://www.robot-hugs.com/pronoun-etiquette.

Appendix C

Sex, Sexuality, and Gender Primer

Many people new to the concept of nonbinary gender have difficulty unpacking the related concepts of sex, sexuality, and gender. This appendix provides a brief overview of each.

SEX

Sex is a bundle of physical characteristics including chromosomes, hormones, reproductive organs, genitals, and secondary sex characteristics. A male person tends to have XY chromosomes, primarily testosterone, testicles, a penis, and heavier body hair. A female person tends to have XX chromosomes, primarily estrogen and progesterone, ovaries and a uterus, a vulva, and breasts and lighter body hair. However, these characteristics are not as binary as they seem. Babies are assigned a sex at birth based upon their genital configuration. This does not always match other sex characteristics; as many as one in one hundred people do not match the standard "male" or "female" categories and are classed as intersex.[1]

SEXUALITY

Sexuality is a person's romantic and/or sexual attraction to others. Men who are attracted to women and women who are attracted to men are generally called straight or heterosexual. Men attracted to men are generally called gay. Women attracted to women are generally called lesbian. People attracted to two or more sexes are generally called bisexual. People who experience low or no sexual or romantic attraction are generally called asexual or aromantic. For nonbinary people, some of these categories can feel false, as they are based on a binary system. That said, nonbinary people can be straight, gay, lesbian, bisexual, queer, asexual, aromantic, or any number of other sexual identity terms.

GENDER

Gender encompasses an inner feeling of identity as well as the outer expression of that identity. Gender includes man/male, woman/female, and nonbinary (and all the identities that fall under the nonbinary umbrella). Many people identify as the sex they were assigned at birth. These people are called cisgender. Some people do not identify as the sex they were assigned at birth. These people are called transgender. Transgender people can be binary (men or women) or nonbinary. Some transgender people transition through legal name or gender change, hormones or surgery, or changing their expression (clothing, hair, gait, etc.). Others do not, for a variety of reasons.

Trans Student Educational Resources has a wonderful resource called the Gender Unicorn that articulates sex, sexuality, and gender in an infographic designed to be filled out with one's identities.[2]

NOTES

1. For more information about intersex characteristics, see http://www.isna.org.

2. See http://www.transstudent.org/gender.

The Gender Unicorn

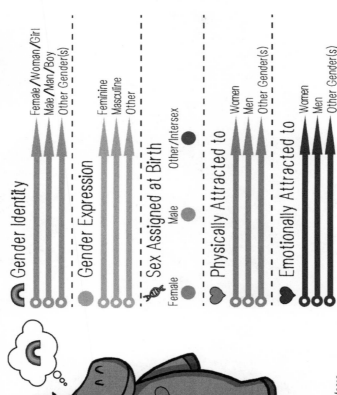

Graphic by:
TSER
Trans Student Educational Resources

Gender Identity
- Female/Woman/Girl
- Male/Man/Boy
- Other Gender(s)

Gender Expression
- Feminine
- Masculine
- Other

Sex Assigned at Birth
- Female
- Male
- Other/Intersex

Physically Attracted to
- Women
- Men
- Other Gender(s)

Emotionally Attracted to
- Women
- Men
- Other Gender(s)

To learn more, go to:
www.transstudent.org/gender

Design by Landyn Pan and Anna Moore

FIGURE A3.1

The Gender Unicorn was designed by Landyn Pan and illustrated by Anna Moore for Trans Student Educational Resources, 2016. Reprinted with permission of Trans Student Educational Resources.

Appendix D
Library of Congress Subject Headings

The Library of Congress Subject Headings is a controlled vocabulary used to describe library materials. Libraries worldwide use this thesaurus when cataloging in order to make resources discoverable. Library users can use subject headings to locate items that best match their search criteria. Because this system is created and maintained by humans, however, many traditionally marginalized topics are poorly represented.[1] Furthermore, updates are slow due to the nature of committee labor. There is not yet a subject heading specifically for nonbinary identities, though there are several that are wider terms (transgender) and some that are narrower terms (Two-Spirit). Library users seeking nonbinary-relevant materials will need to be creative in their searches, using multiple subject headings to capture various elements. The following list encompasses the current most relevant subject headings with which to locate nonbinary materials. For more headings, see Ganin's comprehensive list.[2]

RELEVANT SUBJECT HEADINGS

African American transgender people

African American transsexuals

Androgyny (Psychology)

Butch and femme (Lesbian culture)

Christian transgender people

Christian transsexuals

Drag balls

Female impersonators

Gay liberation movement

Gender expression

Gender identity

Gender identity disorders

Gender identity in advertising

Gender identity in art

Gender identity in dance

Gender identity in education

Gender identity in literature

Gender identity in mass media

Gender identity in motion pictures

Gender identity in music

Gender identity in science

Gender identity in the Bible

Gender identity in the Qur'an

Gender identity in the theater

Gender identity in the workplace

Gender identity on television

Gender minorities

Gender-neutral toilet facilities

Intersex children

Intersex people

Intersexuality

Intersexuality in art

Intersexuality in literature

Jewish transgender people

Jewish transsexuals

Legal assistance to transgender people

LGBT History Month

Libraries and transgender people

Libraries and transsexuals

Male impersonators

Older transsexuals

Queer theology

Queer theory

Radical Faeries (New Age movement)

Sex change

Sex role

Sexual minorities

Sexual minorities in art

Sexual minorities in literature

Sexual minorities on television

Sexual minorities' writings

Sexual minority community

Sexual minority students

Sexual minority youth

Social work with transgender people

Social work with transgender youth

Stonewall Riots, New York, N.Y., 1969

Transgender artists

Transgender athletes

Transgender children

Transgender college students

Transgender musicians

Transgender parents

Transgender people

Transgender people in art

Transgender people in literature

Transgender people in motion pictures

Transgender people's writings

Transgender youth

Transgenderism

Transgenderism on television

Transphobia

Transsexual college students

Transsexualism

Transsexual parents

Transsexual students

Transsexual youth

Transsexuals

Transsexuals in literature

Transsexuals in motion pictures

Transsexuals' writings

Transvestites

Two-spirit people

Two-spirit people in literature

NOTES

1. For a comprehensive look at how oppressive dynamics are reified in subject headings, see Sanford Berman, *Prejudices and Antipathies: A Tract on the LC Subject Heads concerning People* (Jefferson, NC: McFarland, 1993).

2. Netanel Ganin, "Queer LCSH," last updated March 15, 2017, http://www.netanelganin.com/projects/QueerLCSH/QueerLCSH.html.

Bibliography

Alexeyeff, Kalissa, and Niko Besnier. "Gender on the Edge: Identities, Politics, Transformations." In Alexeyeff and Besnier, *Gender on the Edge*, 1–30.

———, eds. *Gender on the Edge: Transgender, Gay, and Other Pacific Islanders.* Honolulu: University of Hawaii Press, 2014.

Als, Hilton. "Life Is a Cabaret." *New Yorker*, January 10, 2011.

Ashenfelder, Mike. "The Average Lifespan of a Webpage." *The Signal* (blog), November 8, 2011. https://blogs.loc.gov/thesignal/2011/11/the-average-lifespan -of-a-webpage.

Audre Lorde Project. http://alp.org.

Australian Passport Office. "Sex and Gender Diverse Passport Applicants." https://www.passports.gov.au/passportsexplained/theapplicationprocess/ eligibilityoverview/Pages/changeofsexdoborpob.aspx.

Beemyn, Brett Genny. "Genderqueer." In *GLBTQ Encyclopedia Project*, edited by Claude Summers, 2005. http://www.glbtqarchive.com/ssh/genderqueer_S.pdf.

Beemyn, Genny, and Susan Rankin. *The Lives of Transgender People.* New York: Columbia University Press, 2011.

Benjamin, Harry. *The Transsexual Phenomenon: A Scientific Report on Transsexualism and Sex Conversion in the Human Male and Female.* New York: Julian, 1966.

Berman, Sanford. "Personal LCSH scorecard." Last modified April 5, 2008. http://jenna.openflows.com/files/lcshscorecard080415.pdf.

———. *Prejudices and Antipathies: A Tract on the LC Subject Heads concerning People*. Jefferson, NC: McFarland, 1993.

Binkley, Collin. "He? She? Ze? Colleges Add Gender-Free Pronouns, Alter Policy." *Seattle Times*, September 18, 2015. http://www.seattletimes.com/nation-world/nation/he-she-ze-colleges-add-gender-free-pronouns-to-forms.

Black and Pink. http://www.blackandpink.org.

Blackless, Melanie, Anthony Charuvastra, Amanda Derryck, Anne Fausto-Sterling, Karl Lauzanne, and Ellen Lee. "How Sexually Dimorphic Are We? Review and Synthesis." *American Journal of Human Biology* 12 (2000): 151–66.

Black Lives Matter PDX. "Unbroken, Black, and Free: A Statement on the Politics and Principles of Black Lives Matter Portland." http://blmpdx.tumblr.com.

Boellstorff, Tom. "Playing Back the Nation: *Waria*, Indonesian Transvestites." *Cultural Anthropology* 19, no. 2 (2004): 159–95.

Bond, Justin Vivian. *Tango: My Childhood, Backwards and in High Heels*. New York: Feminist Press, 2011.

Bornstein, Kate. *Gender Outlaw: On Men, Women, and the Rest of Us*. New York: Routledge, 1994.

———. *A Queer and Pleasant Danger: A Memoir*. Boston: Beacon, 2012.

Bowen, Gary. "Transgendered Warriors: An Interview with Leslie Feinberg." *Lambda Book Report* 6, no. 6 (January 1998): 19.

Bulldagger, Rocko. "The End of Genderqueer." In Sycamore, *Nobody Passes*, 137–48.

Butler, Judith. *Gender Trouble: Feminism and the Subversion of Identity*. New York: Routledge, 1990.

Callender, Charles, Lee M. Kochems, Gisela Bleibtreu-Ehrenberg, Harald Beyer Broch, Judith K. Brown, Nancy Datan, Gary Granzberg, David Holmberg, Åke Hultkrantz, Sue-Ellen Jacobs, Alice B. Kehoe, Johann Knobloch, Margot Liberty, William K. Powers, Alice Schlegel, Italo Signorini, and Andrew Strathern. "The North American Berdache [and Comments and Reply]." *Current Anthropology* 24, no. 4 (August–October 1983): 443–70.

Case, Julia. "Julia's Page." GenderWeb. Last modified May 2, 1998. http://web.
archive.org/web/20000819003830/http://genderweb.org/julie.

Cauterucci, Christina. "How Prince Led the Way to Our Gender Fluid Present."
Slate, April 21, 2016. http://www.slate.com/blogs/outward/2016/04/21/prince_
dead_at_57_embraced_gender_fluidity_ahead_of_his_time.html.

Chiñas, Beverly N. "Isthmus Zapotec Attitudes toward Sex and Gender Anomalies."
In *Latin American Male Homosexualities*, edited by Stephen O. Murray, 293–301.
Albuquerque: University of New Mexico Press, 1995.

Coleman, Eli, Walter Bockting, Marsha Botzer, Peggy Cohen-Kettenis, Griet
DeCuypere, Jamie Feldman, Lin Fraser, Jamison Green, Gail Knudson, Walter
J. Meyer, Stan Monstrey, Richard K. Adler, George R. Brown, Aaron H. Devor,
Randall Ehrbar, Randi Ettner, Evvan Eyler, Rob Garofalo, Dan H. Karasic, Arlene
Istar Lev, Gal Mayer, Heino Meyer-Bahlburg, Blaine Paxton Hall, Friedmann
Pfafflin, Katherine Rachlin, Bean Robinson, Loren S. Schechter, Vin Tangpricha,
Mick van Trotsenburg, Anne Vitale, Sam Winter, Stephen Wittle, Kevan R.
Wylie, and Ken Zucker. "Standards of Care for the Health of Transsexual,
Transgender, and Gender-Nonconforming People, 7th Version." World
Professional Association for Transgender Health. 2012. www.wpath.org.

Collins, Simon. "X Marks the Spot on Passport for Transgender Travellers." *New
Zealand Herald*, December 5, 2012. http://www.nzherald.co.nz/nz/news/article
.cfm?c_id=1&objectid=10852012.

*Collins English Dictionary: Complete and Unabridged 2012 Digital
Edition.* "Professional Association." New York: HarperCollins, 2012.

Costa, LeeRay, and Andrew Matzner. *Male Bodies, Women's Souls: Personal
Narratives of Thailand's Transgendered Youth*. New York: Haworth, 2007.

Crenshaw, Kimberlé. "Mapping the Margins: Intersectionality, Identity Politics, and
Violence against Women of Color." *Stanford Law Review* 43, no. 6 (1991): 1241–299.

Crestodina, Andy. "Website Lifespan and You." *Orbit Media* (blog), March 2010.
https://www.orbitmedia.com/blog/website-lifespan-and-you.

Dancing to Eagle Spirit Society. http://www.dancingtoeaglespiritsociety.org.

Das Wilhelm, Amara. *Tritiya-Prakriti: People of the Third Sex; Understanding
Homosexuality, Transgender Identity, and Intersex Conditions through Hinduism*.
Philadelphia: Xlibris, 2003.

Davidson, Megan. "Seeking Refuge under the Umbrella: Inclusion, Exclusion, and Organizing within the Category *Transgender*." *Sexuality Research & Social Policy: Journal of NSRC* 4, no. 4 (December 2007): 60–80.

Davis, Vaginal, and Lewis Church. "My Womanly Story: Vaginal Davis in Conversation with Lewis Church." *PAJ: A Journal of Performance and Art* 38, no. 2 (May 2016): 80–88.

de Blasio, Abele. *Usi e Costumi dei Camorristi; Gambella, Naples.* 1897. Reprint, Naples, Italy: Edizioni del Delfino, 1975.

"Denmark: X in Passports and New Trans Law Works." Transgender Europe. September 12, 2014. http://tgeu.org/denmark-x-in-passports-and-new-trans-law -work.

Dentice, Dianne, and Michelle Dietert. "Liminal Spaces and the Transgender Experience." *Theory in Action* 8, no. 2 (April 2015): 69–95.

Dolgoy, Reevan. "'Hollywood' and the Emergence of a *Fa'afafine* Social Movement in Samoa, 1960–1980." In Alexeyeff and Besnier, *Gender on the Edge*, 56–72.

Donnelly, Matt. "Jaden Smith's Adventures in Gender Fluidity: What It Means, Who Profits." The Wrap. February 11, 2016. http://www.thewrap.com/jaden-smiths-adventures-in-gender-fluidity-what-it-means-who-profits.

Drescher, Jack. "An Interview with GenderPAC's Riki Wilchins." *Journal of Gay & Lesbian Psychotherapy* 6, no. 2 (2002): 67–85.

Driskill, Qwo-Li. "Doubleweaving Two-Spirit Critiques: Building Alliances between Native and Queer Studies." *GLQ: A Journal of Lesbian and Gay Studies* 16, no. 1–2 (2010): 69–92.

———. "Shaking Our Shells: Cherokee Two-Spirits Rebalancing the World." In *Beyond Masculinity: Essays by Queer Men on Gender & Politics*, edited by Trevor Hoppe, 120–41. Ann Arbor, MI: Self-published, 2008. http://www .beyondmasculinity.com.

———. "Stolen from Our Bodies: First Nations Two-Spirits/Queers and the Journey to a Sovereign Erotic." *Studies in American Indian Literatures* 16, no. 2 (Summer 2004): 50–64.

Ehrensaft, Diane. *Gender Born, Gender Made: Raising Healthy Gender-Nonconforming Children.* New York: Experiment, 2011.

Epple, Carolyn. "Coming to Terms with Navajo *Nádleehí*: A Critique of *Berdache*, 'Gay,' 'Alternate Gender,' and 'Two-Spirit.'" *American Ethnologist* 25, no. 2 (1998): 267–90.

Feinberg, Leslie. *Transgender Liberation: A Movement Whose Time Has Come*. New York: World View Forum, 1992.

———. "Trans Health Crisis: For Us It's Life or Death." *American Journal of Public Health* 91, no. 6 (June 2001): 897–900.

———. *Trans Liberation: Beyond Pink or Blue*. Boston: Beacon, 1998.

Feinberg, Leslie, and Minnie Bruce Pratt. "Leslie Feinberg: 1949–2014." 2014. http://www.lesliefeinberg.net/self.

Feldman, Adam. "Justin Vivian Bond on Art, Gender, NYC and the Future of Kiki and Herb." *TimeOut*, September 16, 2015. https://www.timeout.com/newyork/music/justin-vivian-bond-on-art-gender-nyc-and-the-future-of-kiki-and-herb.

Feldman, Jamie, and Katherine Spencer. "Medical and Surgical Management of the Transgender Patient: What the Primary Care Clinician Needs to Know." In Makadon et. al, *Fenway Guide*, 479–516.

Fink, Marty, and Quinn Miller. "Trans Media Moments: Tumblr, 2011–2013." *Television & New Media* 15, no. 7 (2014): 611–26.

Fulton, Robert, and Steven W. Anderson. "The Amerindian 'Man-Woman': Gender, Liminality, and Cultural Continuity." *Current Anthropology* 33, no. 5 (December 1992): 603–10.

Ganin, Netanel. "Queer LCSH." Last updated March 15, 2017. http://www.netanelganin.com/projects/QueerLCSH/QueerLCSH.html.

Giannini, Melissa. "Hollywood's Most Famous Progeny Is Entering Adulthood as the Key Progenitor of a Boundless Mode of Existence." *Nylon*, July 6, 2016. http://www.nylon.com/articles/jaden-smith-nylon-august-cover.

Gianoulis, Tina. "Androgyny." In *GLBTQ Encyclopedia Project*, edited by Claude Summers, 2004. http://www.glbtqarchive.com/ssh/androgyny_S.pdf.

Gilden, Andrew. "Preserving the Seeds of Gender Fluidity: Tribal Courts and the Berdache Tradition." *Michigan Journal of Gender & Law* 13 (2007): 237–72.

Godfrey, John. "Kiwis First to Officially Recognize Third Gender." *Nonprofit Quarterly*, July 20, 2015. https://nonprofitquarterly.org/2015/07/20/kiwis-first-to-officially-recognize-third-gender.

Goldberg, Carey. "Public Lives: Issues of Gender, from Pronouns to Murder." *New York Times*, June 11, 1999. http://www.nytimes.com/1999/06/11/nyregion/public-lives-issues-of-gender-from-pronouns-to-murder.html.

———. "Shunning 'He' and 'She,' They Fight for Respect." *New York Times*, September 8, 1996. http://www.nytimes.com/1996/09/08/us/shunning-he-and-she-they-fight-for-respect.html.

Halberstam, Judith/Jack. *Female Masculinity*. Durham, NC: Duke University Press, 1998.

Harrison, Jack, Jaime Grant, and Jody L. Herman. "A Gender Not Listed Here: Genderqueers, Gender Rebels, and OtherWise in the National Transgender Discrimination Survey." *LGBTQ Policy Journal at the Harvard Kennedy School* 2 (2011–2012): 13–24.

Independent Lens. "A Map of Gender-Diverse Cultures." PBS, August 11, 2015. http://www.pbs.org/independentlens/content/two-spirits_map-html.

Jaiswal, Anuja. "US Grants Visa to Chhattisgarh Transgender." *Times of India*, May 7, 2015. http://timesofindia.indiatimes.com/city/raipur/US-grants-visa-to-Chhattisgarh-transgender/articleshow/47190053.cms.

Jarvis, Erika. "Ruby Rose: 'I Used to Pray to God That I Wouldn't Get Breasts.'" *Guardian*, July 25, 2014. https://www.theguardian.com/world/2014/jul/25/ruby-rose-video-break-free-gender.

Jimerson, Randall C. *Archives Power: Memory, Accountability, and Social Justice*. Chicago: Society of American Archivists, 2009.

Keatley, Joanne G., Madeline B. Deutsch, Jae M. Sevelius, and Luis Gutierrez-Mock. "Creating a Foundation for Improving Trans Health: Understanding Trans Identities and Health Care Needs." In Makadon et al., *Fenway Guide*, 459–78.

Kerry, Stephen. "'There's Genderqueers on the Starboard Bow': The Pregnant Male in *Star Trek*." *Journal of Popular Culture* 42, no. 4 (2009): 699–714.

Kosciw, Joseph G., Emily A. Greytak, Neal A. Palmer, and Madelyn J. Boesen. "The 2013 National School Climate Survey: The Experiences of Lesbian, Gay, Bisexual and Transgender Youth in Our Nation's Schools." Gay, Lesbian & Straight

Education Network. 2014. http://www.glsen.org/article/2013-national-school-climate-survey.

Krochmal, Shana Naomi. "Exclusive: Miley Cyrus Launches Anti-homelessness, Pro-LGBT 'Happy Hippie Foundation.'" *Out*, May 5, 2015. http://www.out.com/music/2015/5/05/exclusive-miley-cyrus-launches-anti-homelessness-pro-lgbt-happy-hippie-foundation.

Kulick, Don. *Travesti: Sex, Gender, and Culture among Brazilian Transgendered Prostitutes*. Chicago: University of Chicago Press, 1998.

Kumbier, Alana. *Ephemeral Material: Queering the Archive*. Sacramento, CA: Litwin Books, 2014.

Kuwahara, Makiko. "Living as and Living with *Māhū* and *Raerae*: Geopolitics, Sex, and Gender in the Society Islands." In Alexeyeff and Besnier, *Gender on the Edge*, 93–114.

Laframboise, Sandra, and Michael Anhorn. "The Way of the Two Spirited People." Dancing to Eagle Spirit Society. 2008. http://www.dancingtoeaglespiritsociety.org/twospirit.php.

Lang, Sabine. *Men as Women, Women as Men: Changing Gender in Native American Cultures*. Austin: University of Texas Press, 1998.

Lara, Maria Mercedes. "Jaden Smith Wears a Dress to Prom with *The Hunger Games*'s Amandla Stenberg." *People*, May 30, 2015. http://www.people.com/article/jaden-smith-prom-hunger-games-rue-dress.

Leibowitz, Scott, Stewart Adelson, and Cynthia Telingator. "Gender Nonconformity and Gender Discordance in Childhood and Adolescence: Developmental Considerations and the Clinical Approach." In Makadon et al., *Fenway Guide*, 421–58.

Lim, Clarissa-Jan. "New 'Third Gender' Option on Nepal Passports Finally Protects the Rights of LGBT Community." *Bustle*, January 8, 2015. http://www.bustle.com/articles/57466-new-third-gender-option-on-nepal-passports-finally-protects-the-rights-of-lgbt-community.

Limaye, Yogita. "India Court Recognises Transgender People as Third Gender." BBC. April 15, 2014. http://www.bbc.com/news/world-asia-india-27031180.

Lugones, María. "Heterosexualism and the Colonial/Modern Gender System." *Hypatia* 22, no. 1 (Winter 2007): 186–209.

Makadon, Harvey J., Kenneth H. Mayer, Jennifer Potter, and Hilary Goldhammer, eds. *Fenway Guide to Lesbian, Gay, Bisexual, and Transgender Health*. 2nd ed. Philadelphia: American College of Physicians, 2015.

MAP: Movement Advancement Project. http://www.lgbtmap.org.

Matthews, Jeff. "The Femminiello in Neapolitan Culture." Naples: Life, Death & Miracles. December 2011. http://www.naplesldm.com/femm.html.

McCormack, Brian T. "Conjugal Violence, Sex, Sin, and Murder in the Mission Communities of Alta California." *Journal of the History of Sexuality* 16, no. 3 (September 2007): 391–415.

McLeod, Ken. "Visual Kei: Hybridity and Gender in Japanese Popular Culture." *Young* 21, no. 4 (2013): 309–25.

Mead, Margaret. *Male and Female: A Study of the Sexes in a Changing World*. New York: William Morrow, 1949.

Mele, Christopher. "Oregon Court Allows a Person to Choose Neither Sex." *New York Times*, June 13, 2016. http://www.nytimes.com/2016/06/14/us/oregon-nonbinary-transgender-sex-gender.html.

Meyerowitz, Joanne. *How Sex Changed: A History of Transsexuality in the United States*. Cambridge, MA: Harvard University Press, 2002.

Micah. *Neutrois Nonsense: An Intimate Exploration of Identity and Finding Life Wisdom beyond the Gender Binary* (blog). https://neutrois.me.

Mirandé, Alfredo. "Hombres Mujeres: An Indigenous Third Gender." *Men and Masculinities*, September 6, 2015. doi:10.1177/1097184X15602746.

Muñoz, José Esteban. "'The White to be Angry': Vaginal Davis's Terrorist Drag." *Social Text* 52/53 (Autumn–Winter 1997): 80–103.

Nadal, Kevin L., Chassitty N. Fiani, Lindsey S. Davis, Tanya Erazo, and Kristin C. Davidoff. "Microaggressions toward Lesbian, Gay, Bisexual, Transgender, Queer, and Genderqueer People: A Review of the Literature." *Journal of Sex Research* 53, no. 4–5 (May–June 2016): 488–508.

Nanda, Serena. *Gender Diversity: Crosscultural Variations*. Long Grove, IL: Waveland, 2000.

———. *Neither Man nor Woman: The Hijras of India*. Belmont, CA: Wadsworth, 1990.

Nicolazzo, Z. "'Couldn't I Be Both Fred and Ginger?': Teaching about Nonbinary Identities through Memoir." *Journal of LGBT Youth* 11 (2014): 171–75.

Perlson, Hili. "Vaginal Davis Speaks." *Sleek*, September 30, 2011. http://www.sleek -mag.com/2011/09/30/vaginal-davis-interview.

Perrott, Lisa. "Gender Transgression: How Bowie Blurred the Lines." CNN. January 11, 2016 (originally published July 14, 2015). http://www.cnn.com/2016/01/11/ fashion/david-bowie-gender-drag.

Ramberg, Lucinda. "Troubling Kinship: Sacred Marriage and Gender Configuration in South India." *American Ethnologist* 40, no. 4 (2013): 661–75.

Rivas, Jorge. "Native Americans Talk Gender at a 'Two-Spirit' Powwow." Fusion. February 9, 2015. http://fusion.net/story/46014/native-americans-talk-gender -identity-at-a-two-spirit-powwow.

Roscoe, Will. "Bibliography of Berdache and Alternative Gender Roles among North American Indians." *Journal of Homosexuality* 14, no. 3–4 (1987): 81– 171.

———. *Changing Ones: Third and Fourth Genders in Native North America.* Houndmills, UK: Macmillan, 1998.

———. "We'wha and Klah: The American Indian Berdache as Artist and Priest." *American Indian Quarterly* (Spring 1988): 127–50.

———. *The Zuni Man-Woman.* Albuquerque: University of New Mexico Press, 1991.

Rose, Ruby (Producer), and Phillip Lopez (Director). *Break Free* (short film). YouTube. July 14, 2014. https://youtu.be/EFjsSSDLl8w.

Roxie, Marilyn. "Genderqueer History." Genderqueer and Non-Binary Identities. 2011. http://genderqueerid.com/gqhistory.

Senior Correspondent. "'Third Gender' Gets State Recognition," *BD News*, November 11, 2013, http://bdnews24.com/bangladesh/2013/11/11/third-gender -gets-state-recognition.

Shlasko, Davey. "How Using 'They' as a Singular Pronoun Can Change the World." *Feministing*, February 3, 2015. http://feministing.com/2015/02/03/how-using- they-as-a-singular-pronoun-can-change-the-world.

Silvia Rivera Law Project. http://srlp.org.

Singh, Harmeet Shah. "India's Third Gender Gets Own Identity in Voter Rolls." CNN. November 12, 2009. http://edition.cnn.com/2009/WORLD/asiapcf/11/12/india.gender.voting.

Smith, Nathan. "The Queer Legacy of Prince." *Out*, June 7, 2016. http://www.out.com/music/2016/4/22/queer-legacy-prince.

Solway, Diane. "Planet Tilda: When It Comes to Acting—and Dressing—Tilda Swinton, the Star of the Harrowing New Film *We Need to Talk about Kevin*, is Literally Out of this World." *W Magazine*, August 2011. http://www.wmagazine.com/fashion/2011/08/tilda-swinton-cover-story-fashion.

Spade, Dean. "Undermining Gender Regulation." In *Nobody Passes: Rejecting the Rules of Gender and Conformity*, edited by Matt/Mattilda Bernstein Sycamore, 64–70. Emeryville, CA: Seal, 2006.

Spring-Moore, Michele. "Leslie Feinberg." *Lambda Book Report* 14, no. 2 (Summer 2006): 16–17.

Steinmetz, Katy. "The Transgender Tipping Point." *Time*, May 29, 2014.

Stephen, Lynn. "Sexualities and Genders in Zapotec Oaxaca." *Latin American Perspectives* 29, no. 2 (March 2002): 41–59.

Stone, Martha E. "Leslie Feinberg Beheld a World without Gender." *Gay & Lesbian Review Worldwide* 22, no. 2 (March–April 2015): 7.

Stone, Sandy. "The Empire Strikes Back: A Posttranssexual Manifesto." In *Body Guards*, edited by Julia Epstein and Kristina Straub, 280–301. New York: Routledge, 1991.

Stotko, Elaine M., and Margaret Troyer, "A New Gender-Neutral Pronoun in Baltimore, Maryland: A Preliminary Study," *American Speech* 82, no. 3 (Fall 2007): 262–79.

Stryker, Susan. "Transgender Activism." In *GLBTQ Encyclopedia Project*, edited by Claude Summers, 2004. http://www.glbtqarchive.com/ssh/transgender_activism_S.pdf.

———. *Transgender History*. Berkeley, CA: Seal, 2008.

Swanson, Carl. "The Story of V." *New York*, May 16, 2011.

Sycamore, Matt/Mattilda Bernstein, ed. *Nobody Passes: Rejecting the Rules of Gender and Conformity.* Emeryville, CA: Seal, 2006.

Taylor, Tracey. "Supporters Rally for Berkeley Student Set on Fire on Bus." *Berkeleyside*, November 6, 2013. http://www.berkeleyside.com/2013/11/06/ supporters-rally-for-berkeley-student-set-on-fire-on-bus.

ten Brummelhuis, Han. "Transformations of Transgender: The Case of the Thai *Kathoey*." In *Lady Boys, Tom Boys, Rent Boys: Male and Female Homosexualities in Contemporary Thailand*, edited by Peter A. Jackson and Gerard Sullivan, 121–39. New York: Haworth, 1999.

Tobia, Jacob. Jacob Tobia: Speaker—Writer—Advocate. http://www.jacobtobia.com.

——— (jacobtobia). "Feelin cute and pensive in Asheville." Instagram post. August 15, 2016. https://www.instagram.com/p/BJJGcI6jOPi.

Trexler, Richard C. "Making the American Berdache: Choice or Constraint?" *Journal of Social History* (Spring 2002): 613–36.

Vaid-Menon, Alok (DarkMatter). Instagram post. September 3, 2016. https://www .instagram.com/p/BJ52jGphgRQ.

von Kreutzbruck, Vera. "Interview with Actress Tilda Swinton: 'I Am Probably a Woman.'" The WIP. March 20, 2009. http://thewip.net/2009/03/20/interview-with-actress-tilda-swinton-i-am-probably-a-woman.

Walters, Barry. "David Bowie, Sexuality and Gender: A Rebel Who Changed the Face of Music." *Billboard*, January 14, 2016. http://www.billboard.com/articles/ news/magazine-feature/6843021/david-bowie-sexuality-gender-rebellion-changing-music.

West, Isaac. "PISSAR's Critically Queer and Disabled Politics." *Communication and Critical/Cultural Studies* 7, no. 2 (2010): 156–75.

Wilchins, Riki Anne. *In Your Face.* Transexual Menace newsletter, Spring 1995.

———. *In Your Face.* Transexual Menace newsletter, Summer 1999.

———. *Read My Lips: Sexual Subversion and the End of Gender.* Ithaca, NY: Firebrand Books, 1997.

———. "Time for Gender Rights." *GLQ: A Journal of Lesbian and Gay Studies* 10, no. 2 (2004): 265–67.

Williams, Walter L. "Persistence and Change in the Berdache Tradition among Contemporary Lakota Indians." *Anthropology and Homosexual Behavior* (1986): 191–200.

———. *The Spirit and the Flesh: Sexual Diversity in American Indian Culture*. Boston: Beacon, 1986.

Young, Antonia. *Women Who Become Men: Albanian Sworn Virgins*. Oxford: Berg, 2000.

Index

Page references for figures are italicized.

femme, 24, 56, 63, 243, 260; resources
  about, 108, 130–32, 134, 144, 146,
  152, 188, 211–13, 218, 223, 226, 231,
  233, 240. *See also* butch
femminiello, 33, 243
film and television, *45*, 55–57, 73, 76,
  81, 86; resources, 228–36; resources
  about, 137–38, 146–47, 165, 207
Finley, Chris, 86; work by, 142
First Nations, xv, 8–9, 39–41, 43, 86,
  249; resources about, 154, 166, 206.
  See also berdache; Two-Spirit
Fleischman, Sasha, 20

gender confirmation surgery, 7–9,
  14, 24–25, 45–46, 48, 67, 242, 244,
  247–48, 256; resources about, 128,
  139–40, 148, 150, 157, 166, 197–98.
  See also transition
Gender Identity Disorder, 7, 24, 260;
  resources about, 140, 154, 158, 170
gender nonconformity, xii, xv, 11, 13,
  18, 20, 25–27, 55–57, 76, 78, 81,
  83–84, 244; resources about, 134,
  138–40, 142, 147–62, 166–71, 178,
  180, 188, 204–5, 215, 220, 222–24,
  227, 231, 234
genderfluid, xv, 9, 26, 57, 244; resources
  about, 129, 132, 176–80, 215–16, 219,
  229, 234, 237, 239
GenderPAC, 83–84. *See also* Wilchins,
  Riki
genderqueer, xi, xv, xvii, 9, 18–19,
  23–24, 59, 61, 63–65, 71, *72*, 73–74,
  78, 83–84, 94, 244; resources about,
  127–32, 134–35, 140, 143, 146–48,
  151, 153–58, 160–61, 164–74, 179,

  186–88, 199, 202, 208–16, 221–28,
  230, 232–33, 236, 239–40
genitals, 5–6, 8, 14, 23, 44, 46, 48, 242,
  248, 255
Gilley, Brian Joseph, 86; work by, 142
Greenson, Ralph, 16

hair, 7, 9, 23, 25, 46, 56–59, *60*, 61–62,
  241, 244, 246, 255–56
hate crimes, xii, xv, 10–11, 16, 19–21,
  64, 83, 85; resources about, 137, 156,
  162, 188, 212–13, 234
Hawaii. *See* māhū
hijra, xvi, 46, 244–45; resources about,
  136–37, 151, 156, 179, 207–8, 222,
  228–29, 235–36
Hirschfeld, Magnus, 14; archives of, 122
honorifics, 7, 9, 64, 246
hormone replacement therapy (HRT), 7,
  9, 25, 44–45, 48, 67, 248, 256; puberty
  suppression through, 7, 25; resources
  about, 140, 148, 150, 166–67, 197–98,
  235. *See also* transition
Howell, Clare, 84; work by, 135
HRT. *See* hormone replacement therapy

identity documents, xv–xvi, 8, 10, 16,
  20, 29n28, 34, 244; resources about,
  205–7
India, 34; resources about, 140–41, 186,
  228.
See also devadasi; hijra; sādhin
indigenous genders, xv, 13, 33–37,
  38, 39–41, *42*, 43–48; resources
  about, 161, 164, 168, 209–10.
  See also bakla; berdache; biza'ah;
  devadasi; fa'afafine; hijra; kathoey;

About the Author

Charlie McNabb is a folklorist, librarian, and queer activist. They hold a bachelor of arts with a focus in cultural anthropology from the Evergreen State College, a master of arts in folklore from the University of Oregon, and a master of library and information science from San José State University. They have been a cultural consultant and archivist since 2011, providing cultural competency training and research support to faculty, students, non-profits, and corporations. In addition, Charlie has worked as a social sciences librarian at two private colleges, assisting students and faculty with research and scholarship.

Charlie's research focuses on nonbinary identities and experiences, queer and trans reproductive health, disability justice, and bigfoot sightings, though not all at the same time. Charlie runs a DIY archives, which you can learn more about at mcnabbarchives.wordpress.com. They also review queer media at beyondhankycode.wordpress.com.

DISCARD